The Shape of Reason

Over the past three decades, there has been a rapid development of research on human thinking and reasoning. This volume provides a comprehensive review of this topic by looking at the important contributions Paolo Legrenzi has made to the field by bridging the gap from Gestalt ideas to modern cognitive psychology. The contributors, who include some of the most distinguished scholars of reasoning and thinking in Europe and the USA, reflect upon the ways in which he has influenced and inspired their own research, and contributed to modern approaches to human inference.

This volume draws on both traditional and new topics in reasoning and thinking to provide a wide-ranging survey of human thought. It covers creativity, problem solving, the linguistic and social aspects of reasoning and judgement, and the social and emotional aspects of decision making through telling examples, such as the cognitive mechanisms underlying consumers' attitudes towards herbal medicines. It considers a series of key questions, such as how do individuals who are unfamiliar with logic reason? And how do they make choices if they are unfamiliar with the probability calculus and decision theory?

The discussions throughout are placed within a wider research context and the contributors consider the implications of their research for the field as a whole, making the volume an essential reference for anyone investigating the processes that underlie our thinking, reasoning, and decision making in everyday life.

Vittorio Girotto is Professor of Psychology at The University IUAV of Venice and an Honorary Member of the Laboratory of Cognitive Psychology at the CNRS University of Provence.

Philip N. Johnson-Laird is Stuart Professor of Psychology at Princeton University.

The Shape of Reason

Essays in honour of Paolo Legrenzi

Edited by
**Vittorio Girotto and
Philip N. Johnson-Laird**

Ψ Psychology Press
Taylor & Francis Group

HOVE AND NEW YORK

First published 2005 by Psychology Press
27 Church Road, Hove, East Sussex, BN3 2FA

Simultaneously published in the USA and Canada
by Psychology Press
270 Madison Avenue, New York NY 10016

Psychology Press is part of the Taylor and Francis Group

Typeset in Times by RefineCatch Limited, Bungay, Suffolk
Printed and bound in Great Britain by
TJ International Ltd, Padstow, Cornwall
Cover design by Lou Page

British Library Cataloguing in Publication Data
A catalogue record for this book is available from the British Library

Library of Congress Cataloging in Publication Data
The shape of reason : essays in honour of Paolo Legrenzi / [edited by]
V. Girotto & P. N. Johnson-Laird.—1st ed.
    p.   cm.
Includes bibliographical references and indexes.
ISBN 1-84169-344-8 (hardcover)
1. Reasoning (Psychology)   2. Decision making.   I. Legrenzi, Paolo.
II. Girotto, V., 1957–   III. Johnson-Laird, P. N. (Philip Nicholas), 1936–

BF442 .S53   2005
153 .4'3—dc22   2004015973

ISBN 1-84169-344-8

Contents

PART II
Deductive reasoning 49

PART V
Social and emotional aspects of decision making   177

Tables

Figures

Contributors

Céline Buchs, Laboratoire de Psychologie Sociale, Université Pierre Mendes France, BP 47–38040 Grenoble, Cedex 9, France. email: celine.buchs@pse.unige.ch

Fabrizio Butera, Laboratoire de Psychologie Sociale, Université Pierre Mendes France, BP 47–38040 Grenoble, Cedex 9, France. email: fbutera@clio.upmf-grenoble.fr

Ruth M. J. Byrne, Psychology Department, Trinity College, Dublin University, Dublin 2, Ireland. email: rmbyrne@mail.tcd.ie

Erica Carlisle, Department of Psychology, Princeton University, Green Hall, Princeton, NJ 08544, USA. email: ecarlisl@princeton.edu

Nuria Carriedo, Departamento de Psicología Evolutiva y de la Educación, Universidad Nacional de Educación a Distancia, C/Juan del Rosal 10 (Ciudad Universitaria), 28940 Madrid, Spain. email: ncarriedo@psi.uned.es

Jean-Paul Caverni, Laboratoire de Psychologie Cognitive, CNRS-Université de Provence, 29 Avenue R. Schuman, 13100 Aix-en-Provence, France. email: caverni@mailup.univ-mrs.fr

Jonathan St. B. T. Evans, Department of Psychology, University of Plymouth, Drake Circus, Plymouth PL4 8AA, UK. email: J.Evans@plymouth.ac.uk

Juan A. García-Madruga, Departamento de Psicología Evolutiva y de la Educación, Universidad Nacional de Educación a Distancia, C/Juan del Rosal 10 (Ciudad Universitaria), 28940 Madrid, Spain. email: jmadruga@psi.uned.es

Vittorio Girotto, Dipartimento delle Arti e del Disegno Industriale, Università IUAV di Venezia, Dorsoduro 2206, 30123 Venezia, Italy. email: vgirotto@iuav.it

Michel Gonzalez, Laboratoire de Psychologie Cognitive, CNRS-Université of Provence, 29 Avenue R. Schuman, 13100 Aix-en-Provence, France. email: gonzalez@up.univ-mrs.fr

David W. Green, Department of Psychology, University College, Gower Street, London WC1E 6BT, UK. email: d.w.green@ucl.ac.uk

Francisco Gutiérrez, Departamento de Psicología Evolutiva y de la Educación, Universidad Nacional de Educación a Distancia, C/Juan del Rosal 10 (Ciudad Universitaria), 28940 Madrid, Spain. email: fgutierrez@psi.uned.es

Philip N. Johnson-Laird, Department of Psychology, Princeton University, Green Hall, Princeton, NJ 08544, USA. email: phil@princeton.edu

José María Luzón, Departamento de Psicología Evolutiva y de la Educación, Universidad Nacional de Educación a Distancia, C/Juan del Rosal 10 (Ciudad Universitaria), 28940 Madrid, Spain. email: jluzon@psi.uned.es

Laura Macchi, Dipartimento di Psicologia, Università di Milano-Bicocca, Piazza dell'Ateneo Nuovo 1, 20126 Milan, Italy. e-mail: laura.macchi@unimib.it

David Over, Department of Psychology, University of Sunderland, Sunderland SR6 0DD, UK. email: david.over@sunderland.ac.uk

Jean-Luc Péris, Université de Provence, 29 Avenue R. Schuman, 13100 Aix-en-Provence, France. email: peris@up.univ-mrs.fr

Guy Politzer, CNRS-Psychologie Cognitive, Université de Paris VIII, 2 Rue de la Liberté, 93526 Saint-Denis, France. e-mail: politzer@univ-paris8.fr

Sandrine Rossi, Groupe d'Imagerie Neurofonctionnelle, Università de Caen, Batiment Science D, Esplanade de la Paix, 14032, Caen, France. email: rossi@psycho.unicaen.fr

Walter Schaeken, Laboratory of Experimental Psychology, Department of Psychology, University of Leuven, Tiensestraat 102, B-3000 Leuven, Belgium. email: walter.schaeken@psy.kuleuven.ac.be

Eldar Shafir, Department of Psychology, Princeton University, Green Hall, Princeton, NJ 08544, USA. email: eldar@princeton.edu

Jean-Baptiste Van der Henst, Institut des Sciences Cognitive, CNRS, 67 Boulevard Pinel, 69675 Bron, France. email: vanderhenst@isc.cnrs.fr

José Óscar Vila, Departamento de Psicología Evolutiva y de la Educación, Universidad Nacional de Educación a Distancia, C/Juan del Rosal 10 (Ciudad Universitaria), 28940 Madrid, Spain. email: jvila@bec.uned.es

Clare A. Walsh, Cognitive & Linguistic Sciences, Brown University, Providence, RI 02912, USA. email: Clare_Walsh@brown.edu

Preface

This book is dedicated to Paolo Legrenzi, who is a professor at the University of Architecture in Venice. It consists of written versions of most of the papers from a conference that was held on San Servolo in the Venice lagoon in August 2002, to celebrate Paolo's sixtieth birthday. Readers may wonder why a professor at an architectural university is honoured by a set of essays on psychological topics. They may also wonder why the title to the book is: *The Shape of Reason*. The answer to the first question is that Paolo Legrenzi is a distinguished psychologist. The answer to the second question lies in his intellectual biography, which the papers gathered in this volume reflect.

Paolo graduated in a time and place (the early 1960s, Padua) in which Gestalt psychology dominated views about the mind. In his thesis under the supervision of Paolo Bozzi (who died in October 2003, at the age of 73), Paolo reported a phenomenon of temporal dislocation in visual perception. He then began to investigate human reasoning, largely influenced by the early work of Gestalt theorists on thinking and problem solving. When he and his wife Maria Sonino-Legrenzi went to London in the late 1960s to work with Peter Wason and Phil Johnson-Laird at University College London, he surprised many people there by asking them whether they adhered to the Gestalt school. Jonathan Evans, in particular, could not believe that at that time any psychologist could still define himself as a Gestaltist! We should add that at the time we were finishing the editing of this book, Peter Wason died at the age of 78. As the founder of the modern study of reasoning, his work inspired Paolo, the editors of this book, and its contributors.

Paolo's early interests in perception and thinking are reflected in the first chapters of this book. Phil Johnson-Laird (Chapter 1) and Jonathan Evans (Chapter 2) discuss the classical views of the Gestalt school about creativity and insightful problem solving, and outline theories of their own on these matters. Perhaps the central pillar of Paolo's research, however, has been his work on reasoning. The next three chapters focus on this topic. In Chapter 3, Walter Schaeken and Jean-Baptiste Van der Henst report some studies of spatial inference. In Chapter 4, Juan García-Madruga and his colleagues discuss the influence of working memory on conditional reasoning. In Chapter 5, Ruth Byrne and Clare Walsh present their recent research on how individuals reason about contradictions to conclusions that they have inferred. In Paolo's contribution to the pioneering European conference on psycholinguistics, the 1969 meeting at Bressanone, he was the first to show that the linguistic formulation of the premises affects conditional reasoning. More than three decades later, linguistic and pragmatic effects on reasoning are still under intensive investigation. These effects on hypothesis testing are examined in Chapter 6 by Jean-Paul Caverni and his colleagues, and in Chapter 7 Guy Politzer and Laura Macchi consider their effects on probabilistic reasoning. How naive individuals reason about probabilities is indeed a topic that Paolo has investigated over the years. The next two chapters present contrasting views about this research. In Chapter 8, David Over criticises Paolo and the editors' theory of naive probabilistic reasoning based on mental models. A knowledge of history is integral to Paolo's approach to psychology: he was the first professor of the history of psychology in Italy. Hence, it is appropriate that in Chapter 9 Vittorio Girotto and Michel Gonzalez report historical evidence bearing on Paolo's views about probabilistic reasoning.

Only a few people can be both outstanding researchers and successful businessmen. Paolo is one of the few. During his academic career, he was able to found and to manage two consulting companies. Many readers will be surprised to learn that some products they use in their daily life were created by Paolo, e.g., the idea of surrounding Nutella spread with chocolate (a.k.a. Ferrero Rocher). As Paolo himself says: "The invention of a new sort of shampoo or candy can produce the same intellectual pleasure as devising an elegant way to test a theory." Indeed, Paolo has a long history of work in applying psychology to many aspects of everyday life. In addition to his consulting work, he has written on the psychology of exams, on the interpretation of school grades, and on the psychological implications of the euro, the new currency of continental Europe. Lying behind all of this practical work is his interest in social and emotional aspects of decision making. The final three chapters of the book reflect these interests. In Chapter 10, David Green examines how affect and arguments influence human decision making. In Chapter 11, Fabrizio Butera and Céline Buchs review some studies, including those conducted with Paolo himself, showing how reasoning and choice are affected by the social context in which they take place. Finally, in Chapter 12, Erica Carlisle and Eldar Shafir explain how consumers' attitudes towards herbal medicines depend on basic mechanisms of decision making.

Acknowledgements

The editors thank CNR (the Italian National Research Council), MIUR (the Italian Ministry for University and Research) and the Foundation-School for Advanced Studies in Venice for grants to support the conference, and Psychology Press for publishing this volume. We thank all those who attended the conference, including Dan Sperber who was unable to provide a written version of his paper. We are also grateful to Ignazio Musu (Dean of the Venice International University in San Servolo), Marino Folin (Rector of the University IUAV of Venice) and Marco De Michelis (Dean of the School of Arts and Design at the University IUAV of Venice) for their help in making the conference and the volume possible, and Maurizio Riccucci for his editorial help. And, of course, we thank Paolo Legrenzi, who inspired us all.

Vittorio Girotto
Phil Johnson-Laird
August 2004

Part I
Problem solving

1 The shape of problems

Philip N. Johnson-Laird

Tutta la teoria del problem-solving, da Simon ai giorni nostri, può venire considerata come uno sviluppo diretto o indiretto dei lavori dei gestaltisti. [All theories of problem solving from Simon to the present day can be considered as a development, direct or indirect, of the work of the Gestalt psychologists.]
(Paolo Legrenzi, 1978, p. 173)

Introduction

Psychology in Italy during the twentieth century was unique. Vittorio Benussi (1878–1927) initiated an Italian variety of Gestalt psychology, deriving more from Meinong than the great German school; Cesare Musatti (1899–1979) continued the tradition; and Gaetano Kanizsa (1913–1993) brought it to fruition in his startling and original demonstrations of perceptual phenomena, especially illusory contours. Paolo Legrenzi is a crucial figure in this history, because he built the bridge from Gestalt theory in his collaborations with Kanizsa to information-processing psychology (see, e.g., Kanizsa & Legrenzi, 1978; Kanizsa, Legrenzi, & Sonino, 1983). As the epigraph to the present chapter shows, he has never lost sight of the Gestalt origins in the study of thinking. For over 30 years, he and I have carried out research together, usually in collaboration with his wife Maria Sonino, and mostly on deductive reasoning. He is thus both a colleague and a dear friend. In this chapter, my aim is to honour him with an analysis of human problem solving, a topic that goes back to some of his own studies (e.g., Legrenzi, 1994) and to those of his Gestalt forebears (e.g., Duncker, 1945; Katona, 1940; Köhler, 1925; Luchins, 1942; Maier, 1931; Wertheimer, 1945/1959).

A common phenomenon when you are struggling to solve a problem is that you have a burst of inspiration – an *insight* – and the solution suddenly emerges into your consciousness, seemingly from nowhere. "Eureka," you say, like Archimedes: "I have it". Though you do not normally leap from your bath and run stark naked through the streets, shouting the solution to the world. The experience seems very different from the normal process of thought in which you advance step by step towards the solution of a problem, as, say, when you work out your income tax returns. Indeed, the Gestalt psychologists assumed that insight was special. It is a creative process, they argued, that depends on a sudden restructuring (*Umstruktuierung*) or recen-tring (*Umzentrierung*) of the perceptual field (see Kohler, 1929/1947; Wertheimer, 1945/1959). But critics both early (Bulbrook, 1932) and late (e.g., Perkins, 1981; Weisberg, 1986), have argued that there is nothing special about insight. Normal thinking is analogous to a search for the number that opens a combination lock. When at length you stumble on to the solution, it is bound to be sudden, but it does not depend on any processes that differ from those that hitherto failed.

An empirical discovery about problem solving contrasts with such claims. Janet Metcalfe and her colleagues asked participants in an experiment to rate how "warm" they were in their efforts to solve problems (see, e.g., Metcalfe & Weibe, 1987). With some problems, the participants made progress towards the solution, as shown in the increase in their ratings of warmth. But, with other problems – those typically used in studies of insight, there was no increase in ratings of warmth: Individuals felt remote from the solution right up to the moment that it popped into their heads. When the ratings of warmth did grow incrementally for insight problems, they tended to presage a failure to solve the problem. Hence, some problems are solved in a sudden and unexpected way. These solutions, we shall say, depend on *insight*. The question is what are its underlying mental processes?

The short answer is: no one knows. There are, however, three main schools of thought. The first view is the Gestalt account of insight as dependent on restructuring or recentring. The trouble is that these notions are obscure (Ohlsson, 1984a, 1984b): no computer model implementing them exists.

The second school of thought is that insight depends on overcoming an erroneous approach to a problem (see, e.g., Isaak & Just, 1995; Knoblich, Ohlsson, Haider, & Rhenius, 1999; Weisberg, 1993). Individuals become fix-ated on inappropriate methods based on their prior experience, but a period of "incubation" in which they think about other matters allows the misleading cues to become less accessible with a consequent greater chance of recovering the correct cues (Smith & Blankenship, 1991). Such perseverations certainly occur, e.g., designers tend to conform to any initial example that they are given, incorporating its features into their finished designs even when they are asked not to (Jansson & Smith, 1991). The trouble with this approach, however, is its assumption that individuals know the right methods, though cannot access them. The claim may be correct for some problems (see Keane, 1989), but it is false for others. Arguments to the contrary resemble Socrates' leading questions to a slave boy to show that he knew the solution to a geometric problem (see Plato's *Meno*). In fact, a major theme of the present chapter is that attempts to solve a problem can lead to the creative discovery of knowledge.

The third school of thought is based on Newell and Simon's (1972) concept of a "problem space", which is defined as all possible sequences of the mental operations pertinent to the solution of a problem. The problem solver needs to search this space for a sequence of operations leading from the initial state of the problem to its goal. Kaplan and Simon (1990) extended this idea to insight. They argued that it depends on switching from a search in the problem space to a search in the meta-level space of *possible* problem spaces for a new representation of the problem (see also Korf, 1980). In a case of insight, this new representation yields the solution to the problem. For example, most people are at first defeated by the problem of the "mutilated" chessboard. The goal is to cover a chessboard with dominoes, or else to prove that the task is impossible. Each domino is in the shape of a rectangle that covers two adjacent squares on the chessboard. However, the board has been mutilated by the removal of a square at one corner and another square at the diagonally opposite corner. Individuals who imagine laying out dominoes on the board get nowhere. They have the wrong representation of the problem. The key insight depends on constructing a new representation, which concerns parity: Each domino covers one white square and one black square, but the diagonally opposite corners are of the same color. Hence, after they are removed, the remainder do not include an equal number of black and white squares, and so the task is impossible.

Tom Ormerod and his colleagues have formulated an alternative account of insight (see, e.g., Chronicle, Ormerod, & MacGregor, 2001; MacGregor, Ormerod, & Chronicle, 2001; Ormerod, MacGregor, & Chronicle, 2002). They argue that when individuals tackle a problem, they select moves to maximise progress towards a hypothesised goal but to minimise the expansion of the problem space. They relax this constraint only if they have to, but in this way they may discover a new sort of move. This theory postulates that problem solvers can assess whether a putative move does make progress towards a goal, and so they can rely on a "hill-climbing" strategy. The assumption is plausible for certain problems, but perhaps less plausible for others, such as those problems in daily life that call for insight (or those discussed towards the end of this chapter).

The problem with "problem spaces" is that they are irrefutable. Any computable process can be described as a search through a space of possible sequences of operations. At the limit, of course, there is no search at all, because the process follows a deterministic sequence of operations. This limit, however, is merely a special case. To characterise insight as a search through *possible* problem spaces is highly abstract. As Kaplan and Simon remark (1990, p. 381): "The space of possible problem spaces is exceedingly ill-defined, in fact, infinite." What we need is an account of how the mind carries out the search.

In sum, all three schools of thought contain elements of the truth, but none is wholly satisfactory. The present chapter accordingly outlines a new theory of creative problem solving. It begins with an analysis of creativity and an exhaustive set of possible creative strategies. It describes a test bed for the new theory – a domain of "shape" problems – and a process of creative discovery depending on explorations of possible operations in tackling these problems. This process enables individuals to develop strategies for problem solving. It can also lead to insights that overcome the failure of an initial strategy. Finally, the chapter draws some conclusions about the nature of problem solving.

The nature of creativity

Insight is creative, and so to understand it we need to understand how the mind creates. But what is creativity? Science does not advance by a priori definitions, but elsewhere I have offered a working definition of creativity (see, e.g., Johnson-Laird, 2002). This definition depends on five main assumptions:

(1) *Novelty*: the result of a creative process is novel for the individual who carries out the process. Creativity is not mere imitation or regurgitation.
(2) *Optional* novelty for society: the result may also be novel for society as a whole, but this requirement is optional. The mental processes underlying creativity are the same even if unbeknownst to the relevant individual someone else has already had the same idea.
(3) *Nondeterminism*: creativity depends on more than mere calculation or the execution of a deterministic process, such as long multiplication. When you create something, such as the solution to a problem, alternative possibilities can occur at various points in the process. If you could relive your experience with no knowledge of your first effort, then you might make different choices the second time around. Hence, creation does not unwind like clockwork with only one option for you at each point in the process. In computational theory, a machine with this property is known as *nondeterministic*. It can yield different outcomes when it is in the same internal state, and has the same input if any (see, e.g., Hopcroft & Ullman, 1979). No one knows whether human creativity is truly nondeterministic, but at present we have to make this assumption. It allows for our ignorance and, computationally speaking, it costs us nothing. In principle, anything that can be computed nondeterministically can also be computed deterministically.
(4) *Constraints*: creativity satisfies pre-existing constraints or criteria. For a problem in science, art, or daily life, a crucial constraint is that the solution works, i.e., it is viable. There are usually many other constraints on the operations, physical or mental, that are pertinent to the problem. The aesthetic values of a genre constrain the creation of works of art; a knowledge of robust results constrains the creation of scientific theories; and an awareness of practical realities constrains the creation of solutions to everyday problems. The individual creator is not a closed system,

but is influenced by mentors, collaborators, and leaders (Simonton, 1984). In this way, the values of a culture influence individuals' creative processes, which, in turn, may contribute to the values that are passed on to the next generation.

(5) *Existing* elements: you cannot create out of nothing. There must be existing elements to provide the raw materials for even highly original works of art or science. These existing elements include, of course, the system of mental processes that allow creativity to occur.

Novelty, Optional novelty for society, Nondeterminism, Constraints, and Existing elements are the five components of the NONCE definition of creativity. The definition has an unexpected consequence. On the assumption that creativity is a computable process, there can be only three sorts of creative strategy. A *strategy* is a systematic sequence of elementary steps that an individual follows in solving a problem, and is therefore similar to a computer algorithm for solving a problem.

The first sort of strategy is *neo-Darwinian*. It is analogous to the evolution of species according to the neo-Darwinian synthesis of genetics and natural selection. The strategy has two stages: a generative stage in which ideas are formed by an entirely arbitrary or nondeterministic process working on existing elements; an evaluative stage that uses constraints to pass just those results that are viable (see Figure 1.1, p. 8). Whatever survives evaluation, which may be little or nothing, can serve as the input to the generative stage again. The process can thus be repeated ad libitum with the output from one iteration serving as the input to the next. Neo-Darwinist theories of creativity include accounts based on trial and error, and they have often been proposed by psychologists (e.g., Bateson, 1979; Campbell, 1960; Simonton, 1995; Skinner, 1953). An individual produces a variety of responses, and the contingencies of reinforcement, or some other constraints, select those that are viable and eliminate the remainder. It is crucial to distinguish between a single operation of a neo-Darwinian strategy and its iterative or repeated use, which is much more powerful (Dawkins, 1976). Evolution is thus an archetypal *recursive* process: It applies to its own successful results. It is mimicked in the "genetic algorithms" developed by Holland and his colleagues for finding optimal solutions to problems (e.g., Holland, Holyoak, Nisbett, & Thagard, 1986).

A neo-Darwinian strategy is grossly inefficient, but the only feasible strategy if the generative process cannot be guided by constraints, as in the case of the evolution of species (see Mayr, 1982, p. 537). Yet, if constraints are used in the evaluation of ideas, then they could be used instead to constrain their generation in the first place. Unlike species, ideas could evolve using this process. The second sort of strategy is *neo-Lamarckian* in just this way (see Figure 1.1, p. 8). All the constraints acquired from experience govern the generative stage – by analogy with Larmarck's theory of evolution (see Mayr, 1982, p. 354). If an individual has acquired a comprehensive set of

(1) Neo-Darwinian

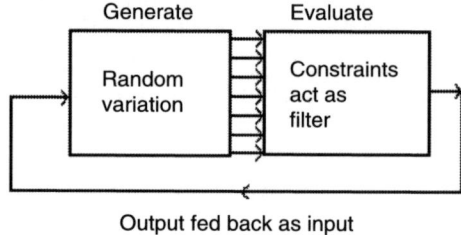

Output fed back as input

(2) Neo-Lamarckian

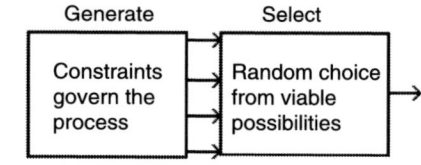

(3) Multistage

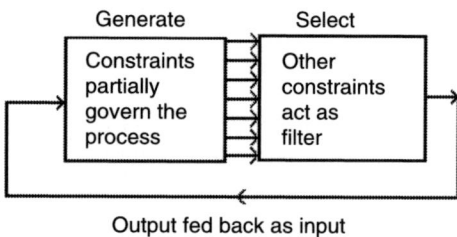

Output fed back as input

Figure 1.1 The three strategies for creativity

constraints guaranteeing the viability of the results, then the generative stage will yield a small number of possibilities, all of which meet the constraints. But because all the constraints are used to generate a result, by definition none are left over for its evaluation. The constraints will sometimes allow more than one possibility, and so the only way to choose amongst them must be nondeterministic, e.g., by making an arbitrary decision. The strategy has just two stages with no need for recursion: (1) the generation of possibilities according to constraints; (2) an arbitrary selection, where necessary, from amongst them. The strategy is highly efficient, because it never yields hopeless results and never calls for recursion.

The third sort of strategy is a compromise. It is *multistage*: The generative stage uses some constraints like a neo-Lamarckian strategy, and the evaluative stage uses some constraints like a neo-Darwinian strategy (see Figure 1.1). The initial generation of possibilities under the guidance of some constraints may leave something to be desired, and so the individual applies further constraints to evaluate the results. They may need further work, and so the process can be recursive.

Figure 1.1 summarises the three strategies. Many creative individuals do indeed repeatedly revise the results of their earlier efforts. Since they are applying constraints at each stage, why do they not apply all of these constraints immediately in the first generative stage? Why the need for a time-consuming division of labour over several recursions? From a computational standpoint, it would be more efficient to apply all the constraints in the generative stage in a neo-Lamarckian way. It seems paradoxical for individuals to waste time making an inadequate attempt if they have the ability to perceive its inadequacy and to set matters right. The resolution of the paradox may lie in the way the mind works. Knowledge for generating ideas is largely unconscious, whereas knowledge for evaluating ideas is largely conscious and embodied in beliefs. This dissociation resolves another puzzle, which Perkins (1981, p. 128) refers to as the fundamental paradox of creativity: People are better critics than creators. Criticism can be based on conscious knowledge that can be acquired easily; whereas the generation of ideas is based on unconscious knowledge acquired only by laborious practice in creating. Hence there are two stages in many sorts of creation: a generative stage and an evaluative stage. Hence the greater ease of criticism over imagination. In creation, no substitute exists for a period of apprenticeship. You learn by emulating successful creators, and by trying to create for yourself in a particular domain. Only in this way can you acquire the tacit constraints for creativity. If this account is correct, then it is a blow to the purveyors of universal nostrums for creativity. There can be no effective recipes for enhancing your creativity across all domains. Creation is local to a particular domain of expertise.

Problems of shape

An important distinction in the problems that arise in daily life and in the psychological laboratory is between what I shall refer to as *one-off* problems and *series* problems. One-off problems are those that occur just once. If you have solved a one-off problem, then provided you have not forgotten the solution you can apply it at once to any other instance of the problem. A classic example of a one-off problem is Duncker's (1945) candle puzzle. You are given a candle and a box of thumb tacks (drawing pins), and your task is to fix the candle to the wall. Most people are stumped, unless and until they have the insight that the box containing the thumb tacks can itself be pinned to the wall and thereby support the candle. Once they have had this insight, they retain it, and so the solution to any other instance of the problem is trivial. The solution to other insight problems may not be so easy to retain. Tom Ormerod et al. (2002) argue that retention depends on how easy it is to recode the solution as a single step or a single idea. One corollary of this analysis is that there is no such thing as an "insight" problem per se, i.e., the quest for a decisive categorization is chimerical (pace Weisberg, 1996). All that can exist are problems that call for most *naive* individuals to have an insight if they are to solve them.

In contrast to one-off problems, water jug problems come in a series of different forms, e.g., using just three jugs, measuring respectively 127, 21 and 3 quarts, your task is to measure a quantity of 100 quarts. Infinitely many water jug problems can be posed; they do not all have the same sort of solution and the acquisition of one sort of solution can inhibit the use of another (see, e.g., Luchins, 1942; Luchins & Luchins, 1950). The distinction between one-off and series problems can also be drawn for problems in mathematics and science. The theoretical problem of relating mass, force, and acceleration was solved by Newton, and later revised by Einstein. Their solutions can be exploited to solve a series of practical problems in mechanics.

The study of one-off problems in the psychological laboratory is intriguing, but it has methodological problems. As Tom Ormerod and I discovered to our cost (in an unpublished study), it is difficult to distinguish between the knowledge that individuals bring to a problem and the knowledge that they discover in trying to solve it. Likewise, it is difficult to observe the development of their strategies for coping with the problem. The main experimental procedure is to give hints of one sort or another in order to trigger the knowledge requisite for the solution. This manipulation, however, tells one little about an individual's strategy. We need to understand how people develop both knowledge and strategies, and the task calls for a series of problems. This section of the chapter accordingly examines a series of *shape* problems in which individuals have to make or to modify a shape by the addition, removal, or rearrangement of its component pieces (see, e.g., Katona, 1940). Here is an example:

Given the following arrangement of five squares:

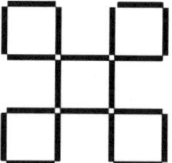

in how many ways can you move three pieces to make exactly seven squares of the same size as the originals and with no loose ends, i.e., additional pieces left over?[1]

---

1 One solution is:

There are seven other ways to solve the problem, i.e., a total of eight.

Infinitely many shape problems can be posed, but there are three main sorts:

- problems calling for the removal of a certain number of pieces
- problems calling for the addition of a certain number of pieces
- problems calling for the rearrangement of a certain number of pieces.

Most shape problems are simple, yet they call for sufficient thought to be a staple of puzzle books (see, e.g., Orleans & Orleans, 1983). Some shape problems, however, are sufficiently difficult that they defeat most naive individuals, where "naive" here means an individual who has not had any relevant experience in solving these problems.

Shape problems illustrate most of the features of human problem solving, and in what follows, the chapter uses them to illustrate a theory of human problem solving. We begin with the simplest possible shape problem:

(1) Given the following five squares, add one piece to make six squares:

The problem is trivial. But, why? There are at least two reasons. First, the symmetry of the figure ensures that the missing piece "pops out" of the display. This missing piece is highly salient. Human perceivers can subitize these squares, i.e., they can apprehend them in a single glance and see that a piece is missing. This ability depends on parallel processing. In contrast, a serial computer program can merely convolve a function for identifying a square (typically a template) with each cell in the visual array, and thereby reveal the presence of five squares and the three sides of a square with a missing piece. The process does not yield an outcome akin to the "pop out" phenomenology of human perception. Second, the addition of only a single piece to a shape makes a neo-Darwinian strategy feasible. You add a piece arbitrarily here or there, and sooner rather than later you will get the right answer.

For a naive participant, who has not seen the previous problem, the following problem is slightly harder:

(2) Given the following six squares, remove one piece to leave exactly five squares with no loose ends, i.e., pieces that are not connected to any other piece at one or other end:

In this case, the solution does not pop out, and naive individuals are likely to try one or two experimental moves at least in their mind's eye using a neo-Darwinian strategy.

The following problem is more interesting:

(3) Given the following six squares, remove five pieces to leave exactly three squares with no loose ends:

You are invited to tackle this problem for yourself before you read on. You are welcome to use matches, tooth picks, or pen and pencil as an aid. A neo-Darwinian strategy can solve this problem, but it is laborious: There are over 6000 different ways to remove five pieces, and only ten of them yield a solution to the problem. A computer program that I have written to model the neo-Darwinian strategy churns away until by chance it derives a solution. The generative stage removes a piece at random, and the evaluative stage checks the result according to a single constraint: Does it solve the problem? Human solvers almost certainly lack the patience and memory to tackle the problem in such a stupid way. They either know what to do in order to solve it (they may be wrong) or they are lost. In the latter case, depending on their motivation, they flail around for some time. In unpublished studies, Louis Lee and I have indeed observed this process of flailing around when individuals first tackle shape problems (see Lee & Johnson-Laird, 2003). They try out seemingly arbitrary choices, which they undo when these moves fail to yield the solution.

Suppose that after you have removed a single piece, you have some way to assess whether your move is a good one moving you towards the solution or a bad one that is not a step towards the solution. With this ability, you could use a neo-Darwinian strategy. You remove a piece at random, and evaluate whether or not your move is a good one. If it is, you retain it, and then return to the generative stage, which removes a second piece at random, and so on. But, if your first move is not good, you abandon it, and return to the generative stage to choose a different first move. You proceed in this way until you have solved the problem. The strategy is neo-Darwinian, but it is tolerably efficient, because you make progress towards the solution move by move, i.e., you are hill climbing (cf. Ormerod et al., 2002). The crux is accordingly whether you can evaluate moves as good or bad without having to solve the problem as a whole.

Let us suppose that you remove a piece at random using a neo-Darwinian strategy:

This move transforms problem (3) into a new one: You now have to remove four pieces from the preceding array to leave exactly three squares with no loose ends. So, is your move a good one or not? You are unlikely to have any way to answer this question without carrying out some further moves and assessing their consequences. Hence, you cannot use a neo-Darwinian strategy based on an evaluative stage using only success as one constraint and goodness of move as another. You must develop more powerful constraints or a more powerful strategy. But how? The next section of the chapter aims to answer this question.

The discovery system

The way people discover how to solve shape problems depends on three mental components that they bring to the task. First, they understand the language in which these problems are posed, and their knowledge includes a grasp of the concepts of *squares* and *pieces*, of *numbers* both cardinal and ordinal, and of the pertinent arithmetical operations of counting, adding, and subtracting. Intelligent adults in some other cultures do not have these concepts, and so they cannot understand, let alone solve, shape problems. Second, people are equipped with the mechanisms of perception and action. They can see squares, and they can envisage the consequences of removing a piece. These mechanisms are unconscious: Introspection does not tell you how you see at once that a piece is missing in problem (1). Third, people are equipped with a *system for discovery*. It enables them both to acquire knowledge about problems from their attempts to solve them, and to develop a strategy for coping with them. Such a strategy exploits the knowledge that they acquire and that can constrain the process of solution. As we will see, the discovery system stores the effects of different sorts of move. It can also shift such a constraint from the evaluative stage of solving a problem to the generative stage.

The process of discovery occurs as individuals explore the effects of different moves in trying to solve a problem. Consider, again, problem (3) in which the task is to remove five pieces from an array to eliminate three squares. You are likely to tackle this problem by removing a piece and assessing the consequences. Suppose you remove a piece from a corner of the shape, then the result is:

It is now necessary to remove the remaining "loose end" to yield the following shape. You have discovered something: One way to eliminate a square is to

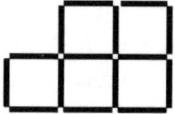

remove the two pieces making up a *corner*. A corner is indeed one of seven sorts of configuration in a shape problem (see Figure 1.2, below).

A further result is that you now have a new problem: to remove three pieces from the preceding shape to eliminate two squares. If you remove another corner, then discounting rotations there are three ways in which you could do so. In each case, your remaining problem is to remove one piece to eliminate one square:

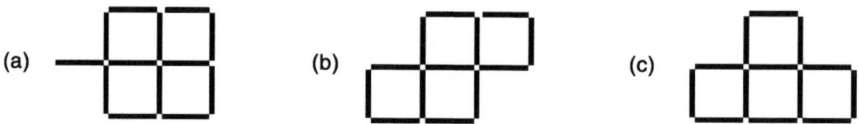

In case (a), you are obliged to remove the loose end, and so you fail to solve the problem. In case (b), you also fail, because here the only way to eliminate a square as a result of removing a single piece is to remove a piece that is common to two squares, thereby eliminating both of them. You have discovered something new: Removing one *middle* piece, i.e., a piece in the middle of two squares, eliminates both the squares. In case (c), you can succeed. You can remove one piece to eliminate one square, as shown here:

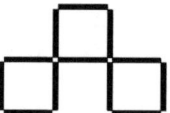

Once more, you have made a discovery: You can eliminate a square by removing an *outer* piece, i.e., a piece in the square that has middle pieces from the same square at both ends, but that is not itself a middle. There are, as we will see presently, quite different solutions to problem (3).

What this analysis has illustrated is how the exploration of possible moves leads to a tactical knowledge of the different sorts of pieces in shape problems, and of the different effects of removing them. As Figure 1.2 shows, there are seven sorts of piece in shape problems. These tactics, in turn, provide constraints on the creative process. When they are first acquired, they are constraints that are discovered in the evaluative stage of trying to create a

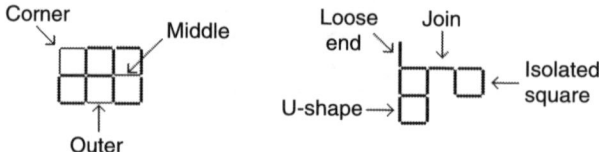

Figure 1.2 Illustrations of the seven sorts of piece in shape problems

solution. A major change occurs, however, when such knowledge is shifted to the generative stage of the process. You no longer have to try out moves in an exploratory way, but, like the participants whom Louis Lee and I have tested experimentally, you can go directly to the solution of at least certain problems with no false moves (Lee & Johnson-Laird, 2003).

The discovery system operates by storing the effects of operations on shapes. The order in which individuals develop a knowledge of the different tactical steps, and the completeness of their knowledge, is likely to differ depending on each individual's experience. Table 1.1 summarises the complete set of tactical steps for shape problems of the present sort.

Table 1.1 The seven tactical steps for a set of shape problems (see Figure 1.2 for illustrations of the different sorts of piece)

---

1. To remove 1 piece and 0 squares, remove a loose end (obligatory).
2. To remove 1 piece and 0 squares, remove a join.
3. To remove 1 piece and 1 square, remove an outer.
4. To remove 1 piece and 2 squares, remove a middle.
5. To remove 2 pieces and 1 square, remove a corner.
6. To remove 3 pieces and 1 square, remove a U-shape.
7. To remove 4 pieces and 1 square, remove an isolated square.

Does the use of visual imagery help you with shape problems? Perhaps. But, it has its limitations. Consider the following problem:

> I take a bunch of thousands of very thin needles, and throw them up into the air, imparting different arbitrary accelerations to each of them. They fall to the ground. As they fall, however, I freeze them in mid-air. Are there likely to be more needles nearly horizontal than nearly vertical, more needles nearly vertical than nearly horizontal, or are the two proportions likely to be roughly equal?

Many people say that the two proportions should be roughly equal. They are wrong. Visual images tend to be two-dimensional. An accurate three-dimensional representation shows that there are many more ways in which a needle can be nearly horizontal than it can be nearly vertical. A horizontal needle can be pointing in any of the 360° compass directions, but a vertical needle must point, in effect, only due North (or due South). Imagery is also difficult in the case of the following figure. You have to imagine that each of the lines that is crossed out has been removed from the figure:

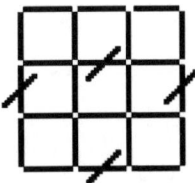

One source of the difficulty is that looking at the figure interferes with your ability to imagine its appearance with the crossed out lines missing. The resulting figure is shown at the end of this section of the chapter.

Does symmetry influence the sequence of tactics that problem solvers adopt? Consider the problem of removing four pieces from the following shape in order to eliminate four squares:

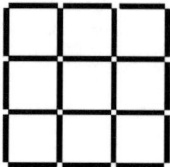

An obvious solution is to remove the symmetrical outer pieces:

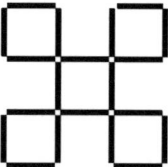

A much less obvious solution is an asymmetrical one:

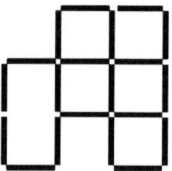

A sequence of the same tactical moves preserves symmetry, and symmetry suggests the use of such a sequence. Indeed, individuals can carry out symmetrical operations in parallel rather than one after the other (pace Newell, 1990). Suppose you are given the following initial shape, and your task is to remove four pieces to eliminate two squares:

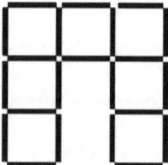

You can envisage removing the two top corners simultaneously:

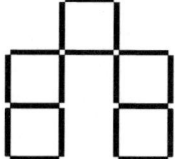

You are quite unlikely to reach the following solution:

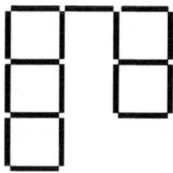

Symmetry is important in solving shape problems. As our unpublished studies show, symmetry makes certain moves salient. If they are indeed part of the solution to a shape problem, the problem is simpler to solve than if they are not part of the solution (Lee & Johnson-Laird, 2003).

The development of strategies

Strategies are the molar units of problem solving, *tactics* are the molecular units, and their underlying perceptual and action *mechanisms* are the atomic units. Tactics alone cannot enable you to solve a complex problem. You have to discover how to combine them into useful sequences that make up a strategy. Van der Henst, Yang, & Johnson-Laird (2002) have investigated how individuals develop strategies in order to make deductive inferences. Our results corroborated the following principle of *strategic assembly*: Naive individuals assemble strategies bottom up as they explore problems using their existing tactics. Once developed, a strategy can control thinking in a meta-cognitive way, i.e., individuals can consciously apply it top down (Van der Henst et al., 2002).

The same principle appears to apply to the development of strategies to solve problems. Hence, in some domains, different individuals are likely to develop different strategies. Likewise, different sorts of problem should inculcate different sorts of strategy. Shape problems, however, are sufficiently simple that the intelligent adults usually converge on a fairly comprehensive knowledge of tactics, which they can use to solve shape problems with few false moves (Lee & Johnson-Laird, 2003).

Instruction has an effect on strategies too. Katona (1940) demonstrated this phenomenon. He tested two groups of participants with shape problems. One group was shown the solution to a few problems, and another group was given a lesson about the relations between numbers of pieces and numbers of squares – a lesson, in effect, about tactics. Only this second group showed a positive transfer to new problems. Yet, for shape problems, individuals are unlikely to develop beyond a multistage strategy in which they use some tactical constraints to generate ideas and other constraints, such as the goal of the problem, to evaluate the outcomes. A deep one-off problem is whether there is a neo-Lamarckian strategy for shape problems, that is, a strategy that solves any shape problem whatsoever without ever making a false move.

Readers familiar with the seminal work of Newell and Simon (1972) may wonder whether a means–ends strategy, in which individuals work backwards from the desired goal, is feasible for shape problems. The answer is: no. The goal state in shape problems is deliberately imprecise. It specifies how many squares should remain, but not how they are arranged. A precise goal with such an arrangement would amount to a solution of the problem. Granted an imprecise goal, it is impossible to use a means–ends strategy. Feasible strategies for shape problems call for a certain amount of working forwards from the initial shape.

An initial strategy that intelligent adults seem to adopt is to work forwards in the way that I sketched in the previous section. As they discover tactical constraints, they adopt them to constrain the possibilities that they envisage. For example, a person whose immediate problem is to remove one piece and thereby eliminate two squares will look at once to see whether the shape contains a *middle* piece. Likewise, a person who has to remove four pieces to eliminate two squares will look to see whether the shape contains two *corners*. A more systematic strategy uses the following sorts of constraint:

- If the number of pieces to be removed is greater than the number of squares to be eliminated, then remove an isolated square, a U-shape, or a corner.
- If the number of pieces to be removed is greater than the number of squares to be eliminated and no further squares are to be eliminated, then remove a loose end or a join.
- If the number of pieces to be removed is smaller than the number of squares to be eliminated, then remove a middle.
- If the number of pieces to be removed is equal to the number of squares to be eliminated, then remove an outer.

Naive reasoners often begin by focusing either on the number of matches to be removed or else the number of squares to be eliminated, and only later realise the need to think about both these numbers at each step.

A more advanced strategy aims to decompose complex problems into tactical moves. It starts by making an inventory of the different sorts of piece in the shape. The shape may contain, for example, four corners (two pieces each), seven middles, and two outers. If the goal is to remove five pieces in order to eliminate three squares, then the solution must satisfy two equations:

5 pieces to be removed = $n_1$2.corners + $n_2$middle + $n_3$outer

3 squares to be eliminated = n_1 + $2n_2$ + n_3

Two simultaneous equations containing three unknowns are ill-formed, i.e., they can have more than one integral solution. Yet, they do constrain the set of possible solutions. One solution, for instance, is $n_1 = 2$, $n_2 = 0$, and $n_3 = 1$. The final stage is to try to construct such a solution. In fact, for problem 3, it yields the familiar answer:

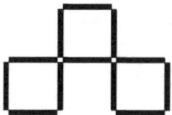

Two difficulties exist for the successful use of this strategy. The first is that naive individuals have to discover how to solve simultaneous ill-defined equations. An insight that yields a solution to this one-off problem is to treat it as an "occupancy" problem, i.e., to compute the different ways in which P pieces can be put into N cells, where P is the number of pieces to be removed, and N is the number of squares to be removed. This step is likely to be beyond many individuals. The second difficulty is that the inventory of a problem can change, not merely quantitatively but also qualitatively, as each piece is removed from a shape. Hence, at each removal step, it is prudent to categorise the remaining pieces in the resulting shape all over again.

One feasible strategy, which I owe to my colleague Uri Hasson, is that individuals think at the level of squares, and so they treat problem (3) as calling for the removal of three squares. There are six squares in the initial shape, i.e., four squares at the corners and a vertical row of two squares in the middle. Hence, individuals think about the different ways of removing individual squares: If they remove three corner squares, they remove six pieces, which fails to solve the problem; if they remove two corner squares and one square in the middle, then they can solve the problem; and if they remove both squares in the middle and one corner square, they can also solve the problem. The details of the solutions, however, call for some careful thought – working forwards from the initial shape – about which particular pieces to remove. We have observed a similar phenomenon: Individuals soon realise that there are higher order configurations than those shown in Figure 1.2. They learn, for example, to remove an E-shape (five matches making up a corner and a U-shape) in a single move (Lee & Johnson-Laird, 2003).

Another sort of strategy depends on reformulating problems. Given problem (3) to remove five pieces and thereby eliminate three squares, a solver can reformulate the problem taking into account the initial shape: Use 12 pieces to make three squares. The tactical knowledge that each isolated square requires four pieces immediately yields the goal of constructing three isolated squares from the initial configuration. This goal in turn yields the familiar solution shown in the preceding diagram.

Still another strategy can be based on a different reformulation of the problem: Remove any five arbitrary pieces, and then move any of the remaining pieces into positions that were previously occupied but that make up three squares. The result of removing the five pieces might be as follows, where the dotted lines show the pieces that were previously in the shape:

It is obvious that moving one or two pieces cannot solve the problem. A move of three pieces, however, can yield the familiar solution illustrated above. A corollary of these observations about strategies is that the verbal framing of a problem may bias individuals to adopt one strategy rather than another (see Van der Henst et al., 2002).

A final note on imagery. The result of removing the lines crossed out in the example earlier in this section is the following shape:

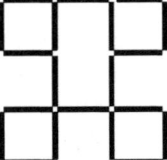

Insight

The previous sections of this chapter have explained how an exploration of problems yields a knowledge of tactics and of ways of sequencing them into problem-solving strategies. The human discovery system appears to lay down a record of the outcome of various operations on problems, and the knowledge cumulates as a result of experience. But what about sudden insights? Do they have no role to play in solving shape problems? Let us consider three further problems:

(4) Given the following shape, remove two pieces to leave two squares with no loose ends (see Levine, 1994, p. 91; Perkins, 2000, p. 111, for versions of this problem):

At first sight, the problem may seem to be impossible, but of course it isn't.

(5) Given the following shape, add two pieces to make five squares, where a square cannot have any pieces inside it:

(6) There are exactly four squares of the same size in a shape. Remove one piece to eliminate all of them with no loose ends.

Before you read on, you should make every effort to solve each of these problems. To solve each of the three problems, most readers are likely to need an insight. The insight for problem (4) is that squares can be of different sizes. This point is normally obvious, but assiduous readers who have tackled all the problems in the chapter may by now have made the tacit assumption that all squares in the solution to a shape problem must be the same size. The solution to problem (4) is indeed the same shape as the starting shape for problem (5): one small square is contained within another larger square. The insight required to solve this problem accordingly calls for you to relax the constraint that all squares are the same size.

Problem (5) is much harder. It depends on a deeper insight. The solution is the following shape:

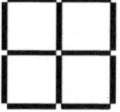

You may object that there are only four squares here, or you may think instead that the fifth square is the large one containing the four smaller squares. This large square, however, is disqualified because the problem specifies that a square cannot contain any pieces inside it. But look closely at the centre of the shape, which is enlarged here:

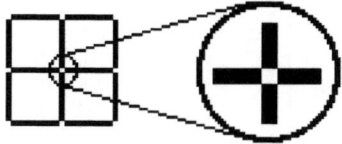

The separate ends of the four pieces meeting at the centre form a tiny square, which is the required fifth one. When I have revealed this solution to people who have given up on the problem, they usually give me the sort of old-fashioned look reserved for perpetrators of a bad pun. Yet, the solution is a genuine one, and it depends on an insight. You have to relax the constraint that only the sides of pieces can be parts of squares: Ends of pieces can make squares too.

At this point, if you have not solved problem (6) then I urge you to try it one last time. Its solution also depends on an insight, which contravenes the nature of all the shape problems that you have so far encountered in the chapter. This solution depends on relaxing the constraint that shapes are two-dimensional. They can also be three-dimensional, and Figure 1.3 shows the required initial shape. If you remove the central vertical piece, then you eliminate all four squares, because they each become a rectangle.

When you have an insight, at one moment you are unable to solve a problem, and then at the next moment you are aware of the solution. The three preceding problems illustrate the present theory's account of insight. It depends on changing the constraints currently governing the problem-solving strategy. The current constraints fail to yield a solution. Indeed, the problem may be provably insoluble given the current constraints. The process of insight accordingly depends on the following steps:

(1)   The current strategy fails to yield a solution.
(2)   There is a tacit consideration of the constraints in the strategy.
(3)   The constraints are relaxed in a new way.
(4)   Many changes in constraints lead nowhere, but, with perseverance, a change may be made that leads at once to the solution of the problem.

For example, the constraint that squares are the same size is relaxed to the constraint that squares can be of different sizes. In some cases, as Kaplan and Simon (1990) argued, the change in constraints can lead to a new representation of the problem. For instance, if squares can be in a three-dimensional arrangement, then four squares (or more) can have a piece in common. Once such an insight has occurred, it may be used henceforth to constrain the generative stage itself: Individuals look at once for a three-dimensional solution when two-dimensional attempts all fail.

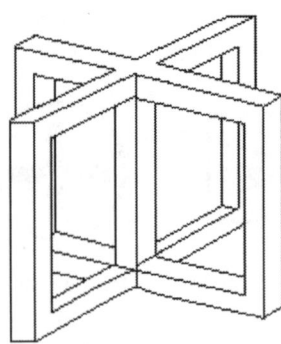

Figure 1.3 A three-dimensional shape that solves problem (6)

Conclusions

This chapter has presented a theory of how people solve problems. According to this theory, as they explore different "moves" in trying to solve a problem, they discover a variety of tactical possibilities. These discoveries can occur even if individuals fail to solve the problem in hand. But once they have acquired a repertoire of tactics, exploration can also lead to the development of a strategy for coping with the problems. The knowledge derived from tactical exploration yields constraints on the process of problem solving. The constraints are used at first in the evaluative stage of thinking. But, this neo-Darwinian strategy is inefficient. Hence, individuals are likely to shift some constraints to the actual generation of ideas to create a multistage strategy. This shift is part of the process of discovering how to solve problems. The problem-solver's dream, however, is to acquire sufficient constraints on the generative process that it never yields any erroneous results. Such a neo-Lamarckian strategy has to be acquired by those who master the improvisation of ideas in real time, e.g., professional jazz musicians (Johnson-Laird, 2002). Whether anyone develops a neo-Lamarckian strategy for shape problems is an open question.

The present theory was illustrated by a series of shape problems, and the reader may wonder whether it also applies to one-off problems, such as Duncker's candle puzzle. For a complex one-off problem, the same process of discovery – yielding a knowledge of tactics – is feasible. But, most one-off laboratory problems call for insight. That is, they are designed so that the problem-solver's initial strategy is almost certain to fail. Insight, on the present account, depends on the discovery of new constraints. They do not always lead to a solution, but when they do yield one suddenly, all the hallmarks of the classic Gestalt phenomenon occur.

The Gestalt psychologists pioneered the study of problem solving. Paolo Legrenzi, to whom this chapter is dedicated, is important because he brought Gestalt ideas into modern cognitive psychology, and showed how they related to mental models (see, e.g., Legrenzi, 1994). The present theory has focused not on this aspect of the representation of problems, but on how individuals acquire tactical knowledge and use it to develop strategic thinking.

Acknowledgements

The research reported in this chapter was supported in part by a grant from the National Science Foundation (Grant BCS 0076287) to study strategies in reasoning. The author thanks Tom Ormerod for many conversations about problem solving, Louis Lee for collaborating in experimental studies of shape problems, Uri Hasson for scholarly advice and thoughts about strategies, and the following colleagues for their helpful criticisms: Vittorio Girotto, Sam Glucksberg, Geoff Goodwin, Cathy Haught, and Sanna Reynolds. He also thanks the participants of the workshop for pointing out some of his errors. And, most of all, thanks to Paolo Legrenzi and Maria Sonino Legrenzi: best friends, outstanding colleagues.

References

Bateson, G. (1979). *On mind and nature*. London: Wildwood House.

Bulbrook, M. E. (1932). An experimental study into the existence and nature of "insight". *American Journal of Psychology, 44*, 409–453.

Campbell, D. (1960). Blind variation and selective retention in creative thought as in other knowledge processes. *Psychological Review, 67*, 380–400.

Chronicle, E. P., Ormerod, T. C., & MacGregor, J. N. (2001). When insight just won't come: The failure of visual cues in the nine-dot problem. *Quarterly Journal of Experimental Psychology, 54A*, 903–919.

Dawkins, R. (1976). *The selfish gene*. Oxford: Oxford University Press.

Duncker, K. (1945). On problem solving. *Psychological Monographs, 58*(5), whole number 270.

Holland, J., Holyoak, K. J., Nisbett, R. E., & Thagard, P. (1986). *Induction: Processes of inference, learning, and discovery*. Cambridge, MA: Bradford Books, MIT Press.

Hopcroft, J. E., & Ullman, J. D. (1979). *Formal languages and their relation to automata*. Reading, MA: Addison-Wesley.

Isaak, M. I., & Just, M. A. (1995). Constraints on thinking in insight and invention. In R. J. Sternberg, & J. E. Davidson (Eds.), *The nature of insight* (pp. 281–325). Cambridge, MA: Bradford Books, MIT Press.

Jansson, D. G., & Smith, S. M. (1991). Design fixation. *Design Studies, 12*, 3–11.

Johnson-Laird, P. N. (2002). How jazz musicians improvise. *Music Perception, 19*, 415–442.

Kanizsa, G., & Legrenzi, P. (1978). *Psicologia della gestalt e psicologia cognitivista*. Bologna: Il Mulino.

Kanizsa, G., Legrenzi, P., & Sonino, M. (1983). *Percezione, linguaggio, pensiero*. Bologna: Il Mulino.

Kaplan, C. A., & Simon, H. A. (1990). In search of insight. *Cognitive Psychology, 22*, 374–419.

Katona, G. (1940). *Organizing and memorizing: Studies in the psychology of learning and teaching*. New York: Columbia University Press.

Keane, M. (1989). Modelling problem solving in Gestalt "insight" problems. *Irish Journal of Psychology, 10* (2), 201–215.

Knoblich, G., Ohlsson, S., Haider, H., & Rhenius, D. (1999). Constraint relaxation and chunk decomposition in insight problem-solving. *Journal of Experimental Psychology: Learning, Memory & Cognition, 25*, 1534–1556.

Köhler, W. (1925). *The mentality of apes*. New York: Liveright.

Köhler, W. (1929/1947). *Gestalt psychology*. New York: Liveright.

Korf, R. E. (1980). Toward a model of representational changes. *Artificial Intelligence, 14*, 41–78.

Lee, L., & Johnson-Laird, P. N. (2003). How individuals learn to solve problems. In preparation.

Legrenzi, P. (1978). Rilettura dei temi della Gestalt in termini di psicologia cognitivista. In G. Kanisza & P. Legrenzi (Eds.), Psicologia della Gestalt e psicologia cognitivista (pp. 165–174). Bologna: Il Mulino.

Legrenzi, P. (1994). Kanizsa's analysis of "prägnanz" as an obstacle to problem solving and the theory of mental models. *Japanese Journal of Psychology*, *36*, 121–125.

Levine, M., (1994). *Effective problem solving* (2nd ed.). Englewood Cliffs, NJ: Prentice Hall.

Luchins, A. S. (1942). Mechanization in problem solving: The effect of einstellung. *Psychological Monographs*, *54*(6), whole number 248.

Luchins, A. S., & Luchins, E. S. (1950). New experimental attempts at preventing mechanization in problem solving. *Journal of General Psychology*, *42*, 279–297.

MacGregor, J. N., Ormerod, T. C., & Chronicle, E. P. (2001). Information-processing and insight: A process model of performance on the nine-dot and related problems. *Journal of Experimental Psychology: Learning, Memory, and Cognition*, *27*, 176–201.

Maier, N. R. F. (1931). Reasoning in humans: II. The solution of a problem and its appearance in consciousness. *Journal of Comparative Psychology*, *12*, 181–194.

Mayr, E. (1982). *The growth of biological thought: Diversity, evolution, and inheritance*. Cambridge, MA: Belknap, Harvard University Press.

Metcalfe, J., & Weibe, D. (1987). Intuition in insight and noninsight problem solving. *Memory & Cognition*, *15*, 238–246.

Newell, A. (1990). *Unified Theories of Cognition*. Cambridge, MA: Harvard University Press.

Newell, A., & Simon, H. (1972). *Human problem solving*. Englewood Cliffs, NJ: Prentice Hall.

Ohlsson, S. (1984a). Restructuring revisited I: Summary and critique of Gestalt theory of problem solving. *Scandinavian Journal of Psychology*, *25*, 65–76.

Ohlsson, S. (1984b). Restructuring revisited II: An information processing theory of restructuring and insight. *Scandinavian Journal of Psychology*, *25*, 117–129.

Orleans, S., & Orleans, J. (1983). *The great big book of pencil puzzles*. New York: Pedigree.

Ormerod, T. C., MacGregor, J. N., & Chronicle, E. P. (2002). Dynamics and constraints in insight problem solving. *Journal of Experimental Psychology: Learning, Memory, and Cognition*, *28*, 791–799.

Perkins, D. N. (1981). *The mind's best work*. Cambridge, MA: Harvard University Press.

Perkins, D. (2000). *The eureka effect: The art and logic of breakthrough thinking*. New York: Norton.

Simonton, D. K. (1984). *Genius, creativity, and leadership: Historiometric inquiries*. Cambridge, MA: Harvard University Press.

Simonton, D. K. (1995). Foresight in insight? A Darwinian answer. In R. J. Sternberg & J. E. Davidson (Eds.), *The nature of insight* (pp. 465–494). Cambridge, MA: MIT Press.

Skinner, B. F. (1953). *Science and human behavior*. New York: Macmillan.

Smith, S. M., & Blankenship, S. E. (1991). Incubation and the persistence of fixation in problem solving. *American Journal of Psychology*, *104*, 61–87.

Van der Henst, J.-B., Yang, Y. R., & Johnson-Laird, P. N. (2002). Strategies in reasoning. *Cognitive Science*, *26*, 425–468.

Weisberg, R. W. (1986). *Creativity: Genius and other myths*. New York: Freeman.

Weisberg, R. W. (1993). *Creativity: Beyond the myth of genius*. New York: Freeman.

Weisberg, R. W. (1996). Prolegomena to theories of insight in problem-solving: A taxonomy of problems. In R. J. Sternberg & J. E. Davidson (Eds.), *The nature of insight* (pp. 157–196). Cambridge, MA: MIT Press.

Wertheimer, M. (1945/1959). *Productive thinking*. Chicago: University of Chicago Press.

2 Insight and self-insight in reasoning and decision making

Jonathan St. B. T. Evans

Introduction

Reasoning and decision making are major topics within the contemporary cognitive psychology of thinking (see Manktelow, 1999, for a recent readable review of these fields). Reasoning research involves studying the ways in which people make explicit inferences from information they are given. Decision research involves asking people to make choices or judgements. Although mostly pursued by different researchers, the two fields are closely connected and confront common issues. For example, in contrast with other areas of cognitive psychology these fields are marked by debate about human rationality. Normative systems for human thought are proposed – such as propositional logic or expected utility theory – and people judged as biased if they fail to conform with them. This has led to major arguments about whether bias implies irrationality (Evans & Over, 1996; Oaksford & Chater, 1998; Stanovich, 1999).

Of more direct relevance to the current chapter, the fields of reasoning and decision making are linked by a debate about whether two distinct mechanisms or styles of thought underlie the behaviour observed. Dual process theories of reasoning have been developing over the past 25 years or so (Evans & Over, 1996; Sloman, 1996; Stanovich, 1999; Wason & Evans, 1975) and have also been discussed in the judgement and decision-making field (Gilovich, Griffin, & Kahneman, 2002; Hammond, 1996). However, related distinctions between thinking that is in some way conscious and sequential on the one hand and unconscious and distributed on the other have appeared many times in the writings of philosophers and psychologists over the centuries. It is not my intention to review these older dual process accounts in this chapter. However, I would like to commence by looking back at some of the earlier contributions to the psychology of thinking, especially those from the Gestalt school in an attempt to draw parallels with the issues that absorb us at the current time.

The psychology of thinking has a long and distinguished history. Debated by philosophers of mind from Aristotle onwards, the subject received much attention from experimental psychologists in the latter part of the nineteenth century and throughout the twentieth century, only eventually being absorbed into the contemporary discipline of cognitive psychology from the 1970s onwards. Introspection was the preferred method of study of the philosophers and early psychologists whose conception of thinking equated it with the mind stuff of consciousness. Yet this stuff of thought proved elusive to the methodology. The systematic introspective experiments of the Wurzburg school at the dawn of the twentieth century often failed to find any conscious thought mediating actions and judgements and sometimes their participants could report only the presence of indescribable feelings (see Humphrey, 1951, for a review of this work). Similarly, Sir Francis Galton's introspective experiments performed on himself led him famously to conclude that the mind was merely a helpless spectator of a huge amount of automatic brain work (Galton, 1879).

The problem of introspection relates to the issue of self-insight to which I shall return. This concerns whether we are able to understand our own behaviour by way of privileged access to our thoughts. Self-insight appears at first sight to be a rather different concept from that of "insight" that was introduced by the Gestalt psychologists working in pre-World War II Germany. We shall see later that the two issues are inextricably entangled.

Gestalt ideas about thinking

Whilst the dominant paradigm of psychology, certainly in American psychology, was that of behaviourism (from the 1920s to the 1950s), Gestalt psychology provided a radically alternative view and one that foreshadowed in many significant ways the cognitive study of thinking developed in the later part of the twentieth century. For example, Duncker's (1945) studies of problem solving anticipated the notions of subgoaling and problem reduction later developed in the information-processing approach of Newell and Simon (1972). Duncker's monograph on problem solving, like much Gestalt writing, was thin on experimental detail and strong on theoretical argument. He relied mostly on what later became known as "think aloud" protocols (Ericsson & Simon, 1984), rather than quantitative analysis, and these were little more than a starting point for his own creative thinking about the processes involved. Generally, Gestalt studies of thinking were supported by minimal quantitative evidence (for example, Maier, 1931) or used methodologies that are subject, in hindsight, to considerable question. However, these methodological shortcomings are of little importance for my present purposes. What we are interested in are the *ideas* of Gestalt psychology and the extent to which these may be relevant today.

The notion of insight (or productive thinking as Wertheimer, 1961, originally published in 1945, preferred) appears in much Gestalt writing about problem solving and is central to their approach. Whilst behaviourists approached thinking from their background in learning, Gestalt psychologists came to it from a study of perception. To solve a problem with insight is to have understanding, but this understanding has a perceptual quality to it. Seeing the relationship of the parts to the whole and productively reformulating the problem are essential ingredients of "good" thinking in Gestalt psychology. "Bad" thinking was of the kind described by the behaviourists – blind, based on trial and error, *lacking* in insight. Gestalt psychologists studied bad thinking as well as good, discovering such fundamental phenomena as *set* (*Einstellung*) and *functional fixedness* (Duncker, 1945; Luchins & Luchins, 1950), characteristic ways in which thought becomes fixated and blind. I will return later to the question of what relation these distinctions bear to contemporary dual process theories of thinking.

How do we find evidence of "insight" according to Gestalt psychologists? One characteristic described was a *sudden* appearance of a solution. This is strongly featured, for example, in the writing of Köhler (1957) in describing his studies of problem solving in apes. The sudden nature of insight was important as the behaviourist opposition described problem solving in terms of trial and error learning processes that were gradual or incremental in nature. A classic example is solving of the "two string problem" as described by Maier (1931). The problem was to tie together two pieces of string hanging from a ceiling. The strings were placed too far apart for the participant to reach one whilst holding the other. The solution of interest was one in which the participant tied a heavy object (for example, a pair of pliers present in the room) to one string and set it in motion like a pendulum. Then moving to the other string, the first string could be caught as its pendulum motion swung it close by.

Maier claimed that the solution usually appeared suddenly and as a complete idea. Moreover, he argued that an effective "hint" for those who were stuck was given by the experimenter brushing against one of the strings and setting it slightly in motion. A number of participants solved the problem shortly after, but none reported noticing the hint. Maier suggested that this was due to the sudden experience of the solution dominating consciousness. It is the idea that we are interested in, not the methodology. (In truth, lack of experimental controls and statistical evaluation means that this study scarcely justifies its many citations as evidence of the effect of unconscious cues in problem solving.) The idea that preconscious process may direct the attention of conscious analytical reasoning processes has certainly been developed in the modern reasoning literature, as in my own "heuristic-analytic" theory (Evans, 1984, 1989).

Whilst the sudden appearance of solutions in consciousness was an important part of the Gestalt idea, it is a difficult criterion to apply to contemporary studies of reasoning and decision making, at least in the great majority of studies where no verbal protocols are collected. A second and more useful criterion of "insight" appears in writings of Wertheimer (1961). In illustrating his idea of "productive thinking", and its contrast "blind thinking", Wertheimer describes a class being taught how to measure the area of a parallelogram (see Figure 2.1(i)). They already know that the area of a

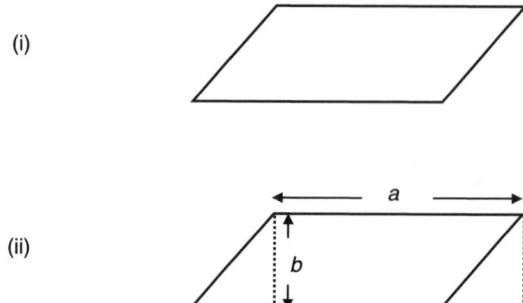

Figure 2.1 Orthodox proof that the area of a parallelogram is equal to $a \times b$ where a is the width and b the vertical height (discussed by Wertheimer, 1961). The dotted lines extended from the top right-hand corner form a triangle with the base line extended to the right which is congruent with the left-hand triangle formed by dropping a perpendicular line from the top left-hand corner of the parallelogram. Students with insight imagine cutting the triangle from the left and moving it to the right to complete a rectangle of known area $a \times b$.

rectangle is the product of the height and width. The teacher tells the children to drop a perpendicular line from the top left-hand corner, extend the base-line to the right and drop a perpendicular from the top right-hand corner to meet it (Figure 2.1(ii)). The teacher then proves that the two triangles created are congruent and that the area of the parallelogram is therefore equal to the rectangular area $a \times b$.

The children proceed to find the areas of parallelograms by this method with a variety of sizes and angles. However, Wertheimer wonders what the children have really learned and whether they have grasped the principle. He therefore draws the parallelogram shown in Figure 2.2(i). The children respond either by saying that they have not been taught how to do this or by applying the original method in a blind way, dropping perpendiculars from the top corners and extending the base line to right, producing the unhelpful figure shown in Figure 2.2(ii). What this shows is that the children have rote learned the proof but failed to understand that one area is compensating for another. If, for example, the parallelograms were cut out of paper and the children allowed to rotate them, cut a triangle off one end and then move it to the other to make a rectangle, they would be much more likely to understand.

The principle for measuring insight that is implicit in Wertheimer's account is that of *transfer*. If the children understood the principle then they should have been able to transfer the method to the new parallelogram, by rotating it or by drawing their additional lines in the appropriate places. Where learning is rote and thinking is blind, people will fail to generalise the principle. In my own experience as a teacher I can relate this to the problem of getting mathematically weak undergraduate psychology students to understand inferential statistics. Weaker students learn the statistical procedures by rote and

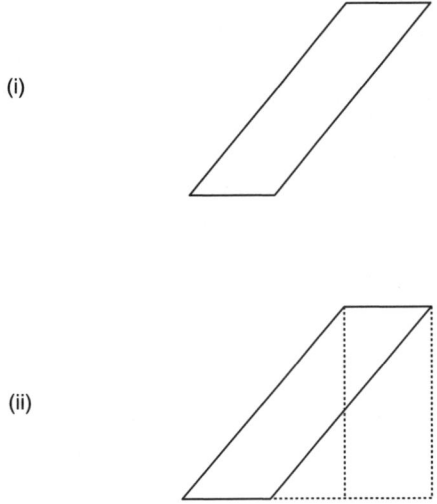

Figure 2.2 If students apply the proof shown in Figure 2.1 to this parallelogram by rote learning then they will drop perpendiculars from the top left and right corners, extend the baseline to the right and be unable to prove that its area is equal to that of the rectangle, as no congruent triangles appear (used by Wertheimer, 1961 to illustrate lack of insight). A student with insight will rotate the parallelogram 90 degrees right and extend the baseline to the *left*.

then, as with Wertheimer's children, fail to recognise their application to problems presented in a slight unfamiliar form.

So far, I have had little to say about *self-insight*. This is the idea that people are aware of their own mental processes and can describe them through verbal reports. The assumption of self-insight was intrinsic to early introspective schools of psychology, but not required by the Gestalt methodology. They demonstrated their cases of insightful and blind thinking by experimental methods and claimed evidence of insight in apes as well as people. Where verbal protocols were used, as in Duncker's (1945) study, they were "think-aloud" protocols of the sort favoured by modern cognitive psychologists and not thought to depend upon the assumption of self-insight in introspective reporting (Ericsson & Simon, 1980, 1984). Indeed, Duncker (1945) argued that causes of insight might be unconscious and unreportable.

Insight and self-insight in reasoning

In this section I will discuss logical reasoning with particular reference to the Wason selection task (Wason, 1966). This is not simply because it is a very extensively researched problem in the psychology of reasoning (for reviews, see Evans, Newstead, & Byrne, 1993; Manktelow, 1999). It is also the case that research on this task has provided more data relevant to the issues of insight and self-insight than other paradigms employed in the study of deductive reasoning. Although a hypothesis testing problem, the Wason selection task is generally regarded also as a test of logical reasoning, and as such one that is remarkable for the very poor performance of most participants who attempt it. In Wason's original task people were shown a pack of cards which had letters on one side and numbers on the other and were told that the following rule applies to four cards selected from the pack and is either true or false:

If there is a vowel on one side of the card, then there is an even number on the other side of the card

They were then shown the four cards lying on a table that on their exposed sides had symbols such as:

E   T   4   7

Note that E is vowel, T a consonant, 4 an even number and 7 an odd number. The task was to decide which cards need to be turned over in order to decide whether the rule was true or false. Wason argued that logically only a card with a vowel and an odd number could disprove the rule and hence people ought to choose the E and the 7. This is generally agreed to be the correct solution provided that people attend to the instruction restricting the application of the conditional to the four cards present in the task. (Some authors, such as Oaksford & Chater, 1994, have suggested that people may interpret that problem as a default case of evaluating a conditional which applies generally, in which case the correct response is debatable.) The E and 7 answer is, however, rarely found and correct solutions are estimated by various authors at 10 per cent or fewer amongst typical university undergraduate participant populations. Common choices are E alone, or E and 4. Since E and 4 constitutes the confirming combination of a vowel with an even number, Wason concluded that most of his participants were falling prey to a confirmation bias.

Now, the question is, do the small number of people who solve the task have *insight*? That is, do they get the problem right for the right reasons and are they aware what these reasons are? An early proposal in the literature was that this was indeed the case (Johnson-Laird & Wason, 1970). That is people who chose correctly understood the falsification principle, whereas those choosing incorrectly lacked insight and followed a faulty verification principle. Early research suggested that this analysis was correct, when insight was measured by people's ability to state explicitly the basis for their card choices. As predicted, correct responders stated that they were trying to falsify the rule and incorrect responders referred to verification (Goodwin & Wason, 1972). The drawback of this method, as later research showed, was that it relied on the assumption of self-insight, that is people's ability to state the true reason underlying their behaviour.

Doubts that correct choices did indeed reflect insight were evinced by research that investigated ways of making the selection task a lot easier to solve. It was discovered quite early on (Wason & Shapiro, 1971) that certain thematic versions of the task might lead to much higher solution rates. These are most reliable when linked to reasoning about rules and regulations, as first demonstrated by Johnson-Laird, Legrenzi, and Legrenzi (1972) using a postal rule. These have become known more recently as *deontic* selection tasks. A well-known example is the drinking age rule (Griggs & Cox, 1982). In this version people are told they are police officers observing people drinking in a bar and asked to check whether the following rule is being obeyed:

If a person is drinking beer then that person must be over 19 years of age.

In this experiment the cards represented drinkers, showing the beverage on one side and the age of the drinker on the other. The four visible sides were:

Beer   Coke   22 years of age   16 years of age

The correct choices map on to those for the original Wason task. People should choose "beer" and "16 years of age" because only discovery of an underage drinker could show that the rule was being violated. Griggs and Cox found a huge level of facilitation, with around 75 per cent correct solutions. So the question is, did this version of the problem give people insight into the task? Griggs (1983) argued that realistic versions of the task did *not* facilitate any process of logical reasoning. Although his review made no reference to Gestalt psychology, he effectively argued that participants lacked insight because they failed to pass the Wertheimer test. Johnson-Laird et al. (1972) had shown that there was no transfer from solving a problem based on a familiar postal rule to the standard abstract task performed after, and the same lack of transfer was later demonstrated with the drinking age problem. This was quite a puzzling result at the time.

The transfer test was also involved in the major argument against the insight model presented by Wason and Evans (1975). Evans and Lynch (1973) had demonstrated a *matching bias* effect in a letter–number version of the task, although one of their main findings had been anticipated by Legrenzi (1970) as follows. Given the rule:

If the card has an A on one side then it has a 3 on the other side

most participants chose the A and 3 cards. However, if a negated consequent was added as in:

If the card has an A on one side then it does not have a 3 on the other side most people still choose the A and the 3 cards. On this second version, how-ever, these choices are logically correct. This rule can only be falsified by finding a card that has an A on one side and a 3 on the other. In both cases people seem to be choosing cards that match those items explicitly referred to in the rules. Evans and Lynch (1973) showed that matching bias affected the selection of antecedent as well as consequent cards, a finding replicated in most but not all later studies (Evans, 1998).

In the early 1970s, I discussed with Peter Wason the apparently conflicting findings of Goodwin and Wason (1972) and Evans and Lynch (1973). There was a genuine puzzle here and its resolution had far-reaching theoretical implications. According to the former paper, people's card choices reflected the degree of insight they held into the falsification principle. According to the latter, people were engaged in a simple matching strategy that seemed to have little to do with reasoning. We came up with a study which could demon-strate matching bias whilst also measuring insight by verbal reports. In this study people attempted one affirmative (If p then q) problem and one nega-tive (If p then not q) problem in a counterbalanced order. The findings were quite clear. Participants predominantly gave matching (p and q) choices on both tasks. Those who completed the negative task first – getting it logically correct – showed *no transfer of performance* at all to the standard affirmative problem presented subsequently.

When the verbal reports were inspected, participants showed the apparent level of insight corresponding to their choices. For example, when given a rule in the form "If A then not 3" most people said they were trying to discover hidden values which could *falsify* the rule – for example: "I am turning over the A card because a 3 on the back would show the rule to be false." The same participant subsequently tackling the affirmative rule might match again and give a classic no-insight response: "I am turning over the A card because a 3 on the back would show the rule to be true." Surely an insight gained could not be so easily lost? Like Griggs (1983) and Johnson-Laird et al. (1972) we had found another case of failure to meet the Wertheimer test.

Wason and Evans (1975) concluded that people were *rationalising* card choices that were actually driven by an unconscious matching bias (see also Evans 1996) and that the verbal reporting of reasons was therefore not a reliable indicator of insight. (Our arguments foreshadowed the famous critique of introspective reporting published by Nisbett & Wilson, 1977.) Thus a paper that was designed to investigate insight turned out to be telling us something important about *self-insight*. Wason and Evans proposed an early version of the dual process theory of thinking that was much developed in years to come (Evans, 1989; Evans & Over, 1996; Sloman, 1996; Stanovich, 1999). That is, there were type 1 (unconscious) processes responsible for behaviour and type 2 (conscious) processes responsible for the verbal reports.

The Wason and Evans (1975) paper gave the impression that conscious thinking was simply rationalising unconsciously motivated behaviour. Later versions of the dual process theory, especially those by Evans and Over

(1996) and by Stanovich (1999), gave a much more substantive role to explicit or System 2 processes as opposed to implicit or System 1 processes. Nevertheless, a methodological problem remains. Whereas psychologists might be able to infer the nature of explicit thought processes from think-aloud protocols, such analysis will be at best incomplete as underlying unconscious causes of behaviour may be unconscious and inaccessible – just, in fact, as Duncker (1945) warned us. Moreover, introspective reports are unreliable because people may use their explicit thinking to theorise about their own behaviour (Nisbett & Wilson, 1977).

Are verbal reports, then, to be taken as reliable indicators of insight (as opposed to self-insight)? Well, yes – and no. If I want to test a student's understanding of an issue (say the mental model theory of reasoning), then I set them an essay or written examination question to test their knowledge. Such verbal accounts should indicate their level of explicit understanding or insight. The self-insight complication is that when we are trying to decide whether an inference or a decision is made *with* insight our attempts to record people's explicit thinking through verbalisations may let us down. What people understand and what they do need not go together. A great snooker player must have a high level of implicit knowledge of the physical reactions of the snooker balls and their interaction with the table. However, I would not expect him to be able to describe the mathematical laws involved any more than I would expect an expert physicist to be able to pot the balls.

Over the years since the studies described above were conducted, there has been much research on the Wason selection task but with little direct reference to the issue of insight. Few studies have used any kind of verbal reporting. Mostly what has been investigated is the many and subtle influences of problem content and context, suggesting subtle influences of pragmatic processes and non-logical processes. Recently, however, a new methodology has been brought to bear which has relevance to our concerns: the investigation of individual differences. Keith Stanovich and Richard West have carried out an extensive research programme to investigate the role of individual differences in cognitive ability and in cognitive style across a wide range of reasoning and decision-making tasks (Stanovich, 1999; Stanovich & West, 2000). One of the studies focused on standard (nondeontic) and deontic versions of the selection task (Stanovich & West, 1998).

Although there have been indications in various studies that performance on the selection task might reflect high ability, Stanovich and West (1998) were the first to carry out a study with psychometrically appropriate sample sizes, bearing in mind that as few as 10 per cent might solve the standard problem. Using SAT scores as a measure of general cognitive ability, they showed that the minority who solve the standard – nondeontic – selection task have much higher scores. Differences were much smaller when correct and incorrect solvers of deontic problems were compared. In fact, when only those who failed to solve the nondeontic version were considered, there was little difference at all. Stanovich and West interpreted these findings with reference to the dual process theory of reasoning presented by Evans and Over (1996). General ability scores reflect differences in System 2 thinking ability – the flexible and general purpose problem-solving system, but are unrelated to System 1 thinking, pragmatic thinking (see also Reber, 1993). Because deontic selection tasks can be solved pragmatically based on experience, they are relatively insensitive to cognitive ability. The standard selection task, however, can only be solved by those who suppress pragmatically cued selections (like matching bias) and use abstract logical reasoning.

If Stanovich and West are right, then it is possible that the minority of people who solve the difficult standard version of the selection task *do* have insight after all. The individual differences results show that they are not guessing or getting lucky. They are, in fact, *reasoning*. Hence, we can say that they are getting the problem right for the right reasons, even though we had no reliable way of telling this from introspective reports. If the dual process theory is right about the explicit nature of such reasoning, then these correct solvers might well be solving the task with insight. On other kinds of reasoning tasks, pragmatic processes might well be expected to interfere with reasoning performance. This is especially true of tasks involving *belief bias* (Evans, Barston, & Pollard, 1983; Klauer, Musch, & Naumer, 2000). Most people when asked to judge whether the conclusion of an argument is logically valid find it very difficult to disregard their prior belief in the conclusion presented. The standard deduction paradigm involves asking people to assume the premises are true, base their reasoning only on these premises and judge whether conclusions follow necessarily from them. These instructions – which have origins in the arguably outmoded view that logic forms the basis for rational thought (Evans 2002) – imply that any influence of prior belief must be regarded as an error. Hence, judging that conclusions which are more believable are more likely to follow is traditionally considered a bias – belief bias.

In general, people will reason on the basis of prior belief if full deductive reasoning instructions are not given. Such instructions, whilst improving logical performance, nevertheless always leave substantial influence of belief bias (Evans, Allen, Newstead, & Pollard, 1994; George, 1995; Stevenson & Over, 1995). Moreover, Stanovich and West (1997) have again shown that ability to resist belief biases is related to general intelligence. Taken together, these results suggest that people may make a conscious strategic effort to reason deductively from the information given when explicitly instructed to do so (Evans, 2000) and succeed to some extent in suppressing pragmatic influences in the process. High ability participants are more likely to succeed in overriding pragmatic responses with those based on formal abstract reasoning.

So what do studies of reasoning tell us about insight in the Gestalt sense? If we equate "insight" with *explicit* understanding, then we might have to conclude that much of the reasoning performance observed in the laboratories is lacking in insight as people are driven by preconscious and pragmatic processes. Such processes are domain sensitive or even domain specific, in that the particular meaning of the content and context and the associated knowledge it elicits can influence directly the responses made. This contrasts with the formal reasoning that the instructions for the tasks require, in which one should attempt to recover the underlying logical structure and base responses only on the form of the argument. I do not think we would wish to use the term "insight" to describe processes of this kind. It would seem that most reasoning is, in the Gestalt sense, blind. We will return to this conclusion after consideration of research on judgement and decision making.

Insight and self-insight in judgement and decision making

It would seem that we can make decisions in two different ways. We can make snap judgements, choosing what "feels" right, or we can engage in conscious deliberation. If judgements are made intuitively then – by definition – they are made without awareness of the processes involved and are lacking in insight. If decisions are made consciously then perhaps they are made with insight. But here again we run into the self-insight problem. Are the reasons people express for their decisions the *real* reasons, or merely rationalisations of some underlying cause?

A great psychological mystery is the popularity of gambling, especially in casinos where the games are mostly of chance (although blackjack has a skill element) and where the odds are fixed in favour of the house. To put it bluntly, all long-term gamblers lose money. There are a variety of theories as to why people persist in gambling in the face of constant loss ranging from psychodynamic approaches through learning theory to cognitive theories. The last tend to emphasise false beliefs that reinforce gambling behaviour, many of which are described by Wagenaar (1988). For example, there are a number of "systems" employed for playing games of pure chance like roulette, all of which incorporate the fallacious belief that one bet can compensate for another, whereas each bet is actually independent and all have an expected loss. It is well established that people misunderstand randomness in ways that support the "gambler's fallacy" although the theoretical explanation for this is controversial (see Falk & Konold, 1997). Even games with a small element of skill like blackjack are accompanied by fallacious beliefs. For example, a common belief is that "a bad player can spoil the game for everyone" (see Wagenaar, 1988, p. 36), even though each player plays independently against the dealer.

These are hardly examples of what Gestalt psychologists would call "good thinking" and yet you could make an argument for "insight" in that gamblers are often explicitly following systems that they can describe. However, it might more appropriately be described as *self-insight* as we would otherwise be describing erroneous decisions as "insightful", something of which the Gestalt psychologists would definitely not have approved. Self-insight simply means that you know what you are doing, not that what you are doing is correct. However, a further interesting point about gambling research relates to the self-insight problem. Can cognitive theories *explain* the paradoxes of gambling behaviour? That is to say, do people gamble because they have false beliefs, or do they have false beliefs because they gamble? It could, for example, be the case that a belief that the player is having a run of bad luck, or that another player is spoiling the game is really *rationalisation* of the gambling behaviour and a justification for continuing.

In reviewing Gestalt work earlier, we noted Duncker's (1945) idea that thinking could be unconsciously directed with solutions appearing in consciousness without awareness of their causes. Although few studies of decision making have employed verbal protocol analysis, there are a number of phenomena reported in the literature that are consistent with Duncker's hypothesis. There are, in fact, numerous demonstrations in the decision-making literature that the framing of problems with identical decision parameters can greatly affect the decisions made. Since the expected utility of the choices is not affected by this problem framing, the variation in decisions is usually regarded as evidence of irrationality.

A number of good examples are discussed by Shafir, Simonson, and Tversk (1993). These authors argue that people make choices where they have reasons to support them, even though this leads to a number of demonstrable violations of the principles of normative decision theory. For example, participants in one group say they would buy an attractively priced video recorder, whereas those in another group shown the same deal together with an equally attractive alternative are inclined to defer making a decision and often end up not buying either. In the second case there are reasons for buying one (good price) and also the other (better quality) which conflict, blocking the decision. Another example arises in a problem (Shafir, 1993) where people are asked in different groups either to choose or to reject options. For example, participants might be asked to imagine that they are holding options on two holiday spots, described as follows:

Spot A	*Spot B*
Average weather	Lots of sunshine
Average beaches	Gorgeous beaches and coral reefs
Medium-quality hotel	Ultra-modern hotel
Medium-temperature water	Very cold water
Average nightlife	No nightlife
	Very strong winds

One group were asked which options they would take up and 67 per cent chose spot B. However, in a separate group asked which option they would *cancel*, only 48 per cent chose B, by cancelling A. This subtle difference in problem framing produces a striking and apparently irrational result. Shafir argued that the Spot B with its variable attributes provides both reasons for preference (sunshine, beaches) and also reasons for rejection (cold water, no nightlife) as compared with A. This result, together with many other phenomena in the decision-making literature, suggests that thinking is being unconsciously directed by subtle pragmatic clues. The account of focusing effects in decision making given by Legrenzi, Girotto, and Johnson-Laird (1993) explains such effects by the argument that people form selective representations (mental models) of problem information inducing them to focus on some information at the expense of others – an account in the spirit of Duncker (1945).

Shafir (1993) refrained from asking participants to state their reasons, due to concern with the problems of interpreting introspective reports identified by Nisbett and Wilson (1977). Had he done so, they would almost certainly have given the reasons that supported their choices. Would this constitute insight, or self-insight? Not insight, because they could hardly be showing understanding of a correct principle in producing such non-normative answers. No more than partial self-insight, either, because they would not be aware that their "reasons" were being manipulated by the experimenter.

An interesting phenomenon in this regard is *hindsight bias*: the tendency to believe after the event that you could have predicted something in advance. In a classic study, Fischoff (1975) gave people an historical battle scenario and asked them to evaluate the probability of the outcome which resulted. What they did not know was that different outcomes (win, loss, stand-off, negotiated peace) were described to different groups. Each group overestimated the prior probability of the outcome that they thought had actually happened, citing selective evidence from the scenario to support their case. For example, if the conventional army won it was because they were well organised, and if the guerrillas won it was because the terrain was hilly and well covered, and so on. This looks like post hoc rationalisation of unconsciously biased behaviour, directly analogous to the selection task behaviour discussed by Wason and Evans (1975). In a later article, Fischhoff (1982) argued that this fundamental hindsight bias makes it hard for us to learn from history and suggested that professional historians often engage in storytelling in which antecedent events are portrayed as leading inevitably to the historically observed outcome. This view seems reinforced by the resistance of most historians to the writing of counterfactual histories (Ferguson, 1997) which speculate on how things might have worked out differently.

There is one tradition of research on judgement and decision making, known as social judgement theory or SJT (Doherty, 1996) where self-insight has been explicitly studied. Using the "lens model" methodology developed by Egon Brunswick (see Doherty, 1996), numerous studies have been conducted to capture people's implicit "policies". The standard methodology involves multicue judgement in which a number of cues are relevant to particular judgements. For example, in a medical diagnosis problem, the cues might give information about a patient's symptoms, medical history, results of diagnostic tests, relevant medical conditions and general demographic data. In response to these multiple pieces of information, the judge is required to make a single wholistic judgement. When a large number of such cases are presented and the responses recorded, it is possible to conduct multiple linear regression from the cues on to the judgements, for each individual judge. The resulting beta weights then reveal what is conventionally termed the implicit *policy*, showing how much weight is given to each cue in the judgement. Whether or not this corresponds with an explicit stated policy is regarded as the self-insight problems in this field. The methodology has been widely applied to a range of expert groups, in particular in the study of medical decision making.

When such studies are conducted, it is quite common for self-reports of cue use to be taken at the end of the study. Comparing self-reports with the beta weights provides a measure of self-insight, that is the correspondence between explicit task knowledge and implicit judgements. Both the methodologies used and a range of typical findings is reviewed by Harries, Evans, and Dennis (2000). Typically self-insight so measured is poor to moderate with fairly low correlations between explicit and implicit cues weights, suggesting that the implicit "policies" are not based upon any set of reasoned principles of which the judge is aware. However, although judges often fail to use cues that they report, they rarely report using cues that are not influencing their judgements (see, for example, Evans, Harries, & Dean, 1995). Also, recognition tests in which judges are asked to pick out their own tacit policy from that of others tend to produce well above chance success rates (Harries, Evans, & Dennis, 2000; Reilly & Doherty, 1992). The issue of self-insight in expert judgement is important for several reasons. First, training of experts such as doctors, may depend heavily on the communication of explicit knowledge via lectures and set reading. If experts rely on implicit judgements that do not directly reflect this knowledge, then they may be both inaccurate and idiosyncratic. Unfortunately, judgement research on expert groups, and especially on doctors, often shows marked differences in tacit policies between experts (Wigton, 1996). Also, if expert judges are not aware of the bases of their judgements, then they may be prone to biases that will prove difficult to detect and eradicate. In fact, research on judgement and decision making, like the work on reasoning, suggests that self-insight is limited at best.

Dual process theory and the problem of insight

How does the Gestalt concept of insight relate to contemporary dual process theories of thinking that were mentioned earlier? These accounts propose two fundamentally different methods of reasoning based on processes that are associative or pragmatic on the one hand and logical and sequential on the other hand (Evans & Over, 1996; Sloman, 1996; Stanovich, 1999). Moreover, it is suggested that these processes reflect two distinct cognitive systems (see also Reber, 1993) which were labelled as System 1 and System 2 by Stanovich (1999). The proposals of Evans and Over (1996) develop and extend the earlier accounts of Wason and Evans (1975) and Evans (1989) in describing

System 1 processes as tacit or implicit and System 2 processes as explicit. Let us develop this distinction a bit more.

Implicit cognitive processes operate unconsciously, posting only their final products into consciousness. It is evident that many of our cognitive processes are of this kind. When someone speaks to us we are aware of hearing their voice and of understanding the meaning of what they say. We have, however, no awareness of the process by which the ear and the brain translate movement of air molecules into sound, sounds into phonemes, and phonemes into words and sentences. We are certainly not aware either of how the syntax and semantics of sentences are processed together with pragmatic and contextual knowledge to deliver the final meaning that we represent. Similarly when we recognise a familiar face we are aware of who they are, not of the many complex visual and inferential processes used to deliver this knowledge from the raw visual input.

What psychologists have less readily recognised is the implicit character of much of our thinking, reasoning and decision making. We often make "intuitive" judgements and decisions on the basis of what "feels" right and in the absence of conscious reasoning or reflection. Dual process theory, however, posits that human beings uniquely possess a second system of thinking and reasoning which is explicit, by which I mean that is makes use of central verbal working memory. Although such thinking is conscious, it is not necessarily accurately reportable, especially when reports are taken retrospectively rather than concurrently, as debated by Nisbett and Wilson (1977) and Ericsson and Simon (1984). This is because the contents of working memory can be rapidly forgotten and because post hoc questioning can often lead to people rationalising or theorising about their own behaviour, in the manner observed by Wason and Evans (1975). Self-insight is also constrained by the fact that much of our cognitive processing is implicit in the first place. For example, in the studies of doctors' decision making referred to above, it seems that doctors may be aware of what information they attend to (contents of working memory) but not of which of this affects their judgements (Harries et al., 2000).

The term "insight" implies "self-insight", that is *explicit* understanding of the basis of one's thinking and reasoning. However, it implies more than this, as we saw when discussing problem gamblers earlier. Insight also implies understanding of the correct principle and the ability to transfer knowledge from one problem to another based on structural similarity. We might also want to add the Gestalt notion of *suddenness* of the appearance of solutions, although I am not convinced that good evidence has ever been offered for this claim. Dual process theory implies that we cannot, by definition, have self-insight when responses are based on System 1 processes. In fact, we can never have better than partial self-insight even when System 2 is engaged, as the attentional focus of System 2 processes is still constrained by System 1.

System 2 is thought to have evolved late and uniquely in human beings (Reber, 1993; Stanovich, 1999) and permits various kinds of *hypothetical thinking* (Evans & Over, 1996; Evans, Over, & Handley, 2003) to occur. We can – and often do – make our decisions based on learning from past experience in System 1, but we *can* – and sometimes do – make decisions with the aid of explicit reasoning about hypothetical possibilities, such as the possible consequences of alternative actions available to us. However, even when we are thinking consciously in this way, the direction of our thoughts is influenced by pre-attentive processes in System 1.

The idea that cognitive biases result from such preconscious cueing of information was the central concept developed by Evans (1989) in the heuristic-analytic theory of reasoning. Essentially, if we think about the wrong aspects of the problem information, or retrieve associative knowledge from memory that does not bear on the logical nature of the problem set, then our inferences and judgements will be biased. Evans (1989) was able to show a number of examples where people have a demonstrable understanding of certain logical principles that they regularly fail to apply when faced with certain logical tasks.

A similar idea lies behind the work of Legrenzi et al. (1993) in their studies of *focusing* effects in reasoning and decision making mentioned earlier. They argued that working memory constraints cause people to represent information highly selectively in mental models and that only the explicit content of these models is then considered when attempting a problem. For example, they asked their participants in one study to decide whether or not they would go to the cinema (or some other specified event) when visiting a foreign city on holiday. Participants were invited to ask questions to gain information relevant to their decision. Almost all the questions asked concerned the specified event – say the quality of singers in an opera – and almost no one asked for information about *alternative* ways they could spend the evening. There is actually a range of evidence to support the idea that people usually consider just one hypothetical possibility at a time when making decisions (Evans et al., 2003).

Gestalt psychologists anticipated some of these ideas, for example, in the notion of unconscious direction of thinking (Duncker, 1945) and in their work on "blind" thinking such as set or *Einstellung* (Luchins, 1942) and functional fixedness (Duncker, 1945). They had the idea here that people could have fixed ways of looking at problems that would inhibit better solutions or creative thinking. For example, in one problem people had to set lighted candles against a wall using only objects available in the room. This could be achieved by pinning boxes to a wall and standing the candles on them. When the candles, tacks and matches were *inside* the boxes, people were less likely to think of using the boxes than if they were lying around empty. The containment function of the boxes became fixed, so that people did not think of using them in another way. This really is quite similar to the idea of focusing or of selective representations by heuristic processes which limit the ability of people to solve problems by analytic reasoning.

From the standpoint of dual process theory, however, the fierce debate between the Gestalt psychologists and the behaviourists can be viewed in a new light. Behaviourists were describing associative learning processes that are now seen as one basis for System 1 thinking, whereas the Gestalt psychologists were emphasising explicit System 2 thinking that may overcome set ways of thinking formed by these associations. If the fundamental and generally adaptive nature of System 1 is as I have described it, we would hardly want to use the Gestalt description of blind or bad thinking to describe it. Nevertheless, we can again find links with contemporary writing on this topic. One is put in mind of Stanovich's (1999) discussion of what he terms the "fundamental computational bias" – the tendency to contextualise all problems at the expense of thinking logically or abstractly. In addition to showing that ability to resist System 1 pragmatics is related to high cognitive ability, Stanovich also showed that dispositional factors, such as cognitive style, are involved. Like the Gestalt psychologists before him, he emphasised the importance of providing education in thinking skills that will assist people to overcome the fundamental computational bias in order to reason effectively in modern society.

As we have already seen, Wertheimer's (1961) transfer test of insight has appeared in the modern literature of reasoning, even if unacknowledged. Another example where it works well is in the study of statistical reasoning and judgement. A series of studies by Nisbett and colleagues, discussed by Evans and Over (1996, Chapter 7) have supported the idea that where explicitly acquired knowledge is transferable, implicit knowledge is not (see also evidence from the literature on implicit learning – Berry & Dienes, 1993; Reber, 1993). For example, where people acquire understanding of the law of large numbers by practical experience in some domain of expertise such as sports coaching it does not generalise to other domains (Jepson, Krantz, & Nisbett, 1983), whereas such statistical knowledge gained from studying formal courses can be applied much more widely (Fong, Krantz, & Nisbett, 1986). Hence, if we equate insight with reasoning that follows rules explicitly, then it does indeed, as Wertheimer (1961) proposed, transfer to other problems involving the same principle.

Conclusions

In this chapter we have seen that Gestalt ideas about thinking are reflected in many ways in the contemporary study of reasoning and decision making. Their writings have both anticipated and influenced modern ideas about problem structuring, preconscious direction of thinking and the distinction between insightful and transferable knowledge on the one hand, and context-specific associate learning on the other. By discussing relationships between Gestalt writing and contemporary dual process theories, we have, however, found reason to question their distinction between good and bad thinking, despite some echoes in contemporary writing. Much behaviour based upon associative learning is adaptive and could even be termed "rational", in the sense of achieving the goals of the organism. This is just as well, since non-human animals are entirely reliant on this form of learning when instinctive behaviours are insufficient. However, in contesting the behaviourist domination of the time and arguing for insightful and productive methods of thinking, the Gestalt psychologists were effectively anticipating the argument that humans have a second distinctive system of thinking (Evans & Over, 1996; Reber, 1993; Stanovich, 1999).

The concept of "insight" has proved somewhat difficult to pin down. It implies solving problems with understanding rather than from habit and seems to correspond roughly to the idea of explicit thinking in dual process theory. Wertheimer's (1961) transfer test of insight is particularly useful and applied in the contemporary literature as we have seen. Much more tricky have been later attempts to infer insight from verbal reports. This is where the self-insight complication comes in. Even when processes are conscious and passing through verbal working memory, people's self-reports of their thinking tend to be both incomplete and misleading, due to post hoc rationalisation. It is therefore to the credit of the Gestalt school that – in contrast with many psychologists preceding them – they neither assumed self-insight nor relied on introspective reports in their studies of thinking.

References

Berry, D. C., & Dienes, Z. (1993). *Implicit learning*. Hove, UK: Lawrence Erlbaum Associates Ltd.

Doherty, M. E. (Ed.) (1996). Social judgement theory. *Thinking and Reasoning, 2*, [2/3].

Duncker, K. (1945). On problem solving. *Psychological Monographs, 58*, whole number 848.

Ericsson, K. A., & Simon, H. A. (1980). Verbal reports as data. *Psychological Review, 87*, 215–251.

Ericsson, K. A., & Simon, H. A. (1984). *Protocol analysis: Verbal reports as data*. Cambridge, MA: MIT Press.

Evans, J. St. B. T. (1984). Heuristic and analytic processes in reasoning. *British Journal of Psychology, 75*, 451–468.

Evans, J. St. B. T. (1989). *Bias in human reasoning: Causes and consequences*. Hove, UK: Lawrence Erlbaum Associates Ltd.

Evans, J. St. B. T. (1996). Deciding before you think: Relevance and reasoning in the selection task. *British Journal of Psychology, 87*, 223–240.

Evans, J. St. B. T. (1998). Matching bias in conditional reasoning: Do we understand it after 25 years? *Thinking and Reasoning, 4*, 45–82.

Evans, J. St. B. T. (2000). What could and could not be a strategy in reasoning. In W. Schaeken, G. De Vooght, & A. d. G. Vandierendonck (Eds.), *Deductive reasoning and strategies* (pp. 1–22). Mahway, NJ: Lawrence Erlbaum Associates, Inc.

Evans, J. St. B. T. (2002). Logic and human reasoning: An assessment of the deduction paradigm. *Psychological Bulletin, 128*, 978–996.

Evans, J. St. B. T., & Lynch, J. S. (1973). Matching bias in the selection task. *British Journal of Psychology, 64*, 391–397.

Evans, J. St. B. T., & Over, D. E. (1996). *Rationality and reasoning*. Hove, UK: Psychology Press.

Evans, J. St. B. T., Barston, J. L., & Pollard, P. (1983). On the conflict between logic and belief in syllogistic reasoning. *Memory and Cognition, 11*, 295–306.

Evans, J. St. B. T., Newstead, S. E., & Byrne, R. M. J. (1993). *Human reasoning: The psychology of deduction*. Hove, UK: Lawrence Erlbaum Associates Ltd.

Evans, J. St. B. T., Allen, J. L., Newstead, S. E., & Pollard, P. (1994). Debiasing by instruction: The case of belief bias. *European Journal of Cognitive Psychology, 6*, 263–285.

Evans, J. St. B. T., Harries, C. H., & Dean, J. (1995). Tacit and explicit policies in general practitioners' prescription of lipid lowering agents. *British Journal of General Practice, 45*, 15–18.

Evans, J. St. B. T., Over, D. E., & Handley, S. H. (2003). A theory of hypothetical thinking. In D. Hardman & L. Macchi (Eds.), *Thinking* (pp. 3–21). Chichester: Wiley.

Falk, R., & Konold, C. (1997). Making sense of randomness: Implicit encoding as a basis for judgement. *Psychological Review, 104*, 301–318.

Ferguson, N. (1997). Virtual history: Towards a "chaotic" theory of the past. In N. Ferguson (Ed.), *Virtual history. Alternatives and counterfactuals* (pp. 1–90). London: Picador.

Fischhoff, B. (1975). Hindsight ≠ foresight: The effect of outcome knowledge on judgement under uncertainty. *Journal of Experimental Psychology: Human Perception and Performance, 1*, 288–299.

Fischhoff, B. (1982). For those condemned to study the past: Heuristics and biases in hindsight. In D. Kahneman, P. Slovic, & A. Tversky (Eds.), *Judgement under uncertainty: Heuristics and biases* (pp. 335–351). Cambridge: Cambridge University Press.

Fong, G. T., Krantz, D. H., & Nisbett, R. E. (1986). The effects of statistical training on thinking about everyday problems. *Cognitive Psychology, 18*, 253–292.

Galton, F. (1879). Psychometric experiments. *Brain, 2*, 148–162.

George, C. (1995). The endorsement of the premises: Assumption-based or belief-based reasoning. *British Journal of Psychology, 86*, 93–111.

Gilovich, T., Griffin, D., & Kahneman, D. (2002). *Heuristics and biases: The psychology of intuitive judgement*. Cambridge: Cambridge University Press.

Goodwin, R. Q., & Wason, P. C. (1972). Degrees of insight. *British Journal of Psychology, 63*, 205–212.

Griggs, R. A. (1983). The role of problem content in the selection task and in the THOG problem. In J. St. B. T. Evans (Ed.), *Thinking and reasoning: Psychological approaches* (pp. 16–43). London: Routledge.

Griggs, R. A., & Cox, J. R. (1982). The elusive thematic materials effect in the Wason selection task. *British Journal of Psychology, 73*, 407–420.

Hammond, K. R. (1996). *Human judgement and social policy*. New York: Oxford University Press.

Harries, C., Evans, J. St. B. T., & Dennis, I. (2000). Measuring doctors' self-insight into their treatment decisions. *Journal of Applied Cognitive Psychology, 14*, 455–477.

Humphrey, C. (1951). *Thinking: An introduction to its experimental psychology*. London: Methuen.

Jepson, D., Krantz, D. H., & Nisbett, R. E. (1983). Inductive reasoning: Competence or skill? *Behavioral and Brain Sciences, 6*, 494–501.

Johnson-Laird, P. N., & Wason, P. C. (1970). A theoretical analysis of insight into a reasoning task. *Cognitive Psychology, 1*, 134–148.

Johnson-Laird, P. N., Legrenzi, P., & Legrenzi, M. S. (1972). Reasoning and a sense of reality. *British Journal of Psychology, 63*, 395–400.

Klauer, K. C., Musch, J., & Naumer, B. (2000). On belief bias in syllogistic reasoning. *Psychological Review, 107*, 852–884.

Köhler (1957). *The mentality of apes* (2nd edn, E Winter, Trans.). New York: Harcourt Brace.

Legrenzi, P. (1970). Relations between language and reasoning about deductive rules. In G. B. Flores d'Arcais & W. J. Levelt (Eds.), *Advances in psycholinguistics* (pp. 322–333). Amsterdam: North-Holland.

Legrenzi, P., Girotto, V., & Johnson-Laird, P. N. (1993). Focusing in reasoning and decision making. *Cognition, 49*, 37–66.

Luchins, A. S. (1942). Mechanisation in problem solving. *Psychological Monographs, 54*, Whole number 182.

Luchins, A. S., & Luchins, E. H. (1950). New experimental attempts at preventing mechanisation in problem solving. *Journal of General Psychology*, 279–297.

Maier, N. R. F. (1931). Reasoning in humans: II. The solution of a problem and its apperance in consciousness. *Journal of Comparative Psychology, 12*, 181–194.

Manktelow, K. I. (1999). *Reasoning and thinking*. Hove, UK: Psychology Press.

Newell, A., & Simon, H. A. (1972). *Human problem solving*. Englewood Cliffs, NJ: Prentice Hall.

Nisbett, R. E., & Wilson, T. D. (1977). Telling more than we can know: Verbal reports on mental processes. *Psychological Review, 84*, 231–295.

Oaksford, M., & Chater, N. (1994). A rational analysis of the selection task as optimal data selection. *Psychological Review, 101*, 608–631.

Oaksford, M., & Chater, N. (1998). *Rationality in an uncertain world*. Hove, UK: Psychology Press.

Reber, A. S. (1993). *Implicit learning and tacit knowledge*. Oxford: Oxford University Press.

Reilly, B. A., & Doherty, M. E. (1992). The assessment of self-insight in judgement policies. *Organizational Behaviour and Human Decision Processes, 53*, 285–309.

Shafir, E. (1993). Choosing versus rejecting: Why some options are both better and worse than others. *Memory and Cognition, 21*, 546–556.

Shafir, E., Simonson, I., & Tversky, A. (1993). Reason-based choice. *Cognition, 49*, 11–36.

Sloman, S. A. (1996). The empirical case for two systems of reasoning. *Psychological Bulletin, 119*, 3–22.

Stanovich, K. E. (1999). *Who is rational? Studies of individual differences in reasoning*. Mahwah, NJ: Lawrence Erlbaum Associates, Inc.

Stanovich, K. E., & West, R. F. (1997). Reasoning independently of prior belief and individual differences in actively open-minded thinking. *Journal of Educational Psychology, 89*, 342–357.

Stanovich, K. E., & West, R. F. (1998). Cognitive ability and variation in selection task performance. *Thinking and Reasoning, 4*, 193–230.

Stanovich, K. E., & West, R. F. (2000). Individual differences in reasoning: Implications for the rationality debate. *Behavioral and Brain Sciences, 23*, 645–726.

Stevenson, R. J., & Over, D. E. (1995). Deduction from uncertain premises. *Quarterly Journal of Experimental Psychology, 48A*, 613–643.

Wagenaar, W. A. (1988). *Paradoxes of gambling behaviour*. Hove, UK: Lawrence Erlbaum Associates Ltd.

Wason, P. C. (1966). Reasoning. In B. M. Foss (Ed.), *New horizons in psychology I* (pp. 106–137). Harmondsworth: Penguin.

Wason, P. C., & Evans, J. St. B. T. (1975). Dual processes in reasoning? *Cognition, 3*, 141–154.

Wason, P. C., & Shapiro, D. (1971). Natural and contrived experience in a reasoning problem. *Quarterly Journal of Experimental Psychology, 23*, 63–71.

Wertheimer, M. (1961). *Productive thinking*. London: Tavistock.

Wigton, R. S. (1996). Social judgement theory and medical judgement. *Thinking and Reasoning, 2*, 175–190.

Part II

Deductive reasoning

3 It's good to be wrong: An analysis of mistakes in relational reasoning

Walter Schaeken and
Jean-Baptiste Van der Henst

Introduction

The difficulty for cognitive scientists is that what they need to hypothesise in order to explain how the mind works is not available to introspection. So, they have to focus on behavioural data. Scientists interested in human reasoning have paid attention to the time it takes for solving a problem (that is, the latencies) and to the answers that reasoners produce. With respect to the latter dependent variable, much attention has been devoted to the rate of correct responses: This rate gives an indication of the difficulty of the problem, which can lead to interesting hypotheses about the underlying reasoning processes. Scientists, however, not only look at the number of correct responses. For instance, numerous studies have examined the type of valid and invalid responses in syllogistic reasoning, discovering that the figure of a syllogism affects the form of the conclusions that reasoners draw, accuracy, and speed (e.g., Johnson-Laird & Bara, 1984)

Strangely, such an analysis of the nature of the valid and invalid responses is absent in the field of relational reasoning. In the present chapter, we want to address this topic. First, we give a brief account of two theories of relational reasoning. Next, we discuss the issue of cognitive economy in reasoning. This will lead to a first experiment about task instructions and an indeterminacy-shortcut strategy. Finally, we describe two experiments that investigate the type of invalid responses to problems for which the correct response is "nothing follows".

Two views of relational reasoning

Many daily deductions depend on relations between things. Suppose you want to make sure that every child in a theatre can easily see the stage. You know that Anna and Candice are sitting in different rows, but in the same seat number, i.e., one of them is seating in front of the other. You also know:

Anna is smaller than Berta.
Berta is smaller than Candice.

On the basis of this information you can infer that Anna is smaller than Candice, so you will place Anna in the seat in front of Candice and not the other way round. People easily make such transitive inferences. There are other sorts of relational inferences (intransitive, e.g., with the relation "father of" and non-transitive, e.g., with the relation "next to"), but in this chapter, we focus solely on transitive inferences.

Early research on transitive relation inferences concerned so-called *three-term series* problems. These are problems in which three terms are introduced, as in the previous example. This approach led to a debate between two views. According to the linguistic model (see, e.g., Clark, 1969a, 1969b), reasoning relies on linguistic principles, and the type of relational terms used in the premises is the main factor of interest. The main idea is that the more difficult it is to represent the information in the problem, the harder the reasoning process is. This approach can be seen as an early precursor to inference-rule theories (e.g., Braine & O'Brien, 1998; Rips, 1994). According to the competing view, i.e., the analogical approach (e.g., DeSoto, London, & Handel, 1965; Huttenlocher, 1968), people construct a representation of the premises, which is isomorphic to the situation portrayed in the premises. Characteristically, this representation takes the form of a mental spatial array that linearly orders the items mentioned in the premises in a way that corresponds to the situation described in the premises. For instance, the information in the previous problem could be mentally represented in the following manner:

Anna
Berta
Candice

All the information is integrated and stored in a single representation. Consequently, reasoning is nothing more than constructing such an integrated representation of the premises and describing it. The difficulty of the reasoning process is mainly determined by the difficulty of the construction of the integrated representation. This approach can be considered as a precursor to the mental model theory (MMT) (Johnson-Laird, 1983).

Although both views anticipated fundamentally different representation and reasoning processes, their predictions turned out to be similar. Therefore, Byrne and Johnson-Laird (1989) took a different route. They designed problems for which the theories are susceptible to make different predictions. We will now describe these new sorts of problems and the adapted theories, starting with the mental model theory.

Consider *Problem 1*:

A is to the right of B
C is to the left of B
D is in front of C

E is in front of A
What is the relation between D and E?

According to Byrne and Johnson-Laird (1989), reasoners first construct a model of the situation referred to by the premises (the model construction stage). Next they formulate a putative conclusion on the basis of this model (the conclusion construction stage). Finally, reasoners search for a falsifying model, that is a model consistent with the information in the premises, but inconsistent with the putative conclusion (the conclusion validation stage). If they find such a model, they return to the second stage. If they do not find such a model, the putative conclusion is accepted as a valid conclusion. Hence, for the example above, the reasoner should construct the following model:

   C B A
   D   E

On the basis of this model it can be inferred that "D is to the left of E" (or "E is to the right of D"). Next, the reasoner tries to falsify this initial conclusion by attempting to build another model compatible with the premises. However, there is no such model; Problem 1 is then called a "one-model" problem and the initial conclusion can be considered as the final conclusion.
   Consider now *Problems 2* and *3*:

Problem 2	*Problem 3*
B is to the right of A	B is to the right of A
C is to the left of B	C is to the left of B
D is in front of C	D is in front of C
E is in front of B	E is in front of A

What is the relation between D and E?

For *Problem 2*, a first model can be built:

   C A B
   D   E

that supports the conclusion "D is to the left of E". However, another model is also compatible with the premises:

   A C B
      D E

However, both models support the same conclusion "D is to the left of E". *Problem 2* is a multiple-model problem. For *Problem 3*, there are also two models, but they do not lead to the same conclusion:

C   A   B   A   C   B
D   E   E   D

Hence, there is no determinate answer and *Problem 3* is called a "no-valid-conclusion" problem.

Given the basic assumption of the model theory (the greater the number of models, the harder the problem), *Problem 2* should be more difficult than *Problem 1*. Moreover, *Problem 3* should be more difficult than *Problem 2* because it necessarily calls for the construction of two models in order to reach the correct answer. Additionally, one has to cope with the inconsistency between the two constructed models concerning the question, which should also make the reasoning harder.

Following Hagert (1984), Byrne and Johnson-Laird outlined a possible rule-based approach to solve these relational problems They argued that such a theory should make the reverse prediction with respect to one-model and multiple-model problems. In order to solve *Problem 1*, reasoners must infer the relation between the pair of items to which *D* and *E* (the items in the question) are directly related. In order to make this inference, they must use a meaning postulate that captures the transitivity of the relations in the premises. Multiple-model problems such as *Problem 2* do not require the use of such a meaning postulate. The first premise is irrelevant, and the second explicitly shows the relation between the pair of items to which *D* and *E* are related. Therefore, according to the rule-based theory, *Problem 2* should be easier than *Problem 1*.

The results in the literature (Byrne & Johnson-Laird, 1989; Carreiras & Santamaria, 1997; Roberts, 2000a; Schaeken, Girotto, & Johnson-Laird, 1998; Schaeken & Johnson-Laird, 2000; Schaeken, Johnson-Laird, & d'Ydewalle, 1996a, 1996b; Vandierendonck & De Vooght, 1996) clearly corroborated the predictions of the model theory: One-model problems are easier than multiple-model problems; no-valid-conclusion problems are the hardest. These findings caused the diminution of the debate between a rule-based approach and the model theory in the field of relational reasoning: At the moment, there are almost no psychologists defending a rule approach for relational reasoning. However, Van der Henst (2002) has argued that one could conceive a rule-based approach able to accommodate the greater difficulty of *Problem 2* over *Problem 1*.

Notwithstanding the support for the model theory, some aspects of the theory need to be completed (see Schaeken, Van der Henst, & Schroyens, in press). We will focus on some of them, whereby we use cognitive economy as a starting point. Furthermore, our focus of analysis will not be the correct answers, but the mistakes. We believe that an analysis of the mistakes can reveal new aspects of relational reasoning.

Cognitive economy and relational reasoning

The view that people try to economise their cognitive resources is robustly established in cognitive psychology. Granted that human beings have limited cognitive resources, a principle of economy must govern cognitive processes.

According to the traditional accounts of the model theory, reasoners aim at elaborating an exhaustive representation by constructing (sequentially or simultaneously) all the models compatible with the premises. When they construct only a subset of the possible models, it is due to the limitation of their cognitive resources. With cognitive resources of greater capacity, more models could be built and the representation would be richer. According to the hypothesis that cognitive processes are driven, to some extent, by a principle of cognitive economy, reasoners aim at solving a problem by maximising cognitive efficiency (see for instance the first principle of relevance by Sperber & Wilson, 1986); that is, deriving a sound and useful conclusion in an economical way. We acknowledge that we stay rather vague with respect to the principle of economy. One more precise view on the principle of cognitive economy is that it is explicitly represented in the mind and used to control processing. Another view is that, as a result of innate factors and/or experience, cognitive processes develop so as to maximise efficiency. In the latter case, efficiency occurs as a result of how processes operate but with no recourse to an explicit principle that guides them to be economic. In the present chapter, we take no decision between these two options.

The search for economy can occur in several ways. We have investigated the possibility of isomeric models The starting point of our analysis in terms of cognitive economy is the observation that some multiple-model problems contain an irrelevant premise. Consider *Problem 2* again. You do not need the first premise in order to solve the problem. Or, in a stronger formulation, if you do not take into account the information in the first premise, the multiple-model problem changes into a one-model problem. However, the trouble is that the participants cannot know in advance that this premise is irrelevant and have no reason to avoid taking it into account (Van der Henst, 2002).

We have argued that it is possible to represent all the information conveyed in *Problem 2* without redundancy (Schaeken et al., in press). Indeed, if one constructs two complete models from *Problem 2*, most of the information in the second model is already present in the first one. Our claim is that when an indeterminacy is encountered, as in *Problem 2*, rather than constructing two fully explicit models, some people construct a single model which captures the indeterminacy. We call this new kind of mental model, an *isomeric mental model*. The isomeric mental model of *Problem 2* could be depicted in the following manner:

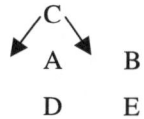

A single model is constructed and the two arrows, which correspond to the annotated part of the model, indicate inside this model that there is an indeterminacy between C and A. The construction of a *single* isomeric model, rather than *two* fully explicit models, provides an illustration of the idea of cognitive economy. An isomeric model contains as much relevant information as two fully explicit models but contains no redundant information as compared to two fully explicit models. However, as suggested by Phil Johnson-Laird (personal communication), the representation of isomeric mental models should call for additional machinery that is not necessary for the representation of standard models. Hence, in supporting the idea of isomeric mental models we trade a greater cognitive economy for a more cognitive complex machinery involving greater load on processing. Our experiments aim at *knowing* whether or not people do construct isomeric mental models.

We gave participants spatial reasoning problems and allowed them to use external aids while they were performing the task. These external aids were either paper and pencil or real instances of the objects named in the problems. An analysis of the diagrams (written or constructed) provided evidence for the existence of such isomeric models.

Another way of being economical consists in using shortcut strategies. Some studies have indeed shown that participants are prone to develop such heuristics when they are highly experienced with problems. Quinton and Fellows (1975) report five shortcut heuristics that participants develop with three-term series problems such as: "Les is bigger than James, Les is smaller than Paul. Who is the smallest?" For instance, the "second premise strategy" consists in applying the question only to the first premise of three-term series problem. If the answer obtained is not present in the second premise, as in the example, then it is treated as the correct answer. Similarly, Wood (1969; Wood, Shotter, & Godden, 1974; see also Johnson-Laird, 1972) shows that after repeated experience with the problems, participants elaborate strategies that rely only on the formal property of the premises but not on their meaning. For instance, with the following premises and question:

> D is taller than E
> C is taller than D
> A is taller than C
> A is taller than B
> B is taller than C
> Who is the taller: B or E?

you can construct a mental model of the premises and answer the question on the basis of this model. But you can also notice that on the one hand B appears once on the left-hand side (i.e., as subject) and once on the right-hand side, but that on the other hand E appears only on the right-hand side. Therefore, B must be the taller. This strategy requires much less effort, and so it is more economical than constructing a mental model. However, the drawback of this strategy is that when the premises have disappeared it is impossible to answer an unexpected question about another relation (see Wood et al., 1974). Hence, an economical shortcut heuristic may be too specialised.

A shortcut strategy is also likely to occur with indeterminate problems that do not support any valid conclusion, such as the following problem: "John is taller than Bob. John is taller than Pete. Who is the shortest?" The correct answer is "no valid conclusion", because you know only that John is the tallest of the three. All "no-valid-conclusion" problems have in common that one relation is indeterminate. Consequently, a possible shortcut heuristic could be that, as soon as reasoners detect an indeterminacy in the problem, they respond: "no valid conclusion". Again this strategy is economical and appropriate for no-valid-conclusion problems, but it is misleading for multiple-model problems that do have a valid conclusion. Clark (1969b) noticed that when participants deal with an indeterminate problem that has a valid conclusion such as: "John is taller than Bob. John is taller than Pete. Who is the tallest?" they tend to answer "nothing follows" because of the indeterminacy. According to Clark, this response occurs because participants do not take enough time to consider the question. They rapidly identify such a problem as an indeterminate one and consequently answer "nothing follows".

In the following section, we report some experimental investigations of such an indeterminacy-shortcut strategy. We examine whether such a strategy can be triggered by manipulating the instructions.

Task instructions and an indeterminacy-shortcut strategy

Schroyens, Schaeken, and Handley (2003) demonstrated that people are more likely to reject invalid inferences when the instructions stress that they are to do so. This sort of procedure was used to investigate the existence of an indeterminacy-shortcut strategy in relational reasoning.

The inspiration for our first experiment was found in a study by Roberts (2000a), which demonstrated a larger difference between one-model and multiple-model problems (e.g., Expt 1, 78 per cent vs. 55 per cent) than traditionally found. Additionally, in this experiment the "no-valid- conclusion" problems were not solved reliably worse than the multiple-model problems with valid conclusions (53 per cent vs. 55 per cent). In most other studies, however, the "no-valid conclusion" problems were solved significantly worse than the multiple-model problems with valid conclusions.

We need to discuss two aspects of the Roberts study in order to give a fair treatment of his theory and data. First, the data we presented here are data from the condition in which all the information was presented simultaneously. Roberts (2000a) was the first study that investigated systematically whether task format (sequential vs. simultaneous presentation) is an important variable for relational reasoning. On the basis of three experiments, Roberts concluded that although multiple model construction is a robust and frequent strategy, changing presentation can result in qualitative changes: It appears that simultaneous presentation leads to a much greater occurrence of multiple-model construction than sequential presentation. Second, Roberts manipulated the instructions. It was this aspect that inspired us. In the instructions of his Experiment 1, Roberts explicitly mentioned that for some problems "no valid conclusion" was the correct answer. In contrast, in most other experiments the participants are instructed that if they thought there was no definite answer, they could write that down as their answer, but they were not told that it is the correct answer for some problems. In the present experiment we will investigate whether or not instructing participants that "no valid conclusion" is a valid conclusion for some problems does influence reasoners.

It might be the case that instructing participants that no valid conclusion is the correct answer for some problems prompts participants to look for a systematic way to identify such problems. Hence, in applying this economical heuristic participants may increase their chances of answering no-valid-conclusion problems correctly, but they also increase their chances of answering incorrectly to multiple-model problems by responding "nothing follows". We investigated this hypothesis by manipulating the task instructions in an experiment in which there were two groups. We told one group of participants (N = 40 undergraduate students at Leuven University) that "nothing follows" was a valid conclusion for some of the problems (the "nothing follows" group). We only told the other group (N = 20 undergraduate students at Leuven University) that they could respond "nothing follows" if they thought that there was no definite answer (the control group), but we did not indicate whether it was ever a correct answer. The premises of each problem were presented simultaneously.

If reasoners use a shortcut heuristic in the "nothing follows" group, they should not respond to multiple-model problems significantly better than to no-valid-conclusion problems. But, there should be such a difference in the control group. Moreover, the type of incorrect answers should be different in the two groups: We should observe a higher rate of "nothing follows" answers for multiple-model problems in the "nothing follows" group than in the control group. Each of the participants received three one-model problems, three multiple-model problems, and three no-valid-conclusion problems. Table 3.1 presents an example of each of the three sorts of problems. All the items mentioned by the premises were fruits or vegetables starting with different letters for a given set of premises. The problems were presented in a random order to each participants.

The percentages of correct responses for the different problems are shown in Table 3.2.

In the "nothing follows" group, one-model problems were easier than multiple-model problems (75 per cent vs. 57 per cent; Wilcoxon's $T = 60.5$, $n = 26$, $p < .005$), and they were easier than the no valid conclusion problems

Table 3.1 An example of each of the three sorts of problems in Experiment 1

Problem type	One-model problem	Multiple-model problem	No-valid-conclusion problem
Premises	The apple is to the left of the kiwi.	The lemon is to the left of the pear.	The lemon is to the left of the tomato.
	The lemon is to the right of the kiwi.	The pear is to the right of the tomato.	The tomato is to the right of the kiwi.
	The pear is in front of the apple.	The apple is in front of the tomato.	The pear is in front of the kiwi.
	The tomato is in front of the lemon.	The kiwi is in front of the pear.	The apple is in front of the lemon.
	What is the spatial relation between the pear and tomato?	What is the spatial relation between the apple and the kiwi?	What is the spatial relation between the pear and the apple?
Correct conclusion	The pear is to the left of the tomato.	The apple is to the left of the kiwi.	No valid conclusion

Table 3.2 The percentages of correct responses in Experiment 1

	One-model problems	Multiple-model problems	No-valid-conclusion problems	Overall
"Nothing follows" group	75	57	67	66
Control group	82	72	60	71

(75 per cent vs. 67 per cent), but the difference was no significant. But as predicted, multiple-model problems were not answered better than no-valid-conclusion problems (57 per cent vs. 67 per cent), and there was a tendency for more correct responses to no-valid-conclusions than to multiple-model problems.

In the control group, one-model problems (82 per cent) were almost significantly easier than multiple-model problems (72 per cent; Wilcoxon's $T = 9$, $n = 9$, $p < .06$) and they were significantly easier than the no valid conclusion problems (60 per cent; Wilcoxon's $T = 12$, $n = 14$, $p < .05$). The multiple-model problems were easier than the no-valid-conclusion problems, but not significantly (72 per cent vs. 60 per cent; Wilcoxon's $T = 24$, $n = 13$, $p < .07$).

In the "nothing follows" group, participants probably erred more on multiple-model models because of the use of an economical shortcut heuristic, which led them to answer "nothing follows" as soon as they detected an indeterminacy. The difference between the one-model and multiple-model problems was larger in the "nothing follows" group (75 per cent vs. 57 per cent) than in the control group (82 per cent vs. 72 per cent), but the difference was not significant. However, if reasoners erred on the multiple-model problems, they answered significantly more often with "nothing follows" in the "nothing follows" group than in the control group (87 per cent vs. 65 per cent; Mann-Whitney $U = 294$, $n1 = 40$, $n2 = 20$, $p < .05$).

The general pattern is in line with our predictions. In the control group, one-model problems were easier than multiple-model problems (but not significantly), and the latter were easier than no-valid-conclusion problems. The "nothing follows" group, were told that "nothing follows" was sometimes a valid answer. We hypothesised that if reasoners follow an economical shortcut strategy, they would be less inclined to unravel the indeterminacy and more likely to conclude that nothing follows. This response is, of course, incorrect in the case of multiple-model problems. Although the difference between one-model and multiple-model problems in the control group was smaller than in the "nothing follows" group, the difference failed to reach significance. However, there were more "nothing follows" answers for the multiple-model problems in the "nothing follows" group than in the control group. Therefore, we can conclude that we observed a small but genuine effect of the instructions. If you explicitly inform reasoners that "nothing follows" is a valid answer, some of them will use a shortcut heuristic: When they notice an indeterminacy, they will automatically decide that there is no definite answer to the question and conclude "nothing follows".

We want to emphasise that we believe instructions can only partly change reasoning strategies. Schroyens et al. (2003) demonstrated this. Additionally, Roberts (2000a) clearly established this in his second experiment (in which only one-model and multiple-models were presented and in which he instructed participants that all problems had a valid conclusion) and his third experiment (in which only one-model and no-valid-conclusion problems were presented, and in which he explicitly told participants that an ambiguous layout meant that there would be no valid answer): These manipulations had almost no effect. Finally, in our experiment, we did not observe a significant difference on the multiple-model problems between the two conditions. Nevertheless, we observed a shift in the nature of the mistakes on the multiple-model problems: Less normal wrong conclusions (e.g., "left" instead of "right"), but more "nothing follows" in the "nothing follows" group. This observation, although small, shows the importance of an analysis of the nature of mistakes. These mistakes reveal that strategies play a role in deductive reasoning. Roberts (2000b) stated that current theories of deductive reasoning have often neglected the topic of strategies, unlike theories concerning other domains (for an overview, see Schaeken, De Vooght, Vandierendonck, & d'Ydewalle, 2000). Experiment 1 shows that certainty in instructions can trigger a shortcut strategy. Reasoners use this strategy independently from the underlying reasoning mechanism. Hence, if such a strategy often occurs in an experiment, its use might obscure the data: Psychologists might conclude that multiple-model problems are as difficult as no-valid-conclusion problems and question the correctness of the mental models' predictions.

Mistakes on no-valid-conclusion problems

The previous section showed that an analysis of the mistakes supports the existence of strategies that bypass the underlying deductive reasoning mechanism. In the present section, we present an analysis of mistakes to no-valid-conclusion problems, which provides evidence about how this mechanism works. Following the analysis in our introduction, we consider in more depth the mental model theory.

The correct response to no-valid-conclusion problems is indeed that there is no valid answer. Nevertheless, a significant proportion of reasoners infer a determinate relation between the two elements in the question. Experimenters typically treat these responses as wrong and do not look further. However, an analysis of these mistakes elucidates the process of building mental models. Consider the problem:

A is to the left of B
C is to the left of B
D is in front of C
E is in front of A
What is the relation between D and E?

On the basis of the first premise, reasoners can construct the following model:

A   B

Unlike the second premise of a one-model problem (which calls for the continuation of the constructed model), the second premise of the no-valid-conclusion problems and multiple-model problems in the present studies calls for the construction of two models. But if reasoners do not construct the two models, how do they tackle the continuation of the existing model?

A straightforward method is to keep the initial model (as a sort of firm foundation) and to put the new item outside (i.e., to the left or to the right of) the two items in the initial model. In this way, the first two items will not be separated by the new item in the second premise. In the preceding example, this procedure leads to the following continuation of the firm foundation of the initial model:

C   A   B

and consequently to the following final model of all the premises:

C   A   B
D   E

This strategy, which we call the "cutting avoidance" procedure, leads to the incorrect determinate conclusion that D is to the left of E.

According to an alternative pragmatic account, suggested to us by Guy Politzer and Ira Noveck, the speaker who communicates the premises is expected to describe the spatial configuration of items in the most appropriate way to the hearer. One could view the premises as an online description by a speaker of a spatial configuration. Imagine that a speaker observes a spatial configuration of items and wants to describe it to the hearer by using spatial expressions such as "to the left of", "to the right of", and "in front of". Initially, the configuration is:

A   B

The speaker can describe this configuration to the hearer by saying that A is to the left of B (or B is to the right of A). Then, a new item, C, occurs so that the configuration is now:

C   A   B

The speaker has two options to describe the configuration to the hearer: One consists in stating the relation between C and A by saying that C is to the left of A; the other consists in stating the relation between C and B by saying that C is to the left of B. However, the second possibility (which occurs in our no-valid-conclusion problem) yields an indeterminate relation between A and C (C could be to the left or to the right of B). The most appropriate way to convey the configuration to the hearer is to choose the first option, which is less ambiguous. Hence, in the context of the premise "A is to the left of B", the subsequent premise "C is to the left of B" conveys a conversational implicature (Grice, 1975) that C is not to the left of A, or, in other words, that C is to the right of A. In short, the indeterminate premises implicate the incorrect determinate conclusion that E is to the left of D.

In sum, we can gain insight into the construction of models from an analysis of the invalid determinate conclusions that reasoners draw from no-valid-conclusion problems. The cutting avoidance procedure uses the initial model constructed from first premise as a foundation, and nothing will be entered in between the items in the model. In contrast, according to the pragmatic hypothesis, reasoners use the first premise as the context in which they interpret the next premise. This context leads to inserting the new element in between the two items in the existing model in the case of no-valid-conclusion problems.

We tested these contrasting hypotheses in two experiments. In Experiment 2, we presented 24 participants (Flemish volunteers with a varying background) with 16 problems, containing four premises. Their task was to answer a question about the two items introduced in the last two premises (i.e., What is the relation between D and E?). There were eight filler items: four one-model problems and four multiple-model problems. There were eight experimental problems, that is eight no-valid-conclusion problems. Four versions of each problem were constructed in the following way: The spatial relations ("to the left", "to the right") in the first and second premise were systematically manipulated so that in one version both premises contained "to the left", in a second version the first premise contained "to the left" and the second "to the right", in a third version the first premise contained "to the right" and the second "to the left", and in a fourth version both premises contained "to the right". From each of these four versions, we constructed a further version in which we switched round the terms in the subject and object keeping the same relational term, i.e., a so-called "mirror" version of the problem. Table 3.3 presents two examples: a left-left problem and its mirror version.

In this experiment, 45 per cent of the no-valid-conclusion problems were solved incorrectly. Of the mistakes, 69 per cent followed the cutting avoidance procedure and 31 per cent followed the pragmatic procedure (Wilcoxon's $T = 22$, $n = 14$, $p < .05$).

In order to get more direct evidence about the nature of the models, we asked participants to draw a diagram of the information in the premises. Various authors, including Huttenlocher (1968) and Larkin and Simon (1987), have proposed that external and internal spatial representations can be viewed as equivalent. Likewise, several researchers (e.g., Bucciarelli & Johnson-Laird, 1999; Van der Henst, Yang, & Johnson-Laird, 2002) also presented participants with paper and pencil and used these data to infer aspects of internal reasoning strategies. We made the supposition that the construction of external diagrams could give some insight about the internal construction of mental models.

In Experiment 3, 35 students from the University of Lyon were assigned to two groups. In the Question group, 17 participants were presented with 16 problems. Among them were four experimental problems. In the Diagram group, 18 participants were presented with the same spatial descriptions but instead of answering a question, their task was to draw the first diagram that came to their mind as they read the premises. They were asked to draw only one diagram even when the premises were compatible with two models.

Table 3.3 Two examples of the no-valid-conclusion problems used in Experiment 2

Problem 1	**Problem 2**
The apple is to the left of the kiwi.	The kiwi is to the left of the apple.
The apple is to the left of the pear.	The pear is to the left of apple.
The lemon is in front of the kiwi.	The lemon is in front of the kiwi.
The tomato is in front of the pear.	The tomato is in front of the pear.
What is the spatial relation between the lemon and the tomato?	What is the spatial relation between the lemon and the tomato?

The no-valid-conclusion problems were similar to those in Experiment 2, but the filler items included four no-valid-conclusion problems and eight one-model problems.

In the Diagram group, 60 per cent of the participants' diagrams followed the cutting avoidance procedure and 26 per cent followed the pragmatic procedure. This finding supports the results of Experiment 2: The evidence points towards the cutting avoidance procedure (Wilcoxon's $T = 21$, $n = 18$, $p < .05$). Therefore, the cutting avoidance procedure may be used by reasoners to continue an existing model in the case of an indeterminacy. Yet this conclusion must be tempered by the fact that the Question group did not perform in line with the previous two sets of data.

In the Question group, there were 60 per cent determinate conclusions to the no-valid-conclusion problems. Of these mistakes, 49 per cent followed the cutting avoidance procedure and 51 per cent followed the pragmatic procedure. In other words, there was no significant difference between the two procedures.

Why did we observe this difference? There are two possible explanations. One reason for the observed difference might be the number of mistakes. Experiment 2 and the Question condition of Experiment 3 are the most comparable: The experimental problems presented to the participants are the same and the task of the participants is also the same. However, there is a huge difference in the number of correct responses. In Experiment 2 there are 55 per cent correct responses, while in the Question condition of Experiment 3 only 16 per cent of the responses were undoubtedly valid (apart from the clear mistakes, there were also 24 per cent vague responses). The higher number of correct responses in Experiment 2 might be an indication of higher cognitive capabilities of these participants. It has been argued that more intelligent reasoners have the capability to decontextualise (e.g., Stanovich & West, 2000), that is, they can suppress pragmatic influences and solve problems by explicit reasoning (Evans, 2000). In other words, future research should investigate whether reasoners with a lesser ability to decontextualise tend to follow the cutting avoidance procedure. Cognitive economy (see Expt 1) is linked to intellectual ability, and so it is likely to influence how individuals construct models.

A second reason for the observed difference might concern the filler items. In Experiment 2, they consisted of four one-model problems and four multiple-model problems. In Experiment 3, they consisted of eight one-model problems and four no-valid-conclusion problems. Hence, in Experiment 3, there were only two categories of problems: those with an indeterminacy and those without an indeterminacy. Perhaps some participants noticed this difference and decided that it was important. However, instead of constructing two models for the no-valid-conclusion problems, they constructed a different kind of single model, in which the new element from the second premise was inserted between the two items in the model of the first premise. If instructions can have a profound effect on the development of shortcut strategies (see Expt 1), then the set of problems, one-model problems, multiple-model problems and no-valid-conclusion problems in Experiment 2 but only the one-model and no-valid-conclusion problems in Experiment 3, can have a comparable effect. Indeed, it is conceivable that the combination of the experimental and the filler items in Experiment 3 triggered a specific shortcut, that is, the pragmatic procedure.

Conclusions

The experiments presented here focused on mistakes in relational reasoning: Experiment 1 concerned invalid "no-valid-conclusion" responses to multiple-model problems, and Experiments 2 and 3 concerned invalid determinate conclusions to no-valid-conclusion problems. Experiment 1 showed the importance of a careful analysis of the instructions, which in turn can yield different strategies in deductive reasoning. Researchers must not only look for evidence for the fundamental deductive reasoning mechanism, but also take potential strategies into account. Indeed, the experiment showed that stating to participants that "nothing follows" is a valid conclusion for some of the problems led to an increase in invalid "nothing follows" responses to multiple-model problems.

Experiments 2 and 3 illuminated the fundamental reasoning mechanism; they revealed information about the construction of models. We hypothesised two possible model construction procedures. The cutting avoidance procedure uses the model constructed on the basis of the first premise as a firm footing, while the pragmatic procedure uses the first premise as the context in which the subsequent premise is interpreted. The results of Experiments 2 and 3 are not decisive. Although the general picture is more in line with a cutting avoidance procedure (which seems to follow quite naturally the general tenets of the mental models theory), pragmatic influences during the model construction phase cannot be ruled out on the basis of our experiments.

References

Braine, M. D. S., & O'Brien, D. P. (1998). *Mental logic*. Mahwah, NJ: Lawrence Erlbaum Associates, Inc.

Bucciarelli, M., & Johnson-Laird, P. N. (1999). Strategies in syllogistic reasoning. *Cognitive Science*, *23*, 247–303.

Byrne, R. M. J., & Johnson-Laird, P. N. (1989). Spatial reasoning. *Journal of Memory and Language*, *28*, 564–575.

Carreiras, C., & Santamaria, C. (1997). Reasoning about relations: Spatial and nonspatial problems. *Thinking and Reasoning*, *3*, 309–327.

Clark, H. H. (1969a). Linguistic processes in deductive reasoning. *Psychological Review*, *76*, 387–404.

Clark, H. H. (1969b). Influence of language on solving three-term series problems. *Journal of Experimental Psychology*, *82*, 205–215.

De Soto, C. B., London, M., & Handel, S. (1965). Social reasoning and spatial paralogic. *Journal of Personality and Social Psychology*, *2*, 293–307.

Evans, J. St. B. T. (2000). What could and could not be a strategy in reasoning? In W. Schaeken, G. De Vooght, A. Vandierendonck, & G. d'Ydewalle, (Eds.), *Deductive reasoning and strategies* (pp. 1–22). Mahwah, NJ: Lawrence Erlbaum Associates, Inc.

Grice, H. P. (1975). Logic and conversation. In P. Cole & J. L. Morgan (Eds.), *Studies in syntax. Vol. 3: Speech Acts* (pp. 41–58). New York: Academic Press.

Hagert, G. (1984). Modelling mental models: Experiments in cognitive modelling spatial reasoning. In T. O'Shea (Ed.), *Advances in artificial intelligence*, (pp. 389–398). Amsterdam: North-Holland.

Huttenlocher, J. (1968). Constructing spatial images: A strategy in reasoning. *Psychological Review*, *75*, 550–560.

Johnson-Laird, P. N. (1972). The three term series problems. *Cognition*, *1*, 58–82.

Johnson-Laird, P. N. (1983). *Mental models*. Cambridge: Cambridge University Press.

Johnson-Laird, P. N., & Bara, B. G. (1984). Syllogistic inference. *Cognition*, *16*, 1–61.

Larkin, J. H., & Simon, H. A. (1987). Why a diagram is (sometimes) worth ten thousand words. *Cognitive Science*, *11*, 65–100.

Quinton, G., & Fellows, B. J. (1975). "Perceptual" strategies in the solving of three-term series problems. *British Journal of Psychology*, *66*, 69–78.

Rips, L. J. (1994). *The psychology of proof. Deductive reasoning in human thinking*. Cambridge, MA: MIT Press.

Roberts, M. J. (2000a). Strategies in relational reasoning *Thinking and Reasoning*, *6*, 1–26.

Roberts, M. J. (2000b). Individual differences in reasoning strategies: A problem to solve or an opportunity to seize? In W. Schaeken, G. De Vooght, A. Vandierendonck, & G. d'Ydewalle (Eds.), *Deductive reasoning and strategies*, (pp. 23–48). Mahwah, NJ: Lawrence Erlbaum Associates, Inc.

Schaeken, W., & Johnson-Laird, P. N. (2000). Strategies in temporal reasoning. *Thinking and Reasoning*, *6*, 193–219.

Schaeken, W., Girotto, V., & Johnson-Laird, P. N. (1998). The effect of irrelevant premise on temporal and spatial reasoning. *Kognitionswissenchaft*, *7*, 27–32.

Schaeken, W., Johnson-Laird, P. N., & d'Ydewalle, G. (1996a). Mental models and temporal reasoning. *Cognition*, *60*, 205–234.

Schaeken, W., Johnson-Laird, P. N., & d'Ydewalle, G. (1996b). Tense, aspect and temporal reasoning. *Thinking and Reasoning*, *2*, 309–327.

Schaeken, W., De Vooght, G., Vandierendonck, A., & d'Ydewalle, G. (2000). *Deductive reasoning and strategies*. Mahwah, NJ: Lawrence Erlbaum Associates, Inc.

Schaeken, W., Van der Henst, J.-B., & Schroyens, W. (in press). The mental models theory of relational reasoning: Premise relevance, conclusion phrasing and cognitive economy. In W. Schaeken, A. Vandierendonck, W. Schroyens, & G. d'Ydewalle (Eds.), *The mental models theory of reasoning: Refinements and extensions*. Hove, UK: Lawrence Erlbaum Associates Ltd.

Schroyens, W., Schaeken, W., & Handley, S. (2003). In search of counterexamples: Deductive rationality in human reasoning. *Quarterly Journal of Experimental Psychology*, *56*, 1129–1145.

Sperber, D., & Wilson, D. (1986). *Relevance: Communication and cognition*. Oxford: Blackwell.

Stanovich, K. E., & West, R. F. (2000). Individual differences in reasoning: Implications for the rationality debate. *Behavioral and Brain Sciences*, *23*, 645–726.

Van der Henst, J.-B. (2002) Mental model theory *versus* the inference rule approach in relational reasoning. *Thinking and Reasoning*, *8*, 193–203.

Van der Henst J.-B., Yang, Y. R., & Johnson-Laird, P. N. (2002). Strategies in sentential reasoning. *Cognitive Science*, *26*, 425–468

Vandierendonck A., & De Voogt G. (1996). Evidence for mental-model-based reasoning: Comparison of reasoning with time and space concepts. *Thinking and Reasoning*, *2*, 249–272.

Wood, D. (1969). Approach to the study of the human reasoning. *Nature*, *223*, 101–102.

Wood, D. J., Shotter, J. D., & Godden, D. (1974). An investigation of the relationships between problem solving strategies, representation and memory. *Quarterly Journal of Experimental Psychology*, *26*, 252–257.

4   Working memory and propositional reasoning: Searching for new working memory tests

Juan A. García-Madruga, Francisco Gutiérrez, Nuria Carriedo, José María Luzón and José Óscar Vila

Introduction

The main theories of deductive reasoning agree on the crucial role of working memory (WM) in the explanation of people's performance (see, for instance, Johnson-Laird & Byrne, 1991; Rips, 1994). However, researchers have paid little attention so far to the role of working memory in reasoning. In this chapter we analyse some theoretical and methodological issues related to the study of working memory and reasoning. Likewise, we examine the role of WM in reasoning from the mental model approach and review previous studies in this field. Finally, we present the main results of two studies in which we used two new tests of working memory for reasoning. In the first study we compare people's performance in Daneman and Carpenter's (1980) classic reading span test (RST) with their performance in two new "reasoning span" tests based on the solving of pronominal anaphora and analogy problems. In the second study we explore the relationship, in disjunctive and conditional inference tasks, between propositional reasoning performance and WM measured by means of the RST and the two new tests.

Basic issues in working memory

Theoretical approaches

Despite its recency, the concept of WM has become central to cognitive psychology. Baddeley and Hitch's (1974; see also Baddeley, 1986) structural model of WM has its roots in Atkinson and Shiffrin's (1968) idea of the active role of short-term memory in cognition. Thus working memory carries out not only the storage of information but also simultaneously the processing of information. According to Baddeley's model, WM consists of three components: a central executive, with a limited capacity, which controls and coordinates the two other components or "slave" systems: the phonological loop and the visuo-spatial sketchpad. One of the main theoretical issues posed by the model is the relation between the two slave systems: Are they different storage modules or just different formats of representation? As

Engle and Conway (1998) hold, there are reasons to favour the second option, because it maintains a consistent view of the structure of the slave systems and postulates variation only in representational format.

Most previous research on WM and reasoning has been conducted in the light of Baddeley and Hitch's model, and has tried to disentangle the role of each of the WM components, typically using a double-task procedure (see Baddeley & Hitch, 1974). In this procedure, a reasoning task is primary and a secondary task loads one of the WM components – central executive, phonological loop or visuo-spatial sketchpad. The rationale is simple: the more the secondary task affects reasoning, the greater the involvement of the WM component in question. Our perspective in this chapter, however, is different. We address the study of the relation between WM and the central executive, and we examine the capacity of that measure to predict performance in reasoning.

The specification of central executive functions in Baddeley and Hitch's (1974) initial model was quite vague and imprecise, and focused on its co-ordination of the two slave systems. But, according to Baddeley (1996, p. 6) it served "as little more than a ragbag into which could be stuffed all the complex strategy selection, planning, and retrieval checking" that subjects perform in simple cognitive tasks. Baddeley's (1986) version of the model incorporates ideas from Norman and Shallice's theory of a supervisory activating system (Norman & Shallice, 1980; Shallice & Burgess, 1993). To clarify the theory, Baddeley (1996) included in his model two new primary functions of the central executive: the role of an attentional controller that either selects or rejects incoming information, and the capacity to select and manipulate information from long-term memory. Recently, however, Baddeley (2000) has argued that the control function of integrating information from the subsidiary systems and from long-term memory is carried out by a fourth component, the "episodic buffer".

The increasing attention paid by European researchers to the central executive coincides with the main trend of North American research. Most researchers across the Atlantic have acknowledged that their conception of WM coincides with the central executive component proposed in Baddeley and Hitch's model (Richardson, 1996). Within this tradition, one of the main contributions is the study of individual differences, using measures of the processing capacity of working memory, such as the reading span test (RST) developed by Daneman and Carpenter (1980).

The key idea underlying the study of individual differences and the central executive is the assumption, evident in Baddeley and Hitch (1974), of the double-sided nature of working memory, which simultaneously stores and manipulates information. North American researchers accordingly stress that working memory has two mutually related components: storage capacity and processing effectiveness (see Just & Carpenter, 1992). The two components are assessed in Daneman and Carpenter's RST, since subjects are asked to read aloud a series of sentences and to recall the final word of each sentence.

The processing part of the task is reading aloud; the storage part of the task is in recalling the final words.

Shah and Miyake (1996) have postulated the existence of two distinct and independent systems of executive functioning, one verbal and the other spatial. Shah and Miyake's proposal introduces the verbal–spatial distinction within the central executive, and discards the possibility of a unitary central executive. Yet, contrary to Shah and Miyake's proposal, we shall see that most of the findings about working memory and thinking appear to support a unitary executive controller that is the main component underlying reasoning.

Methodological problems

Apart from the theoretical issues of WM, there are also methodological problems to measure the processing capacity of individuals' working memory. Three of them are worthy of mention here (see Philips & Forsaw, 1998). First, measures of working memory are diverse, unstandardised, and of uncertain reliability and validity. For example, Waters and Caplan (1996) showed test–retest reliability, with a delay of at least one month, for three reading span measures: two of their own measures and the Daneman–Carpenter measure. The test–retest correlation for the Daneman–Carpenter task was just 0.41, and for the two Waters–Kaplan tasks, 0.65 and 0.66.

Second, the correlations found among the diverse measures of WM, though reliable, are frequently poor (see Gilinsky & Judd, 1994). In one of our studies, for instance, we used three different tests of working memory: a Spanish version of Daneman and Carpenter's (1980) reading span test (RST), a Spanish version of Yuill, Oakhill, and Parkin's (1989) digit span test (DST) in which individuals read aloud a series of three digits and recall the last one of each series, and a new arithmetic span test (AST), in which people recall the result of two simple arithmetical operations, which they say aloud, an addition and a subtraction (for instance, $3 + 2 - 1 =$). The verbal measure of WM (RST) correlated moderately with the equivalent numerical test: RST – DST = 0.47; likewise, the two numerical measures of WM were similarly correlated: DST – AST = 0.46. However, the correlation between the classical verbal measure (RST) and the new arithmetical task (AST) was just 0.23 (Elosúa, García-Madruga, Gutiérrez, Luque, & Gárate, 1997).

Third, the WM concept itself poses some difficulties, since it implies both storage (low-level resource limitations) and processing (high-level cognitive functioning). These two components of WM are tightly intertwined, and cannot easily be split apart. However, our measures assess mainly the storage component. Thus, Daneman and Carpenter (1980) developed their reading span test to elucidate the relation between WM and reading comprehension, and so they loaded the processing component with the task of reading sentences aloud. Their test and others have allowed researchers to show how working memory capacity predicts performance in a variety of cognitive tasks (for a summary see, for example, Engle, 1996). An important example is the highly significant correlations between WM capacity and various measures of reading ability (see, for example, Daneman & Carpenter, 1980, 1983; García-Madruga, Gárate, Elosúa, Luque, & Gutiérrez, 1997). Similarly, as Engle (1996) has shown, the reading span test reveals individual differences important to cognition in many real-life situations, particularly those calling for the acquisition of new information and its subsequent retrieval.

Our aim in this chapter is to examine the relation between WM and reasoning. Hence, we need to assess the capacity of the processing component of WM, and so our measure of its capacity depends on a task calling for an inferential decision. In place of materials that are arbitrarily selected, such as the last word of a sentence, the items that individuals have to recall are a result of an inference. Philips and Forshaw (1998) argue that the selection of such a WM measure is circular. The claim is true in part, because we attempt to explain performance in reasoning tasks from performance in WM tasks that call for an element of reasoning. The amount of reasoning in the WM measure, however, is much smaller than the amount in the reasoning tasks themselves. Moreover, the measure is appropriate. Whether it is useful, however, is an empirical issue, which we examine in due course.

Working memory and reasoning

Working memory and mental models

The mental model theory (MMT) has promoted the study of WM and reasoning. According to mental model theory, reasoning depends on envisaging the possibilities compatible with the premises. It is based on the semantic process of constructing mental models of these possibilities from the meaning of the premises and from knowledge (Johnson-Laird, 1983; Johnson-Laird & Byrne, 1991). A main assumption of the theory concerns working memory: Mental models are constructed, held, and manipulated within WM. This crucial role of WM leads to the principal prediction of the theory: The more models a reasoner must hold in WM, the more difficult the inference should be. A corollary is that inferences which call for the construction of multiple models often err because they overlook models of the premises. Reasoners also tend to construct models of only what is true in a possibility. In general, to avoid overloading working memory, they represent explicitly as little information as possible.

The theory allows us to predict and explain a considerable amount of empirical evidence about propositional reasoning, i.e., reasoning that hinges on sentential connectives, such as "if", "and", and "or". A conjunction of the form *p and q* means that there is only one possibility in which both *p* and *q* hold, and so the conjunction yields only one model. Hence, inferences based on this connective will be very easy. Disjunctions of the form *p or q* call for the construction of at least two models, and so inferences based on them should be harder than those based on conjunctions (see García-Madruga, Moreno, Carriedo, Gutiérrez, & Johnson-Laird, 2001). A conditional of the form *if p then q* is compatible with three possibilities. According to the model theory, however, reasoners construct one explicit mental model (of the possibility in which both *p* and *q* hold) and one implicit mental model (of the possibility, or possibilities, in which the antecedent of the conditional, *p*, does not hold). Individuals do not normally think about the possibilities in which the antecedent is false, but in case they have to, they need to make a mental note that the implicit model represents these possibilities (see Table 4.1). The mental models allow two inferences to be made from a conditional, the valid modus ponens *if p then q; p; therefore, q*) and the invalid "affirmation of the consequent" *if p then q; q; therefore, p*). To make the other two conditional inferences, the valid modus tollens (*if p then q; not q; therefore, not p*), and the invalid "denial of the antecedent" (*if p then q; not p; therefore, not q*), reasoners have to flesh out the implicit model into *fully explicit* models. In this way, the theory accounts for the main empirical results on conditional inferences, and in particular the greater difficulty of modus tollens and denial of the antecedent inferences compared to modus ponens and affirmation of the consequent inferences (see Johnson-Laird, Byrne, & Schaeken, 1992). Finally, the mental models of a biconditional of the form *if and only if p then q* are the same as those for conditionals, but the mental footnote on the implicit model shows that it represents the possibility in which both the antecedent and the consequent are false. Hence, a biconditional has two fully explicit models from which the four inferences may be validly drawn. Table 4.1 summarises the mental models and the fully explicit models of the main sentential connectives.

The model theory has motivated researchers to study the relative involvement in reasoning of the different components of WM. It is sometimes

Table 4.1 The mental models and the fully explicit models of the major sentential connectives

Connective	Mental models		Fully explicit models	
p and q	p	q	p	q
p or q	p		p	¬q
		q	¬p	q
			p	q
If p then q	p	q	p	q
	. . .		¬p	q
			¬p	¬q
If and only if p then q	p	q	p	q
	. . .		¬p	¬q

Note: "¬" denotes negation, and ". . ." denotes a wholly implicit model. Each row represents a model.

supposed that MM are a kind of image-based representation, and therefore that the visual component of WM should be more involved than the verbal one. In this line, Johnson-Laird (1985, p. 190) states that "the ability to construct alternative models . . . should correlate with spatial ability rather than verbal ability". On the other hand, in our opinion mental models are semantic representations that do not imply a particular representational format, and so the crucial component to be checked would be the central executive.

A number of studies on WM and reasoning have been carried out over the last two decades in order to examine the involvement of WM in diverse reasoning tasks, mainly syllogistic and propositional reasoning tasks (see Gilhooly, 1998). These studies can be divided into two groups: those using the dual-task procedure and those based on a correlational approach. In what follows, we review some of these studies, particularly those concerning propositional reasoning. We then present the main results of a study in which we compared the conditional reasoning of individuals with a high and a low WM processing capacity.

Secondary task studies of WM and propositional reasoning

The aim of these studies was to establish the relative involvement of the three main components of WM. The participants had to carry out a propositional reasoning task whilst their working memory was simultaneously loaded with a secondary task. As a secondary task affecting the central executive, researchers have asked subjects to generate random numbers from one to nine (Baddeley, 1996). A secondary task for loading the phonological loop is the repeated speaking of a word or set of words. A secondary task for loading the visual sketchpad is some kind of spatial activity, such as moving a hand in a set pattern.

An early study by Evans and Brooks (1981) used secondary tasks loading the central executive and articulatory loop, but it found no evidence for their involvement in conditional reasoning. However, some authors have claimed that their secondary tasks probably failed to load WM sufficiently (Halford, Bain, & Maybery, 1984). A more comprehensive study, in which the involvement of the three components of WM was checked, was reported by Toms, Warris, and Ward (1993). These authors found clear evidence for the role of the central executive in conditional inferences, but no evidence for the involvement of the visual sketchpad or the articulatory loop. Memory load resulted in poorer conditional reasoning, particularly of the hardest sort: modus tollens inferences.

Klauer, Stegmaier, and Meiser (1997) compared the effects of different secondary tasks affecting the three WM components on propositional (from conditionals and disjunctions) reasoning and on spatial reasoning. Propositional and spatial reasoning were disrupted by the secondary tasks, mainly by those affecting the central executive, and the effects were greater on spatial reasoning. There were no differences in the patterns of disruption between the two kinds of reasoning – only the size of the disruptions differed. For a given load on working memory, the disruption of spatial reasoning was greater than the disruption of propositional reasoning.

Klauer and his colleagues interpreted this result as contradicting the model theory and explained it according to Evans's two-stage theory of reasoning (Evans, 1984, 1989; Evans & Over, 1996). In a first "heuristic" stage some preconscious processes select relevant information and thus direct and focus the working of a subsequent explicit and "analytic" stage. According to Klauer and his colleagues, in propositional reasoning participants use a heuristic strategy that is based on linguistic surface characteristics and that consumes hardly any cognitive resources. The heuristic processing would permit a smaller load on working memory for propositional reasoning than for spatial reasoning. There are, obviously, other possible reasons to explain the differential effects of WM load, e.g., lexical and syntactic differences between two kind of reasoning.

As Klauer et al. (1997) hold, their results may be best understood in the light of the work by Gilhooly and collaborators on working memory and syllogistic reasoning (Gilhooly, Logie, Wetherick, & Wynn, 1993; Gilhooly, Logie, & Wynn, 1999). These authors have found a clear relation between working memory load and the kinds of strategies used by subjects in solving categorical syllogisms. Gilhooly et al. (1999) used two groups of participants: a group that was high in skill and a group that was low in skill at syllogistic reasoning. The accuracy of the high-skilled group was affected by secondary tasks loading the three components of WM, but the low-skilled group was not affected, probably because instead of reasoning they used surface strategies that demanded fewer cognitive resources. Likewise, Gilhooly et al. (1999) found that, under dual-task conditions, both groups of reasoners tended to shift downwards from more competent and demanding strategies to less demanding strategies.

Correlational studies of WM and reasoning

Correlational studies of WM and propositional reasoning have been rare, and so we analyse just three studies. Our own research team (García-Madruga, Gutiérrez, Johnson-Laird, & Carriedo, 1997; Gutiérrez, García-Madruga, Johnson-Laird, & Carriedo, 2002) have studied the relation between working memory capacity, measured by means of Daneman and Carpenter's RST (1980; Spanish version, Elosúa, Gutiérrez, García-Madruga, Luque, & Gárate, 1996), and the ability to reason from multiple conditional premises, e.g.:

If I use mayonnaise then I use lemon
If I use lemon then I use haddock
If I use haddock then I use endive

If I use endive then I use escarole
What follows between lemon and escarole?

Table 4.2 shows the form of the problems, and the number of mental models that the premises should elicit. Hence, some problems call for a single mental model whereas others call for multiple mental models. Since mental models load working memory, or even overload it, it follows that there should be a stronger correlation between WM processing capacity and reasoners' performance with multiple-model problems than with one-model problems. The results tended to confirm the hypothesis, but they were not significant. Percentages of correct responses for one-model and multiple-model problems were 90 per cent and 70 per cent, respectively. Correlations with WM were 0.03 for one-model problems and 0.24 for multiple-model problems.

Previous studies have obtained only weak and unreliable correlations between WM capacity and reasoning with multiple models. The case of conditional inferences is similar, to judge, for example, from the work of Markovits, Doyon, and Simoneau (2002). These researchers gave reasoners the four conditional inference problems with concrete and abstract contents. As measures of WM they used a verbal WM capacity test based on that of Daneman and Carpenter (1980) and a visuo-spatial WM task. They found a number of significant correlations between reasoners' performance for two kinds of content and WM tests, but the correlations were rather low (around 0.20). Moreover, the highest correlation found by Markovits and colleagues was between verbal WM and modus ponens inferences (0.32), while no significant or even positive correlation with modus tollens inferences. These

Table 4.2 Description of multiple conditional problems used by García-Madruga et al. (1997). The representation in terms of mental models is also shown. The actual problems used sensible everyday propositions.

One-model problem	Multiple-model problems	
If e then a	If e then b	If e then b
If a then b	If a then b	If a then b
If b then c	If b then c	If c then b
If c then d	If c then d	If b then d
What follows between a and d?	What follows between a and d?	What follows between a and d?
Conclusion: If a then d	Conclusion: If a then d	Conclusion: If a then d
Representation	*Representation*	*Representation*
1 explicit model (1m)	2 explicit models (2m)	3 explicit models (3m)
e a b c d	e b c d	e b d
. . .	a b c d	a b d
	. . .	c b d
		. . .

findings are particularly unexpected and discouraging, since modus tollens inferences require more cognitive work, and are consequently harder than the direct modus ponens inferences.

One general difficulty in searching for a relation between the capacity of working memory and number of models is that reasoners tend to construct as few models as possible. Indeed, several researchers have proposed that most individuals most of the time construct only a single mental model (see, e.g., Morris & Sloutsky, 2002; Richardson & Ormerod, 1997). Hence, it is crucial for investigators to establish that their participants are constructing multiple models in the relevant condition. Barrouillet and his colleagues have used such a procedure in several developmental studies. They demand that their participants list *all* the possibilities compatible with conditional assertions (see, e.g., Barrouillet & Lecas, 1999).

In their experiment, the participants were three groups of children and young adolescents who were asked to list all the cases compatible with a conditional rule. Working memory capacity was assessed using Case's counting span task. The results confirmed the developmental pattern predicted by mental model theory: The youngest children listed only the case corresponding to the single explicit mental model; slightly older children listed the two cases corresponding to the fully explicit models of a biconditional; only the oldest groups listed the three possibilities compatible with a conditional (see Table 4.1, p. 73). But the results also yielded a reliable and high positive correlation between WM capacity and conditional reasoning (0.648). However, it may not be possible to generalise these results to other tasks or to populations other than children. As diverse studies have shown, the correlation between WM capacity and language comprehension tends to be higher for children than for adults (see, for example, García-Madruga et al., 1997). This phenomenon may be a result of the increasing skill in reasoning as children become more experienced (see Gathercole & Baddeley, 1993). It may also reflect the use of strategies that increasingly rely on envisaging a minimum of possibilities.

Conditional reasoning with high and low WM subjects

A third kind of study about WM and reasoning was carried out by Meilán, García-Madruga, and Vieiro (2000). The main aim of their study was to compare the reasoning of people with high and low WM capacity. They used the Spanish version of Daneman and Carpenter's (1980) RST (Elosúa et al., 1996) to select two groups of participants: those scoring four or more on the RST were the high WM group; those scoring less than three in RST were the low WM group. The reasoning task consisted of four conditional inferences (modus ponens, modus tollens, affirmation of the consequent, denial of the antecedent) for two different sorts of conditional: "if then" and "unless". The participants were asked to write down their own conclusion for each inference problem.

The model theory maintains that some conditional formulations may lead to the construction of two explicit initial models because they make explicit negation, e.g., *p only if q* makes explicit the possibility of *not-p* and *not-q* (see Johnson-Laird & Byrne, 1991). Previous studies suggest that for *not-p unless q* reasoners construct two explicit models: *not-q not-p*, and *q p* (see Carriedo, García-Madruga, Gutiérrez, & Moreno, 1999; García-Madruga, Carriedo, Moreno, & Schaeken, 2002; García-Madruga, Gutiérrez, Carriedo, Moreno, & Johnson-Laird., 2002). For example, a conditional assertion such as:

> *You won't pass the exam unless you study harder,*

tends to elicit two mental models corresponding to the possibilities:

Don't study harder	Don't pass exam
Study harder	Pass exam

There is another relevant feature of "unless" conditionals: They are frequently interpreted as biconditionals. In other words, when we say: *You won't pass the exam unless you study harder*, you will probably understand our assertion to mean that you will pass the exam if and only if you study harder. As a consequence of this usual biconditional interpretation of "unless", the four conditional inferences are all valid.

Table 4.3 summarises the mental models and the fully explicit models for assertions based on "unless" and "if then". These models yield different predictions about the role of WM capacity for the four conditional inferences. From the initial representation of "unless" conditionals, reasoners can draw directly the four conditional inferences, whereas from the initial representation of "if then" conditionals, they can draw only modus ponens and affirmation of the consequent inferences. But because the two mental models for "unless" are both explicit, the percentage of the four conditional inferences should be greater for high WM reasoners than for low WM reasoners. In contrast, as Meilán et al. (2000) predicted, for modus ponens and affirmation

Table 4.3 The mental models and fully explicit models for "if then" and "unless" conditionals

Conditional sentences	Mental models		Fully explicit models			
If p then q	p	q	p	q		
	. . .		¬p	q		
			¬p	¬q		
Not-p unless q	p	q	*One-way*		*Biconditional*	
	¬p	¬q	p	q	p	q
	. . .		¬p	q		
			¬p	¬-q	¬p	¬q

Note: "¬" denotes negation, and ". . ." denotes a wholly implicit model. Each row represents a model.

of the consequent inferences from "if then" conditionals, there should be no differences between high and low WM groups, but the high WM group should draw more modus tollens and denial of the antecedent inferences than the low WM group, because these latter inferences depend on fleshing out mental models into fully explicit models.

A striking result in previous studies of "unless" is that some individuals make an odd "inverse" response. Given, say, premises of the denial of the antecedent form *not-p unless q, p*, they respond *q*. Similarly, given premises of the affirmation of the consequent form *not-p unless q, q*, they respond *not-p*. We assume that a superficial "matching" strategy yields these responses. We therefore hypothesised that they should be made more often by the low WM group than by the high WM group.

Table 4.4 summarises the results from Meilán et al. (2000). They confirmed the predictions. For "if then" conditionals, the decrease in denial of the antecedent and modus tollens inferences for low WM reasoners tends to be greater than in the cases of modus ponens and affirmation of the consequent (though differences were not reliable in any case). For "unless" assertions, there was a clear decrease in all four inferences in the low WM group, and this decrease was significant for affirmation of the consequent (p<0.05), denial of the antecedent (p<0.001) and modus tollens (p<0.01). Likewise, the overall percentage of inferences was significantly greater for high WM reasoners than for low WM reasoners (p<0.01). Finally, as predicted, some inverse responses occurred with "unless" conditionals, and the percentage was greater for low WM (29 per cent) than for high WM participants (10 per cent). This last result confirms previous results showing that some reasoners may be using surface matching that places a lower load on WM than reasoning. This strategy seems to be induced by the difficulty of the problem, the introduction of a secondary task, and low WM capacity.

The dual-task studies presented above, and the research of Meilán et al. (2000), imply that the central executive plays a major role in reasoning. Yet the correlational evidence is not so clear. To bridge the gap between these two

Table 4.4 The percentages of inferential responses for each conditional statement made by the high and low WM participants (adapted from Meilán, García-Madruga, & Vieiro, 2000)

Conditional formulations	WM groups	MP	AC	DA	MT	Overall
If then	High	100	78	23	50	63
	Low	100	68	8	35	53
Unless	High	75	60	48	88	68
	Low	58	33	8	55	38

Note
MP = modus ponens   AC = affirmation of the consequent   DA = denial of the antecedent
MT = modus tollens

types of evidence, we have recently studied working memory capacity and efficiency in the central executive, and we have developed a new measure of working memory capacity pertinent to reasoning. It takes the form of a sort of reasoning span test. The next section presents two new tests of this sort, and some of the findings we have obtained from their use.

Two new measures of working memory capacity for reasoning

The analogy and anaphora tests

The two "Reasoning Span Tests" are based on pronominal anaphora and analogy. In the reading span test of working memory, participants have to remember the last word of an increasing number of sentences that they read aloud in series of two, three, four, five and six sentences. As we saw above, the task has two components: a processing component focused on reading the sentence aloud and choosing the last word; and a storage component consisting of remembering one word from each sentence. Our new measures introduce some modifications in the processing component, whilst maintaining constant the storage component: Participants have to read aloud a sequence of sentences and then infer a word that must be remembered. These two new tests should provide better measures of the central executive's capacity for reasoning.

In the WM anaphora test, people have to remember a word that is the referent of a simple pronominal anaphora. Here is an example:

> *Robert painted **it** white before the summer arrived.*
> – roof
> – *girlfriend*
> – *façade*

The word in bold, façade, is the correct response because it matches the meaning of the sentence and the gender – feminine – of the pronoun (in Spanish: *Roberto **la** pintó de blanco antes de que llegara el verano – tejado – novia – **fachada***).

The participants are given a sequence of such problems. They read the sentence aloud, choose the correct item out of three nouns, read it aloud, and remember it. The foils are either semantically appropriate or grammatically appropriate, i.e., of matching Spanish gender, but not both. At the end of each series, the participants have to recall the correct words for each problem in the correct order.

In the WM analogy test, the participants have to remember a sequence of words, which are the solutions to simple verbal analogies. Here is an example of one such problem:

> *Sun is to dry as water is to*
> – rain
> – *wet*

As in the previous test, the participants read each sentence, choose the correct response from the pair of words, read it aloud, and commit it to memory. The foils are semantically related to the correct response, though not the proper analogy. At the end of each series, the participants have to remember the correct words in the correct order.

The content of the anaphora and analogy problems was based on a normative study in order to ensure that all of them were easy: we used only problems that yielded more than 95 per cent correct responses. Although we expected the new tests to be harder than the standard RST, there should nevertheless be correlations among the various measures.

We tested 89 university students on our two new tests and the standard reading span test (RST), which they carried out in randomised orders. The results confirmed our predictions. Performance in the reading span test (RST) (mean score of 3.15 words) was reliably higher than in the anaphora test – (mean 2.77 words) and the analogy test (mean 2.7 words). The difference between the two new measures was not reliable. The correlations among the three WM measures were as follows:

Reading span and anaphora:	0.46 ($p < 0.001$)
Reading span and analogy:	0.38 ($p < 0.001$)
Anaphora and analogy:	0.35 ($p < 0.001$)

After the main experiment was over, we gave the participants pencil and paper and asked them to solve the anaphora and analogy problems: All the participants solved nearly all the problems.

As the results show, the introduction of simple inference tasks into a test of working memory significantly increases difficulty. The work of inferring the word that has to be remembered increases WM load and reduces the resources for storing the result. However, the correlations among the three WM measures, though reliable, were once again not very high. This result implies that they are measuring different aspects of performance.

A correlational study of WM and propositional reasoning

The aim of this study was to examine the correlations between reasoning with conditionals and disjunctions and the three WM measures (García-Madruga et al., 2003). Thirty participants carried out the three WM tests and a reasoning test that included three sentences, two conditionals and one disjunction. One conditional was of the form *if p then q* and the other was of the logically equivalent form *not p unless q*. The participants had to generate their own conclusions to the four classical inferences (modus ponens, denial of the antecedent, affirmation of the consequent, modus tollens) for both sorts of conditional. The disjunction was of the form *p or q, or both*, and the participants had to generate a conclusion given in addition four categorical premises *p, q, not-p*, and *not-q* respectively.

According to the model theory, reasoners make most inferences from mental models (see Table 4.3, p. 78). Therefore, as in the study reported earlier, the theory predicts that for "if then" inferences modus ponens and affirmation of the consequent should be more frequent than modus tollens and denial of the antecedent. Likewise, there should be no reliable differences among the four inferences for "unless". For this latter conditional, however, there should be some superficial "inverse" responses to which we referred in a previous section.

The inclusive disjunction *p or q, or both* needs a more detailed analysis. Its fully explicit models are as follows (see Table 4.1):

$$p \quad q$$
$$p \quad \neg q$$
$$\neg p \quad q$$

However, this representation is highly demanding, and hence individuals are likely to build only the models they need to reach the conclusion from each premise (Morris & Sloutsky, 2002; Richardson & Ormerod, 1997). Thus, with the categorical premise, *p*, reasoners should build the two models:

$$p \quad q$$
$$p \quad \neg q$$

from which they can make the correct response: "There is no valid conclusion." However, some people may reach an invalid conclusion from the first model (*p*, therefore *q*). A similar process can be hypothesised for the categorical premise, *q*: It yields either the correct "no valid conclusion" response or the invalid conclusion: *q*, therefore *p*.

For the two negative categorical premises *not-p* and *not-q*, the reasoning process may be different. Reasoners probably have to construct the three models:

$$p \quad q$$
$$p \quad \neg q$$
$$\neg p \quad q$$

in order to reach the valid conclusions: *q* from *not-p*, and *p* from *not-q*. These models should block the symmetric responses *not-p*, therefore *not-q*, and *not-q*, therefore *not-p*.

Positive correlations should occur between the WM measures and those responses deriving from a greater cognitive load. Hence, there should be positive correlations with overall correct responses and modus tollens and denial of the antecedent for "if then" conditionals, whereas there should be positive correlations with all four inferences for "unless" conditionals. Granted the usual biconditional interpretation of "unless" all four inferences are valid. Likewise, we predicted a positive correlation among the WM measures and the four valid responses to the inclusive disjunction. The main prediction, however, is that the anaphora and analogy measures of working memory should yield higher and more reliable correlations with inferential performance than the standard reading span measure.

Table 4.5 presents the results for the two sorts of conditional inferences. They confirmed the model theory's predictions about the differences between "if then" and "unless" conditionals. In the former, modus ponens and affirmation of the consequent inferences were reliably easier than denial of the antecedent and modus tollens inferences; in the latter, there was no reliable difference among the four inferences. As in previous studies, inverse responses occurred for "unless" conditionals. These responses are likely to derive from a superficial matching strategy, which, as we maintained above, does not consume many cognitive resources.

Table 4.6 presents the results for the four inferences from the inclusive disjunctions. They also confirm the model theory's predictions. As the first two columns show, the proportion of correct "No valid conclusion" responses to the two positive inferences was around 50 per cent. Likewise, the predicted erroneous symmetric responses did occur. For the two inferences based on negative categorical assertions, the correct "inverse" conclusion was rather difficult, and reasoners preferred the wrong "No valid conclusion" response.

The main aim of this study was to check the correlations among measures of WM and reasoning. Table 4.7 presents these results. The table also shows the correlations among the three WM measures and, on the one hand, responses requiring multiple models and, on the other, those that can be

Table 4.5 The percentages of the various sorts of responses for the four inferences for both conditional statements (correct responses are in bold) (from García-Madruga, Gutiérrez, Carriedo, Luzón, & Vila, 2003)

		MP	*AC*	*DA*	*MT*
If p then q	Inferential responses	**100**	82	54	**53**
	No conclusion	0	**15**	**46**	45
	Inverse responses	0	0	0	2
	Other responses	0	3	0	0
Not p unless q	Inferential responses	**83**	**80**	**71**	**69**
	No conclusion	11	2	7	23
	Inverse responses	5	17	19	8
	Other responses	1	1	3	0

Note
MP = modus ponens   AC = affirmation of the consequent   DA = denial of the antecedent
MT = modus tollens

Table 4.6 The percentages of the various responses for the four inferences from "p or q, or both" disjunctive statement (correct responses are in bold; from García-Madruga, Gutiérrez, Carriedo, Luzón, & Vila, 2003)

	Categorical premise p	Categorical premise q	Categorical premise Not-p	Categorical premise Not-q
Symmetric responses	(q) 38	(p) 29	(not-q) 3	(not-p) 3
No conclusion	**48**	**52**	53	53
Inverse responses	(not-q) 5	(not-p) 9	(q) **43**	(p) **42**
Other	9	10	1	2

Table 4.7 Correlations between WM and diverse reasoning measures (from García-Madruga, Gutiérrez, Carriedo, Luzón, & Vila, 2003)

Measures of working memory	Correct if then	Correct unless	Correct or	Multiple models	Superficial responses
Reading span (RST)	0.05	−0.03	0.27#	0.27#	−0.15
Anaphoric measure	0.37*	0.14	0.25#	0.38*	−0.28#
Analogy measure	−0.04	0.43**	0.39*	0.42*	−0.47**

** $p < 0.01$; * $p < 0.05$; # $p < 0.1$

derived from a superficial "matching" strategy. The kinds of responses included in these categories are as follows:

(1) Multiple model responses:
  • denial of the antecedent and modus tollens inferences, and denial of the antecedent and affirmation of the consequent "No valid conclusion" responses for "if then"
  • the four valid inferences for "unless"
  • the four valid responses for "or"
(2) Superficial responses:
  • Affirmation of the consequent and modus ponens inferences for "if then"
  • Denial of the antecedent and affirmation of the consequent inverse responses for "unless"
  • Symmetric *p*, therefore *q* and *q*, therefore *p* inferences for "or".

In general, the predictions were confirmed. The first three columns of Table 4.7 show a number of positive correlations among WM measures and reasoners' performance. These correlations tended to be higher for the new measures than for the reading span measures. This pattern can be seen clearly in the fourth column, in which the correlations with multiple model responses are shown. However, the most conspicuous results are those in the last column. These were the negative correlations between WM measures and responses involving a small load on WM: those yielded by a superficial "matching" strategy.

These results establish two potentially useful measures of working memory that are pertinent to research on reasoning. The two measures correlate with reasoning to a greater degree than the classical reading span test. In the studies reported here, the analogy test seems to be more sensitive for predicting reasoning performance.

Conclusions

The central executive of working memory is crucial for the maintenance and manipulation of information in thinking. In this chapter, we have described two new measures of the capacity of the central executive. They both introduce a trivial inferential problem as part of the processing required to carry out the test. The participants are forced to regulate their cognitive resources in tasks that require both inference and memory. The inferential component is presumably responsible for the improvement – especially in comparison with the classical reading span task – in the predictions of reasoning performance. Of course, there is an element of circularity in using a measure of WM to predict reasoning ability when the measure itself calls for reasoning (see Philips & Forshaw, 1998). However, the anaphora and analogy problems in the tests are quite different from the propositional reasoning that we have investigated. Moreover, the inferences in the WM measures are trivial: They are typically carried out correctly by every participant.

In this chapter, we have proposed the use of differences between individuals to studying the working memory and reasoning. As we have shown, there are positive correlations between WM and reasoning responses that require high levels of mental work, and negative correlations between WM and reasoning responses that require low levels of mental work. The positive correlations, and especially those with the need to use multiple models, support the model theory and the existence of genuine processes of reasoning. The negative correlations support the idea that some responses are a consequence of superficial strategies. The idea of an automatic superficial representation of premises that underlies reasoning, and that may sometimes affect how reasoners draw a conclusion, was proposed by one of the present authors 20 years ago (García-Madruga, 1981). Perhaps the most interesting suggestion arising from the studies we have presented here is that the use of WM measures can help to clarify the diverse processes through which reasoners reach a conclusion.

Let us end with a personal note. This chapter by Spanish scholars deserves such an explanation. Juan García-Madruga began to work on deductive reasoning in 1971, as a research assistant on a project directed by Professor Juan Delval. The project focused on the acquisition of logical connectives and it investigated Wason's selection task. Juan García-Madruga's first knowledge of Paolo Legrenzi came from reading his well-known paper with his wife, Maria Sonino-Legrenzi, and Phil Johnson-Laird on the effects of content on the selection task. After the 1974 meeting on selection task in Trento, Juan Delval established ties of friendship with Paolo and Maria Legrenzi. In the 1980s, Juan García-Madruga visited Phil Johnson-Laird at the then Applied Psychology Unit in Cambridge, and there he met Paolo Legrenzi. During the last two decades, most of the work in Spanish psychology on reasoning has been influenced by these intellectual and personal ties. With this contribution, we want to express our gratitude to Paolo for his intellect and wisdom from which we have all benefited.

Acknowledgements

We thank Ruth Byrne, Phil Johnson-Laird and Sergio Moreno Ríos for their helpful comments and ideas. The research presented in this paper was begun during the first author's stay in the Department of Psychology at Trinity College, The University of Dublin. This visit was funded by the Spanish Ministry of Education and Science; likewise, the present research is part of a project funded by the Spanish Ministry of Education and Science (PB98-0020-C03-01).

References

Atkinson, R. C., & Shiffrin, R. M. (1968). Human memory: A proposed system and its control processes. In K. W. Spence & J. T. Spence (Eds.), *The psychology of learning and motivation: Advances in research and theory* (Vol. 2, pp. 89–195). New York: Academic Press.

Baddeley, A. D. (1986). *Working memory*. Oxford: Oxford University Press.

Baddeley, A. D. (1996). Exploring the central executive. *Quarterly Journal of Experimental Psychology*, *49A*, 5–28.

Baddeley, A. D., & Hitch, G. (1974). Working memory. In G. A. Bower (Ed.), *The psychology of learning and motivation* (Vol. 8, pp. 47–90). New York: Academic Press.

Barrouillet, P., & Lecas, J. F. (1999). Mental models in conditional reasoning and working memory. *Thinking and Reasoning*, *5* (4), 289–302.

Carriedo, N., García-Madruga, J., Gutiérrez, F., & Moreno, S. (1999). How does content affect "unless" conditional reasoning? *Proceedings of the European Conference on Cognitive Science* (pp. 271–277). Siena.

Daneman, M., & Carpenter, P. A. (1980). Individual differences in working memory and reading. *Journal of Verbal Learning and Verbal Behavior*, *19*, 450–466.

Daneman, M., & Carpenter, P. (1983). Individual differences in integrating information between and within sentences. *Journal of Experimental Psychology: Learning, Memory, and Cognition*, *9*, 561–584.

Elosúa, M. R., Gutiérrez, F., García-Madruga, J. A., Luque, J. L., & Gárate, M. (1996). Versión española del "Reading Span Test" de Daneman and Carpenter. [Spanish version of Daneman and Carpenter's "Reading Span Test"]. *Psicothema*, *2*, 383–395.

Elosúa, M. R., García-Madruga, J. A., Gutiérrez, F., Luque, J. L., & Gárate, M. (1997). Un estudio sobre las diferencias evolutivas en memoria operativa: ¿capacidad o eficiencia? [A study on developmental differences in working memory: Capacity or efficiency?]. *Estudios de psicología*, *58*, 15–27.

Engle, R. W. (1996). Working memory (WM) and retrieval: An inhibition-resource approach. In J. T. Richardson, R. W. Engle, L. Hasher, R. H. Logie, E. R. Stoltzfus, & R. T. Zacks, *Working memory and human cognition*. Oxford: Oxford University Press.

Engle, R. W., & Conway, A. R. A. (1998). Working memory and comprehension. In R. H. Logie & K. J. Gilhooly (Eds.), *Working memory and thinking* (pp. 67–91). Hove, UK: Psychology Press.

Evans, J. St. B. T. (1984). Heuristic and analytic processes in reasoning. *British Journal of Psychology*, *75*, 451–468.

Evans, J. St. B. T. (1989). *Bias in human reasoning: Causes and consequences*. Hove, UK: Lawrence Erlbaum Associates Ltd.

Evans, J. St. B. T., & Brooks, P. G. (1981). Competing with reasoning: A test of the working memory hypothesis. *Current Psychological Research*, *1*, 139–147.

Evans, J. St. B. T., & Over, D. (1996). *Rationality and reasoning*. Hove, UK: Psychology Press.

Farmer, E. W., Berman, J. V. F., & Fletcher, Y. L. (1986). Evidence of a visuo-spatial scratch-pad in working memory (WM). *Quarterly Journal of Experimental Psychology*, *38A*, 675–688.

García-Madruga, J. A. (1981). *Modelos de razonamiento silogístico*. [Models of syllogistic reasoning]. Doctoral dissertation, Facultad de Psicología, Universidad Complutense de Madrid.

García-Madruga, J. A., Carriedo, N., Moreno, S., Gutiérrez, F., & Schaeken, W. (2002). *Conditional reasoning from different formulations: "if", "only if" and "unless"*. Manuscript submitted for publication.

García-Madruga, J. A., Gárate, M., Elosúa, R., Luque, J. L., & Gutiérrez, F. (1997). Comprensión lectora y memoria operativa: un estudio evolutivo. [Reading comprehension and working memory: A developmental study]. *Cognitiva*, *9* (1), 99–132.

García-Madruga, J. A., Gutiérrez, F., Carriedo, N., Luzón, J. M., & Vila, J. O. (2003). *Working memory load and propositional reasoning processes*. In preparation.

García-Madruga, J. A., Gutiérrez, F., Carriedo, N., Moreno, S., & Johnson-Laird, P. N. (2002). Mental models in deductive reasoning. *Spanish Journal of Psychology*, *5*, 125–140.

García-Madruga, J. A., Gutiérrez, F., Johnson-Laird, P. N., & Carriedo, N. (1997). *Los condicionales múltiples*. [Multiple conditionals]. Unpublished manuscript.

García-Madruga, J. A., Moreno, S., Carriedo, N., Gutiérrez, F., & Johnson-Laird, P. N. (2001). Are conjunctive inferences easier than disjunctive inferences? A comparison of rules and models. *Quarterly Journal of Experimental Psychology*, *54A*, 613–632.

Gathercole, S., & Baddeley, A. D. (1993). *Working memory and language*. Hove, UK: Lawrence Erlbaum Associates Ltd.

Gernsbacher, M. (1990). *Language comprehension as structure building*. Hillsdale, NJ: Lawrence Erlbaum Associates, Inc.

Gilhooly, K. J. (1998). Working memory, strategies, and reasoning task. In R. H. Logie & K. J. Gilhooly, *Working memory and thinking* (pp. 23–45). Hove, UK: Psychology Press.

Gilhooly, K. J., Logie, R. H., Wetherick, N. E., & Wynn, V. (1993). Working memory and strategies in syllogistic-reasoning tasks. *Journal of Memory and Cognition*, *21* (1), 115–124.

Gilhooly, K. J., Logie, R. H., & Wynn, V. (1999). Syllogistic reasoning tasks and working memory: Evidence from sequential presentation of premises. *European Journal of Cognitive Psychology*, *11* (4), 473–498.

Gilinsky, A. S., & Judd, B. B. (1994). Working memory and bias in reasoning across the lifespan. *Psychology and Aging*, *9*, 356–371.

Gutiérrez, F., García-Madruga, J. A., Johnson-Laird, P. N., & Carriedo, N. (2002). Razonamiento con condicionales múltiples. La perspectiva de los modelos mentales. [Reasoning with multiple conditionals. The mental models' perspective]. *Anuario de Psicología*, *33* (1), 2–24.

Halford, G. S., Bain, J. D., & Maybery, M. T. (1984). Does a concurrent memory load interfere with reasoning? *Current Psychological Research and Reviews*, *3*, 14–23.

Johnson-Laird, P. N. (1983). *Mental models: Towards a cognitive science of language, inference, and consciousness*. Cambridge: Cambridge University Press.

Johnson-Laird, P. N. (1985). Deductive reasoning ability. In R. J. Sternberg (Ed.), *Human abilities: An information process approach* (pp. 173–194). New York: Freeman.

Johnson-Laird, P. N., & Byrne, R. M. J. (1991). *Deduction*. Hillsdale, NJ: Lawrence Erlbaum Associates, Inc.

Johnson-Laird, P. N., & Byrne, R. M. J. (2002) Conditionals: A theory of meaning, pragmatics, and inference. *Psychological Review*, *109*, 646–678.

Johnson-Laird, P. N., Byrne, R. M. J., & Schaeken, W. (1992). Propositional reasoning by model. *Psychological Review*, *99*, 418–439.

Just, M. A., & Carpenter, P. A. (1992). A capacity theory of comprehension. *Psychological Review*, *99*, 122–149.

Klauer, K. C., Stegmaier, R., & Meiser, T. (1997). Working memory involvement in propositional and spatial reasoning. *Thinking and Reasoning*, *3*, 9–48.

Logie, R. H., & Gilhooly, K. J. (1998). *Working memory and thinking*. Hove, UK: Psychology Press.

Markovits, H., Doyon, C., & Simoneau, M. (2002). Individual differences in working memory and conditional reasoning with concrete and abstract content. *Thinking and Reasoning*, *8*, 97–107.

Meilán, E., García-Madruga, J. A., & Vieiro, P. (2000). Memoria operativa y procesos de razonamiento condicional. [Working memory and conditional reasoning processes]. *Cognitiva*, *12*, 135–151.

Morris, B. J., & Sloutsky, V. (2002) Children's solutions of logical versus empirical problems: What's missing and what develops? *Cognitive Development*, *16*, 907–928.

Norman, D. A., & Shallice, T. (1980). *Attention to action: Willed and automatic control of behavior*. University of California at San Diego (CHIP Report No. 99).

Philips, L. H., & Forshaw, M. J. (1998). The role of working memory in age differences in reasoning. In R. H. Logie & K. J. Gilhooly (Eds.), *Working memory and thinking* (pp. 23–45). Hove, UK: Psychology Press.

Richardson, J. T. E. (1996). Evolving concepts of working memory. In J. T. E. Richardson, R. W. Engle, L. Hasher, R. H. Logie, E. R. Stoltzfus, & R. T. Zacks (Eds.), *Working memory and human cognition* (pp. 3–30). New York: Oxford University Press.

Richardson, J., & Ormerod, T. C. (1997) Rephrasing between disjunctives and conditionals: Mental models and the effects of thematic content. *Quarterly Journal of Experimental Psychology, 50A*, 358–385.

Rips, L. J. (1994). *The psychology of proof: Deductive reasoning in human reasoning*. Cambridge, MA: MIT Press.

Shah, P., & Miyake, A. (1996). The separability of working memory resources for spatial thinking and language processing: An individual differences approach. *Journal of Experimental Psychology: General, 125*, 4–27.

Shallice, T., & Burgess, P. (1993). Supervisory control of action and thought selection. In A. D. Baddeley & L. Weiskrantz (Eds.), *Attention, selection, awareness, and control: A tribute to Donald Broadbent* (pp. 171–187). Oxford: Oxford University Press.

Toms, M., Warris, N., & Ward, D. (1993). Working memory and conditional reasoning. *Quarterly Journal of Experimental Psychology, 46A*, 679–699.

Waters, G. & Caplan, D. (1996). The measurement of verbal working memory capacity and its relation to reading comprehension. *Quarterly Journal of Experimental Psychology*: Human Experimental Psychology, 49A, 51–79.

Yuill, N., Oakhill, J., & Parkin, A. (1989). Working memory, comprehension ability and the resolution of text anomaly. *British Journal of Psychology, 80*, 351–361.

5 Resolving contradictions

Ruth M.J. Byrne and Clare A. Walsh

Introduction

In a story written by Rex Stout in 1949 called "Instead of Evidence", a man is killed by an explosive hidden in a cigar he smokes. When the police examine the cigar box, they find that several of the cigars have been carefully and skilfully rewrapped with explosive hidden inside them. When all of the cigars are taken out of the box, they discover a few strands of long hair. Inspector Cramer suspects that the man's wife, Martha, is the killer. He believes that if Martha's hair is in the box then she's the murderer. And he tells the heroes of the novel, Nero Wolfe and Archie Goodwin, that it is Martha's hair. Inspector Cramer concludes that Martha is the murderer and he wants to arrest her. However, Martha is Nero Wolfe and Archie Goodwin's client. They believe she is not the murderer. Such contradictions are common, not only in fiction but also in real life. A theory predicts a certain observation, but the data reveal otherwise; an economic policy dictates a certain course of action, but the politicians responsible for implementing it take a different course; your memory for where you left your keys indicates they should be in their usual place, but when you look for them, they're not. One of Paolo Legrenzi's most recent important contributions to our knowledge about human reasoning has been to show that people can detect some inconsistencies readily (Legrenzi, Girotto, & Johnson-Laird, 2003) and our interest in this chapter is in how people resolve such contradictions.

Nero Wolfe and Archie Goodwin set about resolving the contradiction in two different ways. Archie Goodwin tackles the facts. He rejects Inspector Cramer's categorical claim that the hair in the cigar box is Martha's. He tells Inspector Cramer that the hair in the cigar box is *not* Martha's. In the pre-DNA analysis days of 1949 his outright rejection of the police chief's "fact" is plausible. Nero Wolfe takes a different tack. He revises Inspector Cramer's conditional hypothesis that if Martha's hair is in the box then she's the murderer. He says if Martha's hair is in box then she is *not* the murderer: "Those hairs, far from being evidence that Martha killed her husband, are instead evidence that she did not kill her husband!" He argues that any murderer so methodical and thorough as to be able to hide explosives in skilfully rewrapped cigars would not be so careless as to leave some strands of hair in the cigar box. Instead he argues that the hairs must have been deliberately planted there to frame his client. To resolve a contradiction, it is equally possible to revise the conditional claim, as Nero Wolfe did, or the categorical claim, as Archie Goodwin did. Our primary aim in this chapter is to examine the circumstances under which people choose to resolve contradictions by revising conditional claims or by revising categorical claims.

Conditional inferences

We will focus on contradictions to conclusions that people have inferred. For example, given the premises:

> If water was poured on the campfire, the fire went out
> Water was poured on the campfire

Most people infer:

> The fire went out

(e.g., Evans, Newstead, & Byrne, 1993 for a review). Given the subsequent information:

> The fire did not go out

they must resolve the contradiction. In fact, people are able to resolve contradictions but very little is known about how they do it (e.g., Elio & Pelletier, 1997).

Inferences from conditionals have attracted probably more attention than any other sort of deductive reasoning, in part because conditional reasoning underlies our ability to think hypothetically (e.g., Johnson-Laird & Byrne, 1991). Hypothetical or suppositional thought is central to most thinking, from planning to problem solving, and from scientific discovery to daily argumentative communication. Some conditional inferences are very easy. For example, given the conditional:

> If Joe puts 50 cents in the machine, he gets a Coke

and the categorical:

> Joe put 50 cents in the machine

Most people can readily infer:

> He got a Coke

This modus ponens inference is so fundamental that we would have great difficulty understanding someone who routinely failed to make it. Given the premises:

> If Joe puts 50 cents in the machine, he gets a Coke
> Joe put 50 cents in the machine

a person would be a mystery to us if they routinely inferred:

> Therefore, he did not get a Coke

an inference dubbed "modus schmonens" by Rips (1986).

Modus ponens seems effortless and automatic and in experiments almost everyone makes it readily. But there are other conditional inferences that are more difficult. Given the conditional information:

> If Joe puts 50 cents in the machine, he gets a Coke

and the categorical information:

> He did not get a Coke

some people consider that nothing follows. Others make the inference to the conclusion:

> He did not put 50 cents in the machine

This *modus tollens* conclusion is logically valid, just as the modus ponens one is. But the modus tollens inference is more difficult for people to make: They make more errors, they take longer to make it, and they subjectively view it as harder (e.g., Evans et al., 1993).

Mental models

Some conditional inferences are easy and some are hard, and theories of reasoning have to be able to explain the difference. A theory of reasoning must explain the competence that underlies reasoning abilities, and that enables people to make some inferences effortlessly. It must also explain the limitations on reasoning abilities, the performance constraints that hamper reasoning, and which can lead to errors. There are several alternative views of reasoning. One view is that people rely on inference rules that operate in virtue of their form (Braine & O'Brien, 1998; Rips, 1994) and another view is that people rely on inference rules sensitive to specific domains (Cheng & Holyoak, 1985; Fiddick, Cosmides, & Tooby, 2000). A third view of conditional reasoning is that people construct mental models (Johnson-Laird & Byrne, 1991, 2002), and it is this view that we will consider further.

What is meant by mental models is simple. People keep in mind true possibilities (Johnson-Laird & Byrne, 2002). When they understand a conditional such as:

If Joe puts 50 cents in the machine he gets a Coke

they think about the possibilities that are true of the conditional. "Joe puts 50 cents in the machine and gets a Coke" is one true possibility, another is "Joe does not put 50 cents in the machine and does not get a Coke":

    50 cents   Coke
    not-50 cents   not-Coke

where "50 cents" represents "Joe puts in 50 cents", "Coke" represents "Joe got a Coke" and "not" is a tag to represent negation (Johnson-Laird, Byrne, & Schaeken, 1992). Different models are represented on separate lines. People may think of other true possibilities depending on the interpretation they have come to of the conditional (the two possibilities here correspond to a "biconditional" interpretation). The important principle is that in general people keep in mind only true possibilities, and not possibilities that make the conditional false, such as "Joe puts in 50 cents and does not get a Coke". In some situations people think explicitly about false possibilities: for example, when they reason counterfactually (e.g., Byrne & Tasso, 1999; Thompson & Byrne, 2002), or when they reason about obligations and permissions (e.g., Quelhas & Byrne, 2003). But in general people think about true possibilities.

A second key principle of the mental model theory is that people do not keep in mind all of the true possibilities. Instead they try to represent as few possibilities as possible (Johnson-Laird & Byrne, 1991, 2002). The constraints of their limited working memories ensure that they construct a minimal representation. Their initial set of models may make explicit only the possibility mentioned in the assertion, that is, "Joe puts 50 cents in the machine and gets a Coke":

    50 cents   Coke
        . . .

Their understanding of the conditional is not merely conjunctive, however, and they keep in mind an implicit model, represented in the diagram by the three dots. They appreciate that there are alternative possibilities to the single explicit possibility they have kept in mind, but they do not think about these alternatives explicitly at this point. The implicit model is essentially an unformed thought. In the computer programs that simulate the theory, the implicit model can be considered to be essentially a means to construct a representation rather than a representation in itself (for a description of such a computer program see Johnson-Laird & Byrne, 1991, chapter 9).

Mental models and conditional inferences

These principles can explain why some inferences are easy and some are hard. When people are given a conditional premise such as:

If Joe puts 50 cents in the machine he gets a Coke

they construct an initial set of models of the conditional that makes explicit one true possibility:

50 cents   Coke
        . . .

When they are given the categorical information:

He put 50 cents in the machine

and they are asked:

What, if anything, follows?

the categorical information matches the true possibility explicitly represented in their initial set of models. They can readily infer the conclusion:

He got a Coke

In contrast when they are given the categorical information:

He didn't get a Coke

it does not match the true possibility represented in their initial models. They may conclude that nothing follows. To make the inference they must flesh out their initial models to be explicit, to think about other true possibilities:

50 cents   Coke
not-50 cents   not-Coke

Once they have thought more deeply about what the conditional means in this way, they can make the modus tollens inference:

He didn't put 50 cents in the machine

However, the modus tollens inference requires extra effort: It requires models to be fleshed out and multiple possibilities to be kept in mind. The model theory explains why the modus ponens inference is easy and the modus tollens inference is hard. The key difference between the two inferences is that the modus ponens inference can be made effortlessly on the basis of the initial superficial understanding of the conditional, that is, a single true possibility consistent with it, whereas the modus tollens inference takes more effort, and requires people to think more deeply about the meaning of the conditional, that is, to think about more of the true possibilities that are consistent with it.

Contradictions

Everyday human inference seems effortlessly to cope with inconsistency, and so to operate in a "non-monotonic" way (e.g., Byrne, Espino, & Santamaria, 1999; Legrenzi, Girotto, & Johnson-Laird, 2003). Given the conditional claim:

If Joe puts 50 cents in the machine, he gets a Coke

the categorical information:

He put 50 cents in the machine

and asked, to say what, if anything, follows, most people infer:

Therefore, he got a Coke

But suppose subsequent information becomes available:

In fact Joe did not get a Coke

What should be believed to be true now? How can the new information be reconciled with the earlier information to resolve the contradiction? That question forms the basis of a series of experiments we have recently completed, and we will describe some of the results here (see Byrne & Walsh, 2003 for further details).

When people encounter a contradiction, it does not cause major chaos within their belief systems. They usually manage to resolve it, often with a minimum of fuss. But how people manage to resolve contradictions is a non-trivial problem. In fact, it has been a stumbling block in the development of artificial intelligence (Gardenfors, 1988). It turns out to be difficult to build computer programs that can deal well with contradictions and there has been a debate on the issue among artificial intelligence researchers since the 1980s. The key problem is that when we encounter a contradiction, it tells us something has gone wrong, but it does not pinpoint what is wrong. The key question is, when we encounter a contradiction between our beliefs, how can we know which belief to hold on to and which to abandon? A major endeavour within artificial intelligence research is the attempt to work out what the best principles for revising beliefs may be (e.g., Gardenfors, 1988).

Given that people are good at belief revision and computers are poor at it, one solution would be for computers to simulate what people do. But therein lies a difficulty: Almost nothing is known about how people revise beliefs. Despite belief revision being a major issue in both philosophy and artificial intelligence (e.g., Gardenfors, 1988; Harman, 1986), very little is known in psychology about it. The problem has only come to the fore in the last few years (e.g., Elio & Pelletier, 1997), and there have been only a handful of experimental studies to address it.

Conditional and categorical beliefs

A key factor addressed in psychological studies is that there are different kinds of beliefs. One sort of belief can be expressed in a conditional assertion, such as "If Joe puts 50 cents in the machine he gets a Coke." Conditionals often express hypotheses, rules, explanations, law-like generalisations, or theories about the world. Another sort of belief can be expressed in a categorical assertion, such as "Joe put 50 cents in the machine." Categoricals often express facts, data or observations about the world (Elio & Pelletier, 1997). Artificial intelligence researchers have debated whether making a change to one sort of belief rather than another will result in the least change overall to the belief system, and thus allow a contradiction to be resolved painlessly. A key factor has been the idea of "epistemic entrenchment", that is, some beliefs may be more embedded within a belief system than others (e.g., Gardenfors, 1988). Arguably, a conditional belief that expresses an explanation, theory or hypothesis may be fundamental to a belief system. Rejecting a conditional rule could cause an entire edifice of beliefs to crumble. One principle of belief revision may be to make minimal changes (e.g., Harman, 1986). To the extent that conditionals describe lawlike generalisations, people may be less likely to revise them than categorical beliefs. Of course, logically it is acceptable to revise either sort of belief, conditionals or categorical beliefs (Revlin, Cate, & Rouss, 2001). And psychologically, either sort of belief can be revised plausibly, as the example about Nero Wolfe and Archie Goodwin illustrates. Which belief do people prefer to revise?

It turns out that they do not focus equally on these two sorts of beliefs. Instead, overall people seem to revise conditional claims more than categorical ones (Elio & Pelletier, 1997). The result may seem surprising in the light of ideas about entrenchment from artificial intelligence. However, there are intriguing hints in recent studies that people revise categorical claims in some situations, and they revise conditional claims in others (Dieussaert, Schaeken,

De Neys, & d'Ydewalle, 2000; Girotto, Johnson-Laird, Legrenzi, & Sonino, 2000; Politzer & Carles, 2001). Our experiments shed further light on the puzzling finding that people revise conditional beliefs.

Revising unfamiliar beliefs

In one of our experiments we gave reasoners the science fiction content used in several previous studies (e.g., Elio & Pelletier, 1997; Politzer & Carles, 2001). We asked people to imagine that they were part of an outer space exploration team that is making new discoveries about the now extinct inhabitants of a distant planet. In this novel and unfamiliar domain, they were told they would be given some initial knowledge that was true and well established at the time they began exploring, and that there were no mistakes at that time. They were told for example:

> If the ruin was inhabited by Pings it had a forcefield surrounding it
> The ruin was inhabited by Pings

Their first task, they were told, was to record in the exploration manual what they could infer, if anything, from this true and established knowledge. Most wrote down the modus ponens conclusion:

> Therefore, it had a forcefield

We took care to ask them to generate their own conclusions. In previous studies reasoners were often simply given conclusions to evaluate, but we wanted to make sure that they had made the inference we thought they would make, so we could be sure in turn that the subsequent information genuinely contradicted their conclusion.

After they had written down their conclusion, reasoners were then told that additional knowledge about the planet had come to light at a later time. This knowledge was also true and well established. The world was still the same but what had happened was that knowledge about it had increased. They were told that:

> The ruin did not have a forcefield

They were told that their task was to try to reconcile the initial knowledge and the additional knowledge. They were told to write down what they now believed to be true of all the knowledge they had at this point.

We gave reasoners the two sorts of inferences, the easy modus ponens inference, and also the more difficult modus tollens inference:

> If the ruin was inhabited by Pings it had a forcefield surrounding it
> The ruin did not have a forcefield

They were asked to write what, if anything, follows. Many of them concluded that:

Therefore, it was not inhabited by Pings

They were then told that:

It was inhabited by Pings

They were asked to say what they should now believe to be true. We will not consider the differences in responses to the modus ponens and tollens inferences here (see Byrne & Walsh, 2002). Instead we will focus on the nature of their revisions, which revealed an interesting asymmetry.

Do people reject a belief or modify it?

Reasoners wrote down the resolution of the contradiction that they generated themselves. We asked them to generate their own resolutions rather than simply to evaluate pre-set resolutions in part because we wanted to examine the different ways reasoners resolve contradictions; for example, whether their revisions consist of outright disbelief or doubt in a premise (e.g., Elio & Pelletier, 1997; Politzer & Carles, 2001). The emphasis in previous research on abandoning beliefs may underestimate the range of possible resolutions of a contradiction naturally available to reasoners (Politzer & Carles, 2001). When reasoners are asked what they believe to be true, they can of course abandon a belief, e.g., they can reject the categorical "it is not the case that the ruin was inhabited by Pings" or they can reject the conditional "it is not the case that if the ruin was inhabited by Pings it had a forcefield surrounding it", or they can reject the contradiction "it is not the case that the ruin did not have a force-field". But past research on conditional inference shows that people can do more than simply disbelieve or doubt a premise, they can reinterpret it (Byrne, 1989; Byrne et al., 1999). In fact, reasoners appear to appreciate as many as ten distinct interpretations of conditionals (Johnson-Laird & Byrne, 2002). Our decision to ask participants to generate their own revisions allowed us to examine whether reasoners ever reinterpreted the premises to reconcile the contradictory information.

In the experiment, we gave reasoners various different science fiction contents. They made inferences based on several modus ponens and modus tollens inferences, and from conditionals that were indicative factual conditionals, or subjunctive counterfactual conditionals. The reasoners were 28 undergraduates from Trinity College, Dublin University, and our primary interest in this chapter is in the nature of their revisions to the conditional or categorical premise.

Overall, we replicated earlier findings that more participants focused on the conditional than on the categorical belief (45 per cent versus 28 per cent).

However, their spontaneous revisions show an interesting asymmetry in their revisions of conditional and categorical beliefs. The results show that reasoners do not simply abandon conditional beliefs. In a few cases they rejected the premise, but often they did more than simply disbelieve or doubt it. Instead they modified their interpretation. In a few cases, people rejected the conditional saying for example, "it is false that if the ruin was inhabited by Pings then it had a forcefield surrounding it" or "the ruin being inhabited by Pings does not imply that it has a forcefield", or simply "the ruin was inhabited by Pings but it did not have a forcefield". Many of their revisions were not rejections however, and were instead modifications. They modified a conditional in a variety of ways, for example, by tagging it as an exception: not all ruins inhabited by Pings are surrounded by a forcefield, or by questioning the necessity of the relationship, e.g., ruins inhabited by Pings do not necessarily have forcefields surrounding them. They sometimes invoked a temporal aspect, e.g., the ruin was inhabited by Pings at one time and no longer has a forcefield surrounding it, or even introduced a new additional feature, e.g., the weather affected the ability of the Pings who inhabited this ruin to construct a forcefield surrounding it. The 45 per cent who focused on the conditional breaks down into 37 per cent of participants generating such modifications and just 8 per cent of them rejecting the conditional. In contrast, when they focused on a categorical fact, they tended to reject it outright, e.g., "Pings did not inhabit this ruin" rather than modify it, e.g., "only a few Pings inhabited this ruin". The 28 per cent who focused on the categorical premise breaks down into 24 per cent who rejected it and 4 per cent who modified it.

The experiment sheds some light on the otherwise surprising result that reasoners tend to revise the more entrenched conditional belief. The experiment shows that when people revise the conditional, they do not reject the belief outright; a step which could cause considerable disruption to related beliefs within a belief system. Instead they make a small adjustment, tweaking this entrenched part of their belief system to accommodate the contradictory information. In contrast, when they focus on the (possibly less entrenched) categorical belief, they tend to simply reject it outright.

The experiment shows that people readily revise their beliefs when they encounter a contradiction. It adds a little to our small store of knowledge about how people revise unfamiliar beliefs. It is important to understand how beliefs about an unfamiliar domain are revised because that is the situation people are in when they are learning something new. When they are acquiring new knowledge or new skills it is often useful to formulate working hypotheses to guide explorations, but these hypotheses by their very nature in an unfamiliar domain are tentative and can be falsified by subsequent information. People need to be able to revise their beliefs as they acquire more knowledge about the domain. Modifying conditional hypotheses in an unfamiliar domain may be a useful strategy to ensure that new knowledge can be assimilated. Understanding more about how people revise unfamiliar beliefs is crucial to understanding how they learn.

Equally important, however, is the need to understand how people revise *familiar* beliefs (Dieussaert et al., 2000; Dieussaert, Schaeken, & d'Ydewalle, 2002; Elio, 1997; Politzer & Carles, 2001). Familiar beliefs are, of course, more entrenched beliefs. We may expect that familiar beliefs, especially familiar conditional beliefs, will be so entrenched that they will be resistant to change. Revising such beliefs may be a mistake as it may cause a radical overhaul of a belief system. Changing fundamental beliefs may cause a whole set of related beliefs to topple. Our aim in another of our experiments was to examine how people revise familiar beliefs.

Revising familiar beliefs

We gave reasoners scenarios based on familiar causal and definitional domains. An example of the one of the familiar causes is:

If water was poured on the campfire the fire went out

And an example of one of the familiar definitions is:

If the animal was a labrador it was a dog

The causes and definitions were chosen carefully to control for various factors such as the necessity and sufficiency of the antecedents (Thompson, 1994). We gave reasoners modus ponens and modus tollens inferences based on causes, definitions and also the science fiction content of the previous experiment, once again based on either indicative or subjunctive conditionals. The participants were 40 undergraduates from Trinity College, Dublin University, and members of the psychology department's participant panel, who are members of the general public recruited through national newspaper advertisements. Once again we gave them information which we described as an initial set of knowledge about a specific situation that they were to assume was true and well established and there were no mistakes in it, for example:

If water was poured on the campfire the fire went out
Water was poured on the campfire

Their first task was to record what they could infer, if anything, from this true and established knowledge about the situation. They were then presented with what was described as additional knowledge about the situation that had come to light at a later time. This knowledge was also true and well established. The situation was still the same, but what had happened was that knowledge about it had increased. Then we gave them information which contradicted their conclusion, for example:

The fire did not go out

Their task was to try to reconcile the initial knowledge and the additional knowledge. They were asked to write down what they now believed to be true of all the knowledge they had at this point.

The experiment showed that people rarely revised the causal or definitional conditionals, which are likely to be entrenched within their beliefs. Instead they tended to focus on the categorical fact. They focused on the categorical fact after a contradiction to a definitional inference more than on the conditional (48 per cent versus 15 per cent). For example, when they were told the conditional "if the animal was a labrador then it was a dog" and the categorical "it was not a dog", they inferred "it was not a labrador". The contradiction "it was a labrador" was incorporated by simply rejecting outright the categorical fact "it was not a dog". A few reasoners modified the conditional instead, e.g., not all labradors are dogs (some are people from the place Labrador), but mostly reasoners rejected the categorical fact. Likewise, they focused on the categorical fact after a contradiction to a cause, more than on the conditional (48 per cent versus 19 per cent). For example, when they were told the conditional "if water was poured on the campfire the fire went out" and the categorical fact "water was poured on the campfire" they inferred "the fire went out". The contradiction "the fire did not go out" was incorporated again by simply rejecting the categorical fact "water was poured on the campfire". A few reasoners modified the conditional instead, e.g., if *enough* water is poured on the campfire the fire goes out, but mostly, they rejected the categorical fact.

Once again, as in the previous experiment, when reasoners focused on a categorical they tended to reject it outright rather than modify it. The 48 per cent who focused on the categorical for the causal content breaks down into 29 per cent rejections and 19 per cent modifications; likewise, the 48 per cent who focused on the categorical for the definitional content breaks down into 46 per cent rejections and 2 per cent modifications. In contrast, when they focused on a conditional, they tended to modify it. The 19 per cent who focused on the conditional for the causal content breaks down into 15 per cent modifications and 4 per cent rejections; the 15 per cent who focused on the conditional for the definitional content breaks down into 8 per cent modifications and 7 per cent rejections.

The experiment shows that for familiar beliefs people tend to focus on the categorical facts and reject them outright. They did not tend to revise the conditional in this familiar domain where the conditional is likely to be entrenched within their beliefs. Instead, they incorporated the contradiction by rejecting the categorical fact.

Belief revision

People are readily able to resolve contradictions to conclusions they have reached, better then current artificial intelligence programs can. But we know very little about how people manage to deal with contradictions so readily.

One possibility is that people hold on to their more entrenched beliefs. Yet earlier studies have shown that people tend to revise conditionals more than categorical beliefs, and conditionals may be more entrenched given that they often express rules or generalisations about the world. Our results replicate this puzzling finding and shed some light on it. Conditionals in an unfamiliar domain are revised more than categorical beliefs, but the revisions carried out on them are modifications to their interpretation, rather than outright rejections of them. Adjusting a working hypothesis in an unfamiliar domain may be a very useful strategy for continuing to amass knowledge rather than having to start again from scratch.

Our results also show that people revise beliefs somewhat differently in a familiar domain. People revise categorical beliefs more than conditional beliefs in a familiar domain. They revise familiar beliefs by rejecting the categorical facts in a familiar domain, regardless of whether the domain concerns causal or definitional beliefs. Conditionals in a familiar domain may express laws or rules which are more deeply entrenched than the hypotheses expressed by conditionals in an unfamiliar domain, and so people do not revise familiar conditionals so readily. The experiments show that, regardless of whether the domain is familiar or unfamiliar, people tend to reject facts outright but they modify conditional beliefs. People do not incorporate contradictions simply by adopting some beliefs and abandoning others. Instead they engage in a more flexible strategy of modifying their beliefs to genuinely resolve the contradiction.

The process of belief revision is vital in helping people to maintain a consistent set of beliefs. A decision about which belief to revise helps to advance knowledge in scientific discovery; e.g., in accommodating data that disconfirms the predictions of a theory, should we abandon the theory or modify it? Our results suggest that people tend to prefer modifications to conditional beliefs. The finding is consistent with field studies of scientific discovery. At university lab meetings, Dunbar (2001) found that scientists' first tendency was to attribute an unexpected finding to a methodological error. The strategy may be useful, because if theories are rejected too readily it will be difficult for knowledge to advance. Our experiments show that in dealing with contradictions, people have mastered a careful balance in updating their beliefs.

Epilogue

Readers may wonder whether Archie Goodwin was right to reject Inspector Cramer's categorical fact, the hair at the bottom of the cigar box was Martha's, to claim instead that the hair was not Martha's, or whether Nero Wolfe was right to reject Inspector Cramer's conditional belief that if the hair was Martha's then she was the killer, and to claim instead that if the hair was Martha's then she was not the killer. In fact, in this rare instance Nero Wolfe and Archie Goodwin were both wrong. Martha did kill her husband. The hairs in the box were hers. However, Nero Wolfe *was* right that the killer was too methodical and skilled to have carelessly left behind the strands of hair, and that their presence indicated that they had been placed there deliberately to frame Martha. In fact, Martha had planted them there herself to throw everyone off her trail.

Acknowledgements

Thanks to Michelle Cowley and Michelle Flood for help with the experiments, Suzanne Egan and Aisling Murray for comments, and Kristien Dieussaert, Renee Elio, Uri Hasson, Phil Johnson-Laird and Guy Politzer for discussions of belief revision. The research was supported by awards from Trinity College Dublin's Berkeley Fellowship fund, and Arts and Social Sciences Benefactions fund, and by a grant from Enterprise Ireland EI-SC-2000–014

References

Braine, M. D. S., & O'Brien, D. (1998). *Mental logic*. Mahwah, NJ: Lawrence Erlbaum Associates, Inc.

Byrne, R. M. J. (1989). Suppressing valid inferences with conditionals. *Cognition, 31*, 61–83.

Byrne, R. M. J., & Tasso, A. (1999). Deductive reasoning with factual, possible and counterfactual conditionals. *Memory and Cognition, 27*, 726–740.

Byrne, R. M. J., & Walsh, C. (2002). Contradictions and counterfactuals: Generating belief revisions in conditional inference. In W. D. Gray & C. D. Schunn (Eds.), *Proceedings of the 24th Annual Conference of the Cognitive Science Society* (pp. 160–165). Mahwah, NJ: Lawrence Erlbaum Associates, Inc.

Byrne, R. M. J., & Walsh, C. (2003). *Belief revision and counterfactual conditionals*. Unpublished manuscript.

Byrne, R. M. J., Espino, O., & Santamaria, C. (1999). Counterexamples and the suppression of inferences. *Journal of Memory and Language, 40*, 347–373.

Cheng, P. W., & Holyoak, K. J. (1985). Pragmatic reasoning schemas. *Cognitive Psychology, 17*, 391–416.

Dieussaert, K., Schaeken, W., De Neys, W., & d'Ydewalle, G. (2000). Initial belief state as a predictor of belief revision. *Current Psychology of Cognition, 19*, 277–288.

Dieussaert, K., Schaeken, W., & d'Ydewalle, G. (2002). A study of the belief revision process: The value of context and contra-evidence. Technical report No. 291, University of Leuven.

Dunbar, K. (2001). What scientific thinking reveals about the nature of cognition. In K. Crowley, C. D. Schunn, & T. Okada (Eds.), *Designing for science: Implications from everyday, classroom, and professional settings.* (pp. 115–140). Hillsdale, NJ: Lawrence Erlbaum Associates, Inc.

Elio R. (1997). What to believe when inferences are contradicted. In M. Shafto & P. Langley (Eds.), *Proceedings of the 19th Annual Conference of the Cognitive Science Society* (pp. 211–216). Hillsdale, NJ: Lawrence Erlbaum Associates, Inc.

Elio, R., & Pelletier, F. J. (1997). Belief change as propositional update. *Cognitive Science, 21*, 419–460.

Evans, J. St. B. T., Newstead, S., & Byrne, R. M. J. (1993). *Human reasoning: The psychology of deduction.* Hove, UK and Hillsdale, NJ: Lawrence Erlbaum Associates, Inc.

Fiddick, L., Cosmides, L., & Tooby, J. (2000). No interpretation without representation: The role of domain-specific representations and inferences in the Wason selection task. *Cognition, 77,* 1–79.

Gardenfors, P. (1988). *Knowledge in flux.* Cambridge, MA: MIT Press.

Girotto, V., Johnson-Laird, P. N., Legrenzi, P., & Sonino, M. (2000). Reasoning to consistency: How people resolve logical inconsistencies. In J. García-Madruga, N. Carriedo, & M. J. González-Labra (Eds.), *Mental models in reasoning* (pp. 83–97). Madrid: UNED.

Harman, G. (1986). *Change in view.* Cambridge, MA: MIT Press.

Johnson-Laird, P. N., & Byrne, R. M. J. (1991). *Deduction.* Hove, UK: Lawrence Erlbaum Associates Ltd.

Johnson-Laird, P. N., & Byrne, R. M. J. (2002) Conditionals: A theory of meaning, pragmatics, and inference. *Psychological Review, 109,* 646–678.

Johnson-Laird, P. N., Byrne, R. M. J., & Schaeken, W. S. (1992). Propositional reasoning by model. *Psychological Review, 99,* 418–439.

Legrenzi, P., Girotto V., & Johnson-Laird, P. N. (2003). Models of consistency. *Psychological Science, 14,* 131–137.

Politzer, G., & Carles, L. (2001). Belief revision and uncertain reasoning. *Thinking & Reasoning, 7,* 217–234.

Quelhas, A. C., & Byrne, R. M. J. (2003). Reasoning with deontic counterfactual conditionals. *Thinking & Reasoning. 9,* 43–65.

Revlin, R., Cate, C. L., & Rouse, T. S. (2001). Reasoning counterfactually: Combining and rending. *Memory & Cognition, 29,* 1196–1208.

Rips, L. J. (1986). Mental muddles. In M. Brand & R. M. Harnish (Eds.), *The representation of knowledge and belief* (pp. 258–286). Tucsok: University of Arizona Press.

Rips, L. J. (1994). *The psychology of proof.* Cambridge, MA: MIT Press.

Thompson, V. (1994). Interpretational factors in conditional reasoning. *Memory & Cognition, 22,* 742–758.

Thompson, V. A., & Byrne, R. M. J. (2002). Making inferences about things that didn't happen. *Journal of Experimental Psychology: Learning, Memory and Cognition, 28,* 1154–1170.

Part III

Pragmatics, hypotheses, and probabilities

6 How to defocus in hypothesis testing: Manipulating the initial triple in the 2–4–6 problem

Jean-Paul Caverni, Sandrine Rossi, and Jean-Luc Péris

Introduction

One of the most widely used tasks for studying hypothesis testing in inductive reasoning is Wason's (1960) 2–4–6 problem. In this task, the experimenter tells the participants that he has a rule in mind concerning triples of numbers. The triple 2–4–6 is presented as satisfying the rule, and the participants' task is to discover this rule by proposing triples. For each proposed triple, the experimenter says whether or nor it follows the rule. The participants are asked to write down each triple, the hypothesis under test, and the experimenter's response. Whenever the participants think they have discovered the rule, they state it, and the experimenter says whether it is correct or incorrect. If incorrect, the participants continue to propose triples until they either discover the rule or give up. Two phenomena have been observed in the task. In general:

(1) Participants propose triples that are positive examples of the hypothesis they claim they are testing (e.g., the "increasing linear series" hypothesis is tested with triples such as 10–12–14, 10–20–30, etc.).
(2) Participants start by hypothesising the most specific rules (e.g., "an increasing series of numbers which differ by 2"), whereas the rule to be discovered is more general ("an increasing series of numbers").

Since 1960, this task has been extensively investigated (for recent reviews, see Gorman, 1995; Poletiek, 2000), and the aforementioned results have been replicated even in studies where the task instructions were changed ("Be disconfirming!" as in studies by Mynatt, Doherty, & Tweney, 1977, 1978) or where the task was transformed (by specifying that the provided feedback may sometimes be erroneous, as in Gorman, 1986). The only ways to induce disconfirming behaviour seem to be to tell participants explicitly to test negative examples (e.g., Gorman & Gorman, 1984), or to tell them that the initial triple is a counterexample rather than an example of the tested rule (Rossi, Caverni, & Girotto, 2001), or to ask them to find two rules, one that is satisfied by "dax" triples and one that is satisfied by "med" triples (Tweney, Doherty, Warner, & Pliske, 1980).

The prevailing interpretation for quite some time was that participants are prone to confirmation bias: They would rather verify (or confirm) their hypotheses than falsify (or disconfirm) them. For Evans (1983), however, this bias is not caused by a participant's deliberate choice, but by a cognitive difficulty in processing negative information: "It is not that participants do not wish to falsify, it is simply that they cannot think of the way to do it" (p. 143). In this case, then, we are not dealing with a confirmation bias, but with a positivity bias. This idea conforms to the Wason's original work (e.g., 1959, 1965), which yielded evidence that individuals have difficulties in processing negation.

There seems, however, to be another way to describe the phenomenon. What information does the participant use to interpret the problem statement? One important piece of information here is that the particular triple "2–4–6" is presented to exemplify the rule to be discovered. Suppose a participant is taking an intelligence test and has to complete the series 2–4–6. Obviously, the simplest correct answer is 8–10–12. Hence, in Wason's task, the initial triple is typical of an obvious rule (numbers increasing in intervals of 2) that is more specific than the one to be discovered (increasing numbers). It is neither socially conventional nor didactically efficient to choose examples having conspicuous properties that do not suggest the law they are supposed to illustrate (see Armstrong, Gleitman, & Gleitman, 1983). As Girotto and Politzer (1990) remarked, the fact that the 2–4–6 triple evokes a more specific rule than the experimenter's one can be considered as a violation of the Gricean maxim of quantity (Grice, 1989). According to this view, we hypothesise that the example used in the original task misleads the participants by implicitly introducing irrelevant assumptions or constraints. This phenomenon is similar to the focusing process proposed by Legrenzi, Girotto, and Johnson-Laird (1993): The initial premise presented to the participants leads them to focus on certain mental models rather than others, so they restrict their thoughts to what is explicitly represented in their mental models.

What would happen if participants could be led to think that 2–4–6 is not necessarily a well-chosen example of the rule to be discovered? If their behaviour stems from their overconstraining the problem because of their knowledge of the properties of "good" examples, then it should be modified by the knowledge that the example provided is not necessarily a "good" one.

How could participants be led to think that 2–4–6 is not necessarily a well-chosen example of the rule? The experimental instructions for the task usually stipulate that the experimenter "has a rule in mind" and that the triple 2–4–6 conforms to the rule. They do not, however, specify the ways in which the experimenter selected the rule or the initial triple. Hence, it is natural for the participants to assume that the experimenter has chosen the rule, and chosen the triple to be a good example of the rule (with the usual properties described above). But, if the rule and the triple are said to have been "randomly drawn" from sets of rules and triples, then there is no implied guarantee about the quality of the initial triple.

In the real world, when somebody is trying to discover a natural rule, two possibilities exist. Either the rule is generated by a natural process (such as a natural law), or it has been chosen by somebody (as in a parlour game). Given a rule to be discovered, whatever its provenance, then another problem concerns the origin of the initial instance of the rule. Once again, there are two possibilities: either the initial instance is picked at random from all the possible examples, or a human being has selected it with a particular intention in mind.

In the standard 2–4–6 problem, the instructions imply to the participants that both the rule and the example have been selected by the experimenter (i.e., with a goal in mind). In our view, the different ideas that participants have about the selection of the rule and its initial instance should induce different strategies for formulating and testing their hypotheses. When the participants think that both the rule and the initial instance have been selected at random, they should have no reason to prefer one possible rule to another; i.e., they should have no reason to focus on one rule rather than another. Hence, they should try to reject hypotheses with the goal of eliminating all but the correct one at the end. It follows that the participants should use a strategy of disconfirming their hypotheses more often in this condition than in the standard one.

One potential problem concerns the respective roles of the rule and the initial triple in eliciting a strategy of disconfirmation. To answer this question we used three experimental conditions. The instructions stated

(1) Both the rule and the triple were randomly selected.
(2) Only the rule was randomly selected.
(3) Only the initial triple was randomly selected.

The control condition used the instructions from the original classic version of the task.

For the sake of simplicity, we told the participants that the rule was selected before the triple. A similar effect should occur if the opposite were true: If the triple is selected first, it is the selection of the rule that should have an effect. On the one hand, if the triple is chosen by a presumably co-operative experimenter, then it should be a "good" example, whatever the rule or its origin. On the other hand, if the triple is picked at random, there is no reason to assume that it is a "good" example of the previously selected rule, even if this rule has been carefully chosen by the experimenter. Thus, a demonstration of an effect of the way the rule and the triple were selected would show that the classic confirmation strategy is caused, at least in part, by the participants' expectations induced by the human origin of the rule.

Before we describe our experiment, we have to explain the way we traced the participants' strategies. The mere fact that participants try a triple that conforms to the hypothesis that they are testing does not show that they are

Table 6.1 The four sorts of trial revealing a strategy of confirmation or disconfirmation

Test	Expected feedback	Strategy
Positive hypothesis test (+HT)	Positive (+FB)	Confirmation
Negative hypothesis test (−HT)	Negative (−FB)	Confirmation
Positive hypothesis test (+HT)	Negative (−FB)	Disconfirmation
Negative hypothesis test (−HT)	Positive (+FB)	Disconfirmation

trying to confirm the hypothesis. There are, at least, two lines of reasoning supporting this view.

First, as Klayman and Ha (1987, 1989) and Klayman (1995) pointed out, if the rule is more specific than the hypothesis being tested, the hypothesis can be rejected only by testing a triple that is an instance of the hypothesis but not of the rule. For example, if the rule is "three consecutive even numbers" and the participant tests the hypothesis "three increasing even numbers" using the triple 4–8–10, then the feedback "no" from the experimenter disconfirms the participant's hypothesis. It is only because of the particular relation between the participant's hypothesis, which is very specific, and the rule, which is very general, that this strategy turns out to be ineffective in Wason's original task.

Second, a reason calling for a reconsideration of the categorisation of participants' trials is the nature of the feedback, *not that they get* but that they expect (Wetherick, 1962). In this way, four trial types can occur, according to (1) whether the participant attempts to confirm or to disconfirm the actual hypothesis; (2) whether the triple is consistent or inconsistent with the actual hypothesis (Caverni, Rossi, & Péris, 2000). When the participant expects a positive feedback of a triple consistent with the hypothesis, or when he expects a negative feedback of a triple inconsistent with the hypothesis, then the participant attempts to confirm the actual hypothesis. Conversely, when the participant expects a negative feedback for a triple consistent with the hypothesis, or when he expects a positive feedback for a triple inconsistent with the hypothesis, then the participant attempts to disconfirm the actual hypothesis. The four trial types are summarised in Table 6.1. Indeed, participants do not necessarily always expect a specific feedback. They have even been known to propose triples without having any particular hypothesis in mind to test (Tukey, 1986). As long as such cases are rare, however, they do not vitiate this analysis of performance.

Experiment

The purpose of the experiment was to show that when participants are led to think that the initial 2–4–6 triple or the rule to be discovered have been picked at random, then they use a disconfirmative strategy more often than in the original procedure.

Method

Participants

Eighty-three volunteers who were psychology undergraduates at the University of Burgundy in Dijon, France participated in the experiment.

Design

Participants were given the 2–4–6 task (Wason, 1960). They had to discover a rule by proposing triples. The experimenter presented an initial triple "2–4–6", which he stated was an instance satisfying the rule that the participants had to discover. Each participant was randomly assigned to one of the four experimental groups, with 20 participants in each group. Two of the groups were told that the rule was "in the experimenter's mind", and two of the groups were told that the rule was "drawn at random by the experimenter from the set of possible rules concerning triples of numbers". One of each pair of these groups was told that the 2–4–6 triple "satisfied the rule" and other group in each pair was told that the triple was "drawn at random from the set of all the triples satisfying the rule". Thus, the design manipulated two variables: the status of the rule and the status of the triple, to yield four groups. Participants wrote down each triple they declared aloud, their hypothesis, the reply they were expecting from the experimenter, and the experimenter's actual reply, all on the same sheet of paper. The experimenter answered "yes" if the proposed triple conformed to the rule, and "no" if it did not. During the experiment, the experimenter did not know what the participants wrote down apart from the triple. The participants continued the task until they either discovered the correct rule or gave up. Three independent judges scored the participants' protocols. The scoring was done according to the principles described above.

Results

Table 6.2 presents the percentages of the four sorts of trial disconfirmation, depending on whether the triple was an instance of the participants' hypothesis and expectation about feedback, in each of the four experimental groups. We rejected a total of three participants' data because their triples could not be classified in a uniform way by the three judges.

Number of hypotheses

The mean number of hypotheses tested by each participant was not reliably affected by the randomness of the rule, or the randomness of the initial triple, or by an interaction between the two (all three F ratios <1).

Table 6.2 The percentages of the four sorts of trial disconfirmation in each experimental group

		Experimental groups				
		1	*2*	*3*	*4*	
				Rule		
		Uns		Rand		
			Triple			
Strategy	*Trial type*	*Uns*	*Rand*	*Uns*	*Rand*	*Overall*
Confirmation	+HT/+FB	82	67	66	60	69
	−HT/−FB	5	8	22	6	10
Disconfirmation	+HT/−FB	13	22	11	33	20
	−HT/+FB	0	3	1	1	1

Group 1: The way both the rule and the initial triple were selected was unspecified (UNS).
Group 2: The way the rule was selected is unspecified; the initial triple was presented as selected at random (RAND).
Group 3: The way the rule was selected was said "at random"; the way the initial triple was selected was unspecified.
Group 4: The way both the rule and the initial triple were selected was said "at random"
+HT: the proposed triples (T) were positive (+) examples of the proposed hypotheses (H)
−HT: the proposed triples (T) were negative (−) examples of the proposed hypotheses (H)
+FB: the expected feedback (FB) were positive (+) feedback
−FB: the expected feedback (FB) were negative (−) feedback

Expected feedbacks

The percentage of trials on which the participants expected negative feedback was 30 per cent (10 per cent were triples that were counterexamples to the hypothesis to which the participants expected negative feedback, and 20 per cent were triples that were examples of the hypothesis to which the participants expected negative feedback). The percentage was reliably higher when the rule was said to be selected at random than when its provenance was unspecified (36 per cent vs. 24 per cent, F (1,76) = 4.86, p < 0.03). The provenance of the initial triple, i.e., whether or not it was selected at random (F (1,76) = 2.35) and interaction between the two factors (F (1,76) = 0.38) did not reliably modify the percentage of triples on which the participants expected negative feedbacks.

When the participants tried to disconfirm, they did it almost exclusively, by expecting negative feedback with triples that were positive instances of their hypotheses. Only 1.5 per cent of the participants' trials were attempts to disconfirm a hypothesis using triples that were counterexamples to the hypothesis under test. In other words, when participants do try to falsify their hypotheses, they are 13 times (20/1.5) more likely to do so by expecting negative feedback to an instance of their hypothesis than by testing a triple that violates their hypothesis.

Randomness of rule and triple

The origin of the initial triple has a reliable effect on the percentages of attempts to confirm hypotheses (71 per cent when the triple chosen at "random" as opposed to 88 per cent when its origin is unspecified, $F(1,76) = 12.26$, $p < 0.001$). Neither the origin of the rule nor the interaction between these two factors had a reliable effect on the confirmation rate (both $F < 1$).

Discussion

When the experimenter attributed a random origin to the initial triple, the participants were more likely to try to disconfirm their hypotheses. That means when participants can find good reasons to consider alternative hypotheses (i.e., not to focus on the more salient properties of the initial triple), they do so more often. The origin of the rule that they have to discover, however, does not modify this rate. The results fit nicely with our "goodness-of-the-example" hypothesis. If the participants have reasons to believe that the initial triple contains only relevant properties, then manipulating factors that induce this belief may improve performance. On the other hand, since we told participants that the rule was picked out before the triple, the way the rule was chosen has no relation to the goodness of the triple, and so the participants' performance should not be affected by the status of the rule.

The present results can be compared with those reported by Gigerenzer, Hell, and Blank, (1988), which showed that random sampling of a description is crucial to the participants' internal representation of a problem as it lead them to use or to neglect bases rates in estimating probability. Our results must also be compared with those reported by Van der Henst, Rossi, & Schroyens (2002), who designed the 2–4–6 problem in such a way that there was no presumption of relevance accompanying the triple 2–4–6. Their participants performed better when the salient characteristics of the 2–4–6-triple resulted from a random procedure (a jackpot) than when a presumption of relevance. However, our results differ from the previous ones in at least one way: Both Gigerenzer et al. (1988) and Van der Henst et al. (2002) argued that random sampling was effective when performed and observed by participants, but we showed that random sampling may be effective too, when it is only declared to participants: so a "pragmatic" way is not necessary.

Our findings about what can determine confirmatory or disconfirmatory strategies must be also compared with those obtained by Paolo Legrenzi himself. He showed that confirmatory behaviour arises from the constraints of the task and the particular social situation in which it is performed (cf. Butera & Buchs, chapter 11 in this book). Butera, Legrenzi, and Oswald

(1997) showed that when hypothesis testing takes place in situations of social confrontation, a minority source induced defocusing, whereas a majority source induced focusing.

We end with some reflections on the shape of reasoning as it has been traced in our experiment. When the participants were asked to express what feedback they expected, they expected negative feedback on a fair proportion (30 per cent) of their trials. It therefore seems wrong to assume that when participants do not have to express their expectations they always expect positive feedback. Hence, the usual coding in terms of "confirmation" or "disconfirmation", which is based on this implicit assumption, may not reflect reality.

A further problem with the usual coding of the task is that the only pattern it calls "disconfirmation" is a negative example with an (assumed) positive expected feedback. This pattern is the least common in our data (1 per cent), whereas the participants' preferred way to disconfirm was a triple satisfying their current hypothesis but with a negative expected feedback (20 per cent). An apparent paradox in our data is the fact that the confirmation rate is the same as the rate usually obtained using the classical coding (about 80 per cent). This result seems rather puzzling: To take the participants' expected feedback into account reveals previously unnoticed disconfirmations, and so the confirmation rate should be lower in our experiment than in usual studies. The comparison, however, is not appropriate, because the procedure in which the participants state their expected feedback also defines differently some trials as confirmation instead of disconfirmation; i.e., in the case of a triple that is a counterexample to the current hypothesis but the participants expects negative feedback.

What do we know about the shape of reason? We know only what the tool we use to study reason reveals about it. If the tool is wrong, the results are misshapen. There is only one way to try to avoid such mistakes: Researchers must search systematically for alternatives. Paolo has long recognised this principle, which may explain why he has influenced so many psychologists and made so many friends.

Acknowledgements

We thank Phil Johnson-Laird and Vittorio Girotto for helpful comments. While we were writing this chapter, Peter Wason died. We want to pay homage to his exceptional contribution to cognitive psychology.

References

Armstrong, S. C., Gleitman, L., & Gleitman, H. (1983). What some concepts might not be. *Cognition, 13,* 263–306.

Butera, F., Legrenzi, P., & Oswald, M. (1997). Is context a bias? *Swiss Journal of Psychology, 56,* 59–61.

Caverni, J.-P., Rossi, S., & Péris, J. L. (2000). The alternatives taken into account in hypotheses testing: Two new paradigms for investigating strategies. In J. A. García-Madruga, N. Carriedo, & M. J. Gonzalez-Labra (Eds.) *Mental models in reasoning* (pp. 133–141). Madrid: UNED.

Evans, J. St. B. T. (1983). Selective processes in reasoning. In J. St. B. T. Evans (Ed.), *Thinking and reasoning: Psychological approaches* (pp. 135–163). London: Routledge & Kegan Paul.

Gigerenzer, G., Hell, W., & Blank, H. (1988). Presentation and content: The use of base rates as a continuous variable. *Journal of Experimental Psychology: Human Perception and Performance, 14*, 513–525.

Girotto, V., & Politzer, G. (1990). Conversational and world-knowledge constraints in deductive reasoning. In J.-P. Caverni, J.-M. Fabre, & M. Gonzalez (Eds.), *Cognitive biases* (pp. 87–107). Amsterdam: North Holland.

Gorman, M. E. (1986). How possibility of error affects falsification on a task that models scientific problem-solving. *British Journal of Psychology, 77*, 85–96.

Gorman, M. E., & Gorman M. E. (1984). Comparison of disconfirmatory, confirmatory and control strategies on Wason's 2–4–6 task. *Quarterly Journal of Experimental Psychology, 36A*, 629–648.

Gorman, M. E. (1995). Hypothesis testing. In S. E. Newstead & J. St. B. T. Evans (Eds.), *Perspectives on thinking and reasoning* (pp. 147–176). Hove, UK & Hillsdale, NJ: Lawrence Erlbaum Associates, Inc.

Grice, H. P. (1989). *Studies in the way of words*. Cambridge, MA: Harvard University Press.

Johnson-Laird, P. N. (1983). *Mental models*. Cambridge: Cambridge University Press.

Klayman, J. (1995). Varieties of confirmation bias. In J. R. Busemeyer, R. Hastie, & D. L. Medin (Eds.), *Decision making from the perspective of cognitive psychology* (pp. 385–414). New York: Academic Press.

Klayman, J., & Ha, Y-W. (1987). Confirmation, disconfirmation and information in hypothesis testing. *Psychological Review, 94*, 211–228.

Klayman, J., & Ha, Y-W. (1989). Hypothesis testing in rule discovery: Strategy, structure and content. *Journal of Experimental Psychology: Learning, Memory, and Cognition, 15*, 596–604.

Legrenzi, P., Girotto, V., & Johnson-Laird, P. H. (1993) Focusing in reasoning and decision-making, *Cognition, 49*, 37–66.

Mynatt, C. R., Doherty, M. E., & Tweney, R. D. (1977). Confirmation bias in a simulated research environment: An experimental study of scientific inference. *Quarterly Journal of Experimental Psychology, 24*, 326–329.

Mynatt, C. R., Doherty, M. E., & Tweney, R. D. (1978). Consequences of confirmation and disconfirmation in a simulated research environment. *Quarterly Journal of Experimental Psychology, 30*, 85–96.

Poletiek, F. H. (2000). *Hypothesis-testing behaviour*. Hove, UK: Psychology Press.

Rossi, S., Caverni J.-P., & Girotto, V. (2001). Hypothesis testing in a rule discovery problem: When a focused procedure is effective. *Quarterly Journal of Experimental Psychology, 54A* (1), 263–267.

Tukey, D. D. (1986). A philosophical and empirical analysis of subjects' modes of inquiry in Wason's 2–4–6 task. *Quarterly Journal of Experimental Psychology, 38A*, 5–33.

Tweney, R. D., Doherty, M. E., Warner, W. J., & Pliske, D. B. (1980). Strategies of rule discovery in an inference task. *Quarterly Journal of Experimental Psychology, 32,* 109–124.

Van der Henst, J.-B., Rossi, S., & Schroyens, W. (2002). When participants are not misled they are not so bad after all: A pragmatic analysis of a rule discovery task. In W. D. Gray & C. Schunn (Eds.), *Proceedings of the Twenty-Fourth Annual Conference of the Cognitive Science Society* (pp. 902–907). Mahwah, NJ: Lawrence Erlbaum Associates, Inc.

Wason, P. C. (1959). The processing of positive and negative information. *Quarterly Journal of Experimental Psychology, 11,* 92–107.

Wason, P. C. (1960). On the failure to eliminate hypotheses in a conceptual task. *Quarterly Journal of Experimental Psychology, 12,* 129–137.

Wason, P. C. (1965). The contexts of plausible denial. *Journal of Verbal Learning and Verbal Behavior, 4,* 7–11.

Wetherick, N. E. (1962). Eliminative and enumerative behaviour in a conceptual task. *Quarterly Journal of Experimental Psychology, 14,* 246–249.

7 The representation of the task: The case of the Lawyer–Engineer problem in probability judgement

Guy Politzer and Laura Macchi

Introduction

Numerous studies have investigated the use of base rates in probabilistic reasoning. Early results of these studies suggested that people generally ignore or neglect base rate probabilities. A famous problem initially proposed by Kahneman and Tversky (1973, pp. 237–238) was the following:

> A panel of psychologists have interviewed and administered personality tests to 30 engineers and 70 lawyers, all successful in their respective fields. On the basis of this information, thumbnail descriptions of the 30 engineers and 70 lawyers have been written. You will find on your forms a description, chosen at random from the 100 available descriptions. For each description, please indicate your probability that the person described is an engineer, on a scale from 0 to 100.

This information was followed by a personality description that presented the stereotype of an engineer:

> Jack is a 45-year-old man. He is married and has four children. He is generally conservative, careful, and ambitious. He shows no interest in political and social issues and spends most of his free time on his many hobbies which include home carpentry, sailing, and mathematical puzzles.
>   The probability that Jack is one of the 30 engineers in the sample of 100 is__per cent.

This description was followed in turn by four other descriptions that varied in their degree of representativeness (one of which, the *null* description, was completely nondiagnostic between the Engineer and the Lawyer stereotypes). These texts were submitted to one group of participants (the *low* base rate group) whereas a second group of subjects (the *high* base rate group) received identical texts except that the proportion of engineers and lawyers, which defines the base rate, differed (70 engineers vs. 30 lawyers). The aim of the study was to check the effect of the two different base rates on the probability judgement by comparing the evaluations given by the two experimental groups. The difference should indicate how wide the use of the base rate was. The prediction followed the representativeness hypothesis which posits that people "select or order outcomes by the degree to which the outcomes represent the essential features of the evidence" (Kahneman & Tversky 1973, pp. 237–238). A consequence of this hypothesis for the description above is that the difference between the evaluations made by the two groups should be very small, because the participants should mainly consider the description that was identical for the two groups.

The answer considered normatively correct follows from Bayes's theorem. Its statement in terms of odds shows that the ratio of the posterior odds for the two groups depends on the base rate but is independent of the likelihood ratio, so that it is the same for all descriptions. Pooling across descriptions (except the null), the average of the mean probability estimate for each participant was only slightly higher for the *high* base rate group (55 per cent) than for the *low* base rate group (50 per cent). The authors concluded that, as the representativeness hypothesis predicted, the participants largely ignored base rates.

The concept of representativeness has been the target of much criticism (Evans & Pollard, 1982; Gigerenzer, 1991; Gigerenzer, Hell, & Blank, 1988; Olson, 1976). It has been shown that the neglect of the base rate lacks robustness (for a review see Koehler, 1996). This question has been hotly debated (e.g., Gigerenzer, 1996; Kahneman & Tversky, 1996) and the standard experimental paradigm might be clarified by a different approach. The present chapter is devoted to such an approach.

The pragmatic approach to the psychology of thinking and reasoning (Hilton, 1995; Politzer, 1986; Politzer, in press; Politzer & Macchi, 2000) has proved fruitful in various areas. It sheds new light on classic tasks (see: Macchi, 1995 for Kahneman & Tversky's cab problem. Dulany & Hilton, 1991; Mosconi & Macchi, 2001; Politzer & Noveck, 1991 for the conjunction fallacy. Politzer, 2003 for conditional reasoning in context. Van der Henst, Rossi, & Schroyens, 2002 for Wason's 2–4–6 task). It raises and solves new questions about old paradigms (see: Van der Henst, Sperber, & Politzer, 2002 for relational reasoning. Mosconi, 1990 for problem solving at large). It even changes our understanding of some tasks altogether (see Politzer, 1993 for the class inclusion question in children. Girotto, Kemmelmeier, Sperber, & Van der Henst, 2001; Sperber, Cara, & Girotto, 1995 for Wason's Selection Task). By the "pragmatic approach", we do not refer to the mere acknowledgement of, or concern about, the effects of context or of world knowledge: It is now widely agreed that such factors affect performance. Our view is more radical: We believe that experimental tasks for which a normatively correct response can be defined should be submitted to a double examination. One, carried out at a micro-structure level, consists of a linguistic analysis of the premises or of the problem statement in order to make sure that they convey the meaning intended by the experimenter: A typical outcome of such an analysis is the identification of different possible interpretations due to the generation of conversational implicatures (Grice, 1989), either particularised (that is, implicatures generated in a specific context), or generalised (that is, implicatures that may accompany connectives or quantifiers). The other examination, at a macro-structure level, consists of identifying the representation of the task that participants are likely to build: A typical outcome of this examination is the identification of the kind of skill, knowledge, or ability that participants think they must exhibit in order to satisfy the experimenter's request. This latter analysis takes a serious view of the special relationship between experimenter and participant (akin to the one between teacher and student in testing situations). It is common knowledge that what is of interest to the experimenter is not the informational content of the answer, but its normative correctness. But what is of interest to the experimenter is not always clear to the participant. The participant may engage in a process of attribution whose outcome may be different from the experimenter's expectations. If this occurs without being detected by the experimenter, the participant's interpretation of the task will cause the experimenter to misinterpret the results. In this chapter, we argue that such a misinterpretation is the case for the Lawyer–Engineer problem. In the 1950s and 1960s, some social psychologists were concerned about the demand characteristics of the task (Orne, 1969) but unfortunately, with few exceptions, investigators of thinking and reasoning have not paid enough attention to such worries. One exception is due to some educational psychologists who have introduced the notion of a *didactic contract*, that is, an implicit set of rules based on mutual knowledge between teacher and pupils that regulate the interpretation of the question and the type of responses that are appropriate (see Schubauer-Leoni & Perret-Clermont, 1997).

Another notable exception is the work of Schwarz (1996) which highlights the importance of the conversational approach and its implications for the design of experiments. Norenzayan and Schwarz (1999) asked participants to attribute reasons for a crime. One group was offered cues to identify the experimenter as a social scientist, and the other group as a personality psychologist. The first group gave more situational attributions than dispositional attributions, whereas the second group showed the reverse pattern. This result demonstrates the role of the epistemic goals that the participants attribute to the experimenter.

Schwarz, Strack, Hilton, and Naderer (1991) applied the same approach to the Lawyer–Engineer problem. They presented the psychological description either as a profile written by a psychologist or as a piece of information formulated by a computer. The probability estimate that the description was that of an engineer was higher in the former case than in the latter, indicating that participants relied more on the individuating information in the former case. According to the authors, these results show that the participants' use of information depends on the communicative intention of the experimenter.

While we agree with these authors' conversational approach, their dependent variable – as in most investigations of the problem – (the mean probability estimate) is not fully satisfactory. It yields only indirect conclusions such as "the higher probability evaluation indicates greater use of individuating information" without allowing the measurement of the size of the effect. Hence, if one aims to show that pragmatic factors are the main determinants of performance in this task, it is necessary to use a different method based on a different dependent variable.

In this chapter, we adopt the theoretical framework of Sperber and Wilson's (1995) relevance theory. The Lawyer–Engineer problem has an evident heterogeneous structure in that the base rate is in the form of a percentage while the individuating information is in the form of a description. Participants assume that the information provided to them is relevant. Indeed, the processing of the description has cognitive effects at a relatively low cost in terms of effort: It yields an estimate of typicality that is necessary for solving the problem. This estimate shows the ability of the participants to exploit a stereotype. Such an estimate, the participants will suppose, is of interest to the experimenter, and so, by providing a numerical value that reflects their estimate of typicality, they will be satisfied that they have fulfilled their task. Our hypothesis, in brief, is that the participants take their task to be one in which they should infer a typicality estimate based solely on the description.

Following our hypothesis, it should be possible to alter performance by designing a situation in which participants would receive equivalent individuating information but without inferring it themselves. For example, if they were provided with just an evaluation of typicality without a psychological description, participants should correctly view the task as mathematical, which would lead them to use the numerical information available in combination with the indicated typicality. In the usual condition, however, many participants stop their reflection after they have worked out a typicality value of their own because, as claimed earlier, they think that, in exploiting the description, they have fulfilled their task.

Experiment

Method

Materials and design

Each participant received a form that contained the problem statement followed by the usual request to indicate the probability that the file under consideration was that of one of the engineers.

Four kinds of forms were prepared, defining four conditions (three controls and one experimental condition). For all conditions, the base rate was defined by the same ratio: 30 per cent of engineers and 70 per cent of lawyers. The four conditions were the following (see Appendix pp. 132–133):

- *Diagnostic description* condition (a) presented a translation and adaptation of Kahneman and Tversky's original problem,
- *Nondiagnostic description* condition (b) is a control presenting a psychological description that could fit various professions and is nondiagnostic between the engineer and the lawyer stereotypes.

There were two novel conditions:

- *No description* + *Statement of Typicality* condition (c) repeated the story about the panel of psychologists making evaluations and about choosing files randomly, but *did not present any psychological description. In its place*, it contained this statement: "The description is typical of an engineer".
- *Diagnostic description* + *Statement of Typicality* condition (d) was a combination of the standard condition (a) and of the crucial statement used in condition (c). In other words, it presented both the statement "the description is typical of an engineer" and the psychological description. It was used as a control for the comparison between conditions (a) and (c). (The authors are indebted to Phil Johnson-Laird for suggesting this condition.)

Predictions

The probability estimates should not only reflect the relative extent to which participants rely on the individuating information, but should also indicate an absolute measure of this extent. An objective and accurate measure can be obtained in the case where the individuating information is totally disregarded in favour of the base rate, in which case the participants give the proportion of engineers (30 per cent) as their answer. Conversely, this answer indicates that the participant is sensitive to the base rate exclusively. We chose a value commonly used in other studies. Likewise, the choice of 30 per cent was motivated by the fact that an answer equal to 0.30 can unambiguously be attributed to the exclusive use of the base rate because a high probability estimate derived from the typical description is unlikely to yield the 0.30 value. This would not be the case with the 70 per cent value (or any value higher than 50 per cent).

Assuming that the only two sources of information for participants to work out their response are the base rate and the individuating information, when a response differs from 0.30 it can be inferred that the individuating information has been taken into account at least to some extent. In brief, the dependent variable, which will be called r, is the frequency of exact reproduction of the base rate. Readers might object that an estimate of 50 per cent does not indicate a non-exclusive use of base rate but rather a "don't know" response. But the results of a pilot study in which participants were asked to justify their answers indicated that an estimate of 50 per cent was a numerical way to express uncertainty based on a lack of cues.

The following predictions were made:

(1) The value of *r* should be lower with (a) (*Diagnostic description*) than with (b) (*Nondiagnostic description*), that is, there should be a greater use of the description in (a) than in (b). This prediction follows from the fact that the description is more relevant in (a) than in (b), i.e., the diagnostic description suggests the stereotype of one of the two professions. The use of this description yields an estimate of typicality and justifies the presumption of its relevance. In contrast, the nondiagnostic description is not the source of an estimate of typicality, which could be used as a basis for answering the question: It is less relevant in the technical sense, that is, few, if any, inferences can be made from it.

(2) The value of *r* should not differ between (a) (*Diagnostic description*) and (d) (*Diagnostic description + Statement of Typicality*). In both conditions, the description is relevant because it enables one to make an inference: Producing an inference in condition (a) and verifying an inference in condition (d). The difference is that, in the latter condition, the description is information attesting to the reasonableness of the judgement of typicality. The inference is directed by given information. But, in the former condition, no such direction is provided: The description is information from which a judgement of typicality has to be inferred. Hence, in both cases, the description is roughly equally relevant because the participant makes use of it either to produce an inference or to make a verification. The values of *r* should accordingly be comparable in both conditions.

(3) The main prediction is that the conditions that present a diagnostic description ((a) and (d)) will elicit a greater use of the individuating information (and therefore a less exclusive use of the base rate) than condition (c) (*No description + Statement of Typicality*). This is because in the conditions with a description, participants may suppose that the essence of their task is to infer a typicality value. If so, they will tend to focus on this value, which represents the end of the task (and consequently overlook the base rate). In contrast, the experimental condition contains no individuating information for participants to work out a typicality estimate. They cannot view the task as calling for such an estimate. They should represent the task as closer to a mathematical exercise than to a request for displaying their psychological skills, and consequently they will tend to look for numerical information. Also, this condition is crucial to distinguish the relevance explanation from the typicality explanation. From the relevance point of view, a typicality value worked out from a description is not equivalent to one that is passively read. Only in the former case does the high degree of typicality render the description relevant for the task, which should be represented as an assessment of the typicality of the description. In the experimental condition, the task has a different representation, as the typicality value is given: The typicality description is relevant for estimating the prob-

ability that an engineer is in the sample. In contrast, for the typicality approach, the two conditions (with or without an explicit statement) are just two alternative ways of giving the same final information to the effect that the typicality value is high.

Participants and procedure

Participants were 113 undergraduate students of psychology at the University Bicocca in Milan. Each of them was randomly allocated to one of the four conditions.

Results

Table 7.1 indicates the frequency of responses equal to the base rate for each condition. The *No description + Statement* condition (c) yielded more productions of the base rate, that is, less use of the individuating information, than the *Diagnostic description* condition (a) (chi-square = 29.9, p <0.001), and also than the *Diagnostic description + Statement* condition (d), (chi-square = 16.2, p <0.001). In addition, the results corroborated the prediction that the *Diagnostic description* condition (a) would give rise to more use of individuating information than the *Nondiagnostic description* condition (b) (chi-square = 8.58, p <0.01). Likewise, as we predicted, performance with the *Diagnostic description* (a) and with the *Diagnostic description + Statement* (d) did not differ significantly.

In brief, the main prediction was confirmed: Participants who received the individuating information indirectly in the form of a psychological description (the standard *Diagnostic description* condition (a)) from which they had to infer a judgement of typicality used this information more often than those who received it in the form of an explicit statement of typicality (in the

Table 7.1 Percentage of responses equal to the base rate for each condition and level of significance of the differences in frequency

Statement of typicality			
Present (novel condition) description		*Absent description*	
none (c)	diagnostic (d)	nondiagnostic (b)	diagnostic (a)
(N = 26)	(N = 29)	(N = 28)	(N = 30)
0.85	0.31	0.54	0.17

<··················p <0. 001··················>

<····p <0. 001····>

<·········p <0.01··········>

<·····················N.S.·····················>

No description + *Statement* condition (c)). This result is paradoxical: One would expect the information that is less explicit and harder to exploit to be used less frequently, so that after the description, participants would use it less often (because the typicality must be inferred) than those to whom this information is explicitly offered in a direct statement. The contrary occurred, and our theoretical approach explains why: When they are presented with a psychological description, participants' representation of the task is that of a test of their own ability to identify the psychological features of a description that can distinguish an engineer from a lawyer. They are consequently diverted from making use of the other sources of information such as the base rate which belongs to a task which is a mathematical exercise: The representation of the two kinds of task are alien to each other.

Readers might object that the less frequent use of individuating information in the *No description* + *Statement* condition as compared to the *Diagnostic description* condition could be attributed to the presence of the typicality statement rather than to the absence of a description. But on the one hand, it is hard to see how a statement of typicality could decrease the use of individuating information: If it had any effect in isolation, it could only increase it. On the other hand, the absence of a significant difference between the *Diagnostic description* and the *Diagnostic description* + *Statement* conditions indicates that the presence of the typicality statement had no effect of its own.

One result is at variance with the results originally reported by Kahneman and Tversky (1973) and replicated in other studies (e.g., Gigerenzer et al., 1988) concerning the nondiagnostic descriptions. These studies found that exactly the same median estimate was given by the groups that had different base rates (30–70 and 70–30) and they took this observation as evidence that the base rates are totally disregarded. But this is a very coarse indicator that conceals the distribution of the participants' answers. The value of the median is compatible with the earlier interpretation, but there is another interpretation that is at least as likely: The same median value was observed because participants have used the base rate in the same manner (*not* because they did not use it). A possible source for the discrepancy with our results (in which the exclusive use of the base rate for the nondiagnostic condition was 54 per cent) could be the difference in the procedure: Our participants received only one description whereas in the standard procedure participants received the nondiagnostic description mixed with diagnostic ones. The results of a number of studies (in Ginossar & Trope, 1980, 1987) point to the existence of order effects. They support the view (equally endorsed by Bar-Hillel, 1983) that Kahneman and Tversky's (1973) result for the nondiagnostic description was due to the repeated measures design that they used, so that participants focused their attention on the descriptions that varied across problems. Likewise, Fischhoff, Slovic, and Lichtenstein (1979) showed that when the base rate is varied within-subjects instead of the description performance reflected the base rates.

General discussion

Three main conclusions can be drawn from the experiment. They concern the relevance-based explanation of performance, the integration of information, and the representativeness explanation. We take up these issues in turn.

Relevance and alternative explanations

Our first conclusion is that the use of the base rate depends on how the task is mentally represented, which in turn depends on considerations of relevance. Knowledge of the typicality of the psychological description is exploited only to the extent that participants consider it to be relevant. About three-quarters of the participants (in the *Diagnostic description* and *Diagnostic description + Statement* conditions) took the diagnostic information into account when they had to extract it from a typical description. However, when the diagnostic information was condensed in the form of a verbal statement (*No description + Statement* condition), only 15 per cent of the participants took it into account. The percentage was intermediate (about 50 per cent) for those who were presented with the nondiagnostic description (suggesting that up to one half of this latter group assumed it was diagnostic in order to render it relevant). These results extend the observations made by Schwarz et al. (1991). While the size of the effect of the manipulation reported by these authors cannot be assessed, the present experiment reveals a shift of about two-thirds of the population in the use of individuating information between the two critical conditions, namely the *Diagnostic description* and the *No description + Statement* conditions.

Is there an alternative explanation of the performance in the experimental group? It may be tempting to attribute the results to the difference in salience of the individuating information between the conditions with a description and the *No description + Statement* condition. There are two reasons to reject this hypothesis. First, in order to accommodate all the results, the salience hypothesis should also explain why most participants apparently disregarded the statement in the *No description + Statement* condition. An explanation in terms of a lack of salience seems highly implausible because it implies that nearly all participants presented with the two sentences "A description has been chosen at random from the 100 available descriptions. The psychological description is typical of an engineer" systematically overlooked the second sentence. Rather, we believe that participants did process the second sentence, but in the end discarded it because its content makes the problem question irrelevant. In effect, participants are facing a request to express numerically the probability that a typical description of an engineer is that of an engineer. For those who understand the difference between likelihood and posterior probability, the question is trivial (although awkward to answer numerically). For those who mix up these concepts, the question contains the answer: In both cases, the problem question lacks relevance. In such a situation, participants will try to reinterpret the question. The most relevant way (which follows a least effort path to producing an answer) is to exploit any other cue provided by the experimenter: The base rate is the most conspicuous piece of information to use. The second and more important reason why the salience hypothesis fails is that it does not make a distinction between the diagnostic (salient) information and the typicality estimate. The diagnostic information, whether it is salient or not, is not the basis for the final probability estimate. The probability estimate is inferred from the typicality estimate, which acts as a mediator between the diagnostic information (whatever its degree of salience may be) and the probability estimate.

There is an alternative version of the salience hypothesis that *does* take into account the distinction between diagnostic information and typicality estimate. It claims that participants who have paid attention to salient information will attach greater importance to the subsequent typicality estimate. But this claim is just an imprecise and pre-theoretical version of the relevance explanation which says that the description carries with it a presumption of relevance; that is, a guarantee for the reader that it is worth processing the description in order to infer new information (or in the present case, in order to arrive at the solution). So, not only does the relevance approach have much to say about the task, it also explains the effect of information salience.

Another possible explanation of the results is based on the notion of vividness: The *Diagnostic description* presented information that is vivid, concrete and specific, whereas the *No description* condition presented pallid, abstract and general information. The salience hypothesis concerns the focusing of attention. But the difference in vividness concerns the subjective weight of the information, which should be greater when there is a description than when there is no description. There are two consequences. First, up to here the analysis of the evidence could result in a degree of belief in the typicality of the description that is greater in the *description* conditions than in the *No description* condition. But it is not sure at all that a belief inferred by the participant's own consideration of the information should be greater than the belief in a statement provided by the experimenter: one could claim quite the contrary. Second, the typicality estimate itself would be higher; for instance, participants in the *description* conditions would infer a belief that the description is *highly* typical, while those in the *No description* conditions were just told that "the description is typical". But it is very doubtful that a necessarily limited difference of this sort (given that "typical" is linguistically marked) could account for the sharp difference in performance that was found. Finally, if the vividness hypothesis has something to say about the belief in the typicality of the description, it cannot explain, contrary to the relevance explanation, performance in the *No description* condition for the same reasons that the salience hypothesis fails: The statement must be processed, unless it is passed unnoticed, which is very implausible.

Integration of information

The second conclusion has two facets, one of which sheds new light on an old paradigm. On the one hand, in the pilot study referred to earlier, in which justifications were asked for (and that was otherwise nearly identical to the present experiment), the analysis indicates that nearly all the responses that differ from the base rate (that is, responses that take the individuating information into account) were justified without any reference to the base rate: This confirms the base rate neglect but our explanation of it differs sharply from the heuristic explanation. In our view, the neglect does not imply an intrinsic bias, but an effect of the interpretation of what the task is about. Actually, the base rate is widely considered when the participants are not diverted from the objective of the task as is the case in the standard problem. On the other hand, the experiment has revealed a symmetrical effect that seems to have passed unnoticed so far. In effect, the proportion of responses equal to the base rate, that is, the proportion of responses showing disregard of the individuating information, is surprisingly high. In the two conditions that had a diagnostic description (with or without the statement of typicality) the proportion of responses equal to the base rate reached about one quarter of the responses, even though the description instantiated the social stereotype. In the pilot study in which a justification was asked for, about three-quarters of the estimates equal to the base rate were justified by a mention of the proportion of engineers (or by an appeal to a procedure of computation); that is, without any reference to the individuating information which, it is noted, was always present either in the form of a description, or in the form of a statement of typicality, or both. In other words, the present manipulation has revealed a mirror effect to the neglect of the base rate, namely the neglect of the individuating information. We claim that this occurs because the individuating information becomes irrelevant when it is realised that it looks like a direct answer to the question. There is a slight asymmetry between the two cases: In one case, the base rate is considered irrelevant because participants think that they have fulfilled the task; in the other case, the individuating information is considered irrelevant because if it were taken into consideration there would be no task to fulfil. Upon being told that the description is typical, participants infer a probability estimate commensurate with the value verbally provided to them. But then, this too easy inference looks very much like an answer to the question, which makes it lack relevance. Except for those who were sophisticated enough to try to combine this qualitative information with the quantitative one, they reinterpreted the question as a request for an unconditioned probability, which enabled them to render the base rate information relevant and to fulfil the task, so that they gave the base rate as their response.

The notion that information should be perceived as relevant in order to be used has already been considered to explain base rate neglect (Bar-Hillel, 1980; Krosnick, Li, & Lehman, 1990). In our opinion, this notion applies to the individuating information as well. The present investigation contributes to redress the balance in a paradigm traditionally considered from a single point of view, demonstrating both the neglect of the base rate and the neglect of the individuating information.

We believe that these neglects are the two sides of the same coin: They reflect *the lack of integration of two disconnected sources of information.* The individuating information is qualitative and actively extracted because covertly provided. The base rate information is quantitative and passively exploited because overtly provided. The one or the other neglect occurs depending on the task representation, that is, presumed relevance. In the original problem, the emphasis is put on the description, so that participants interpret the task as a request to act as a psychologist and once they have extracted the individuating information and inferred a typicality estimate, the implicit contract by which they are linked with the experimenter has been fulfilled. Further information, especially mathematical, is irrelevant, both in the intuitive and theoretical senses. Similarly, in the new version of the problem introduced here, which resembles a mathematical problem, the statement of typicality provided to participants looks like an answer to the question, which would break the same contract if it were taken into consideration; they consider it as irrelevant, and fall back on the numerical information (the base rate) which, in turn, they fail to combine with the other source of information.

The notion that there is a lack of integration of different sources of information is not new. Ginossar and Trope (1987) obtained an increased use of base rate when the base rate value and the description were integrated and presented in the form of a list. But their data, based on the traditional dependent variable (the mean probability estimate), do not indicate what proportion of participants was affected by the manipulation. Kahneman and Tversky (1973, p. 243) themselves commented on the lack of integration:

> Our subjects, however, failed to integrate prior probability with specific evidence . . . The failure to appreciate the relevance of prior probability in the presence of specific evidence is perhaps one of the most significant departures of intuition from the normative theory of prediction.

We concur with this quote; but whereas its authors just made a correct *description* using the pre-theoretical term of *relevance*, we have offered an *explanation* for this observation using the same term in its technical, theoretical sense.

Representativeness

Could representativeness account for the difference in performance between participants in the *No description + Statement* condition and those in the *Diagnostic description* condition? If the operation of the representativeness

heuristic consists in the "assessment of the degree of correspondence between
. . . an outcome and a model" (Tversky and Kahneman, 1983, p. 295), performance in the *No description* + *Statement* condition clearly contradicts this
view. All the participants in this condition were provided with an explicit
statement of strong correspondence between the outcome and the model.
Therefore all of them should have opted for a high probability and in particular none of them should have given an answer equal to 0.30. Of course, one
might object that there is a difference between (a) basing the judgement of
correspondence with the model on a synthetic statement that provides the
assessment ready made (as was necessarily the case in the *No description* +
Statement condition if representativeness is to be used); (b) *working out* the
degree of correspondence by considering the various diagnostic features. In
this view, representativeness would require to actively work out the final
judgement of similarity, and would be blocked otherwise. But it is not
quite clear why. Furthermore, this is close to our main claim that needs no
representativeness hypothesis: People who have been active in exploiting the
description do not feel the need to use extra information.

There are further reasons which render the representativeness explanation
inadequate. As we have shown, it cannot explain the neglect of the individuating information: The representativeness explanation is incomplete and not
parsimonious. More seriously it begs the question because in order to solve
the Lawyer–Engineer problem, it is *necessary* to make a comparison between
the description and the stereotype: The most serious conceptual flaw in this
approach is the use of the *description* of a necessary step in the resolution of
the problem as an *explanatory* concept.

A tentative outlook of how people solve the problem

We will propose an overview of how participants process the problem.
Although it has not been directly tested, the results are compatible with the
idea that solving the standard problem requires a two-step process.

Step one requires people to decide to what extent the set of features is
characteristic of an engineer. It results in a degree of typicality, which all
participants can arrive at. Step two consists in answering the question proper,
that is, given the degree of fit to the stereotype worked out at step one, what is
the probability that the description is that of an engineer? Once participants
have arrived at a high estimate of typicality (step one), the question can
receive two different interpretations.

(1) The high typicality value suggests that the description is that of an engin-
     eer; in other words the question seems to have been answered. Partici-
     pants stop on the way and the typicality value is taken to be the final
     response. This is possible because participants feel that, in exploiting the
     description, they have fulfilled the task requirement and satisfied the
     presumption of relevance of the description. The base rate neglect

reflects a lack of interest in further information that is viewed as irrelevant. Notice that once the response is given, step one can be *described* in terms of the representativeness heuristic since the response is based on the working out of a typicality estimate. But we believe that this step is a necessary (and insufficient) step on the way to the solution, *the bias which consists in, and is explained by, stopping at this step being artificially induced by the task representation.*

(2) The question amounts to asking what is the probability that a description typical of an engineer is that of an engineer: It is viewed as pointless or tautological. But the question can be normalised into "What is the probability of drawing the description of an engineer?". Participants readily find an answer in the base rate which has not been used, and this satisfies the presumption of its relevance. They make an exclusive use of the base rate, failing to integrate the two sources of information. Again their lack of interest in one of the sources of information (the individuating information) stems from its apparent irrelevance. The classic control problem (the nondiagnostic description) leads, after step one, to the absence of a typicality value. This cannot provide the basis for an answer and participants interpret the question as "What is the probability that the description is that of an engineer?" based on no other information than the base rate. The problem in the present *No description* condition leads participants to step two directly and to the second interpretation of the question.

Of course, the lack of integration of the two sources of information that results from task representation depends on an inherent difficulty in integrating them. Participants untutored in probability theory have difficulty in coping with problems that require probabilistic revision: Performance on less deceptive tasks is not perfect, even after the defects in their formulation have been corrected (Macchi, 1995, 2000). One can only regret that so much research has been devoted to a task that artificially enhances a difficulty, the origin of which could be studied better by trying to control it, for instance, by drawing, to various degrees, participants' attention to the necessity of combining the information.

Our theoretical approach is based on the notion of task representation. This notion hinges upon processes of attribution made by the participant to the experimenter, which is but a specific example of the effects of social factors on thinking and reasoning. In view of Paolo Legrenzi's long-standing interest and contribution to that stream of research, we are happy to dedicate the present work to him.

Appendix

A panel of psychologists have interviewed and administered personality tests to 30 engineers and 70 lawyers, all successful in their respective fields. On the basis of this information, thumbnail descriptions of the 30 engineers and 70 lawyers have been written.

Condition (a): Diagnostic description

You will find below a description, chosen at random from the 100 available descriptions. Read this description and indicate your probability that the person described is an engineer.

> Paolo is a 45-year-old man. He is married and has two children. He is generally conservative, careful, and ambitious. He does not care very much about his looks. He shows no interest in political and social issues and he is addicted to his computer. He designed his hi-fi set himself. He spends most of his free time on his many hobbies which include home carpentry, sailing, and mathematical puzzles.

The probability that the description is that of an engineer is—(indicate a numerical value).

Condition (b): Nondiagnostic description (control)

> Andrea is a 30-year-old man. He is married with no children. A man of high ability and high motivation, he promises to be quite successful in his field. He is well liked by his colleagues.

Condition (c): No description + Statement of Typicality

A description has been chosen at random from the 100 available descriptions. The psychological description is typical of an engineer. Indicate your probability that the person described is an engineer.

Condition (d): Diagnostic description + Statement of Typicality (control)

You will find below a description, chosen at random from the 100 available descriptions. The psychological description is typical of an engineer, as you can see. Indicate your probability that the person described is an engineer (*description follows as in condition* (a)).

References

Bar-Hillel, M. (1980). The base-rate fallacy in probability judgements. *Acta Psychologica*, *44*, 211–233.

Bar-Hillel, M. (1983). The base rate fallacy controversy. In R. W. Scholz (Ed.), *Decision making under uncertainty* (pp. 39–61). Amsterdam: North-Holland.

Dulany, D. E., & Hilton, D. J. (1991). Conversational implicature, conscious represen-tation, and the conjunction fallacy. *Social Cognition, 9*, 85–110.

Evans, J. St. B. T., & Pollard, P. (1982). Statistical judgement: A further test of the representativeness construct. *Acta Psychologica, 51*, 91–103.

Fischhoff, B. Slovic, P. & Lichtenstein, S. (1979) Subjective sensitivity analysis. *Organizational Behavior and Human Performance, 23*, 339–359.

Gigerenzer, G. (1991). How to make cognitive illusions disappear: Beyond "heuristics and biases". *European Review of Social Psychology, 2*, 83–115.

Gigerenzer, G. (1996). On narrow norms and vague heuristics: A reply to Kahneman and Tversky (1996). *Psychological Review, 103*, 592–596.

Gigerenzer, G., Hell, W., & Blank, H. (1988). Presentation and content: The use of base rates as a continuous variable. *Journal of Experimental Psychology: Human Perception and Performance, 14*, 513–525.

Ginossar, Z., & Trope, Y. (1980). The effects of base rates and individuating information on judgements about another person. *Journal of Experimental Social Psychology, 16*, 228–242.

Ginossar, Z., & Trope, Y. (1987). Problem solving in judgement under uncertainty. *Journal of Personality and Social Psychology, 52*, 474–484.

Girotto, V., Kemmelmeier, M., Sperber, D., & Van der Henst, J.-B. (2001). Inept reasoners or pragmatic virtuosos? Relevance and the deontic selection task. *Cognition, 81*, B69–B76.

Grice, P. (1989). *Studies in the way of words*. Cambridge, MA: Harvard University Press.

Hilton, D. J. (1995). The social context of reasoning: Conversational inference and rational judgement. *Psychological Bulletin, 118*, 248–271.

Kahneman, D., & Tversky, A. (1973). On the psychology of prediction. *Psychological Review, 80*, 237–251.

Kahneman, D., & Tversky, A. (1996). On the reality of cognitive illusions: A reply to Gigerenzer's critique. *Psychological Review, 103*, 582–591.

Koehler, J. J. (1996). The base rate fallacy reconsidered: Descriptive, normative, and methodological challenges. *Behavioral and Brain Sciences, 19*, 1–53.

Krosnick, J. A., Li, F., & Lehman, D. R. (1990). Conversational conventions, order of information acquisition, and the effect of base rates and individuating information on social judgements. *Journal of Personality and Social Psychology, 59*, 1140–1152.

Macchi, L. (1995). Pragmatic aspects of the base-rate fallacy. *Quarterly Journal of Experimental Psychology, 48A*, 188–207.

Macchi, L. (2000). Partitive formulation of information in probabilistic problems: Beyond heuristics and frequency format explanations. *Organizational Behavior and Human Decision Processes, 82*, 217–236.

Mosconi, G. (1990). *Discorso e pensiero*. [Discourse and thought]. Bologna: Il Mulino.

Mosconi, G., & Macchi, L. (2001). The role of pragmatic rules in the conjunction fallacy. *Mind and Society, 3*, 31–57.

Norenzayan, A., & Schwarz, N. (1999). Telling what they want to know: Participants tailor causal attributions to researchers' interests. *European Journal of Social Psychology, 29*, 1911–1020.

Olson, C. L. (1976). Some apparent violations of the representativeness heuristic in human judgement. *Journal of Experimental Psychology: Human Perception and Performance, 2*, 599–608.

Orne, M. T. (1969). Demand characteristics and the concept of quasi-controls. In

R. Rosenthal & R. I. Rosnow (Eds.), *Artifact in behavioral research* (pp. 143–179). New York: Academic Press.

Politzer, G. (1986). Laws of language use and formal logic. *Journal of Psycholinguistic Research, 15,* 47–92.

Politzer, G. (1993). *La psychologie du raisonnement: lois de la pragmatique et logique formelle.* [The psychology of reasoning: Laws of pragmatics and formal logic.] Doctoral dissertation, University of Paris VIII.

Politzer, G. (2003). Premise interpretation in conditional reasoning. In D. Hardman & L. Macchi (Eds.), *Thinking: Psychological perspectives on reasoning, judgement, and decision making* (pp. 79–93). Chichester: Wiley.

Politzer, G. (in press). Reasoning, judgement, and pragmatics. In I. Noveck & D. Sperber (Eds.), *Experimental pragmatics.* London: Palgrave.

Politzer, G., & Macchi, L. (2000). Reasoning and pragmatics. *Mind and Society, 1,* 73–93.

Politzer, G., & Noveck, I. A. (1991). Are conjunction rule violations the result of conversational rule violations? *Journal of Psycholinguistic Research, 20,* 83–103.

Schubauer-Leoni, M. L., & Perret-Clermont, A.-N. (1997). Social interactions and mathematics learning. In T. Nunes & P. Bryant (Eds.), *Learning and teaching mathematics. An international perspective* (pp. 265–283). Hove, UK: Psychology Press.

Schwarz, N. (1996). *Cognition and communication: Judgmental biases, research methods, and the logic of conversation.* Mahwah, NJ: Lawrence Erlbaum Associates, Inc.

Schwarz, N., Strack, F., Hilton, D. J., & Naderer, G. (1991). Base rates, representativeness, and the logic of conversation: The contextual relevance of "irrelevant" information. *Social Cognition, 9,* 67–84.

Sperber, D., Cara, F., & Girotto, V. (1995). Relevance theory explains the selection task. *Cognition, 57,* 31–95.

Sperber, D., & Wilson, D. (1995). *Relevance: Communication and cognition* (2nd edn). Oxford: Blackwell.

Tversky, A., & Kahneman, D. (1983). Extensional versus intuitive reasoning: The conjunction fallacy in probability judgement. *Psychological Review, 90,* 293–315.

Van der Henst, J.-B., Sperber, D., & Politzer, G. (2002). When is a conclusion worth deriving? A relevance-based analysis of indeterminate relational problems. *Thinking and Reasoning, 8,* 1–20.

Van der Henst, J.-B., Rossi, S., & Schroyens, W. (2002). When participants are not misled, they are not so bad after all: A pragmatic analysis of a rule discovery task. *Proceedings of the 24th Annual Conference of the Cognitive Science Society.* Mahwah, NJ: Lawrence Erlbaum Associates, Inc.

Part IV
Probabilistic judgement

8   Naive probability and its model theory

David Over

Introduction

Johnson-Laird, Legrenzi, Girotto, Legrenzi, and Caverni (1999) formulate a mental model theory of what they call extensional reasoning about naive probability. They say that they "take *extensional* to mean inferring the probability of an event from the different possible ways in which it could occur" (p. 63). The different ways in which an event could occur are the logical possibilities, or models, of the theory. It spite of the reference Johnson-Laird et al. make to the occurrence of events in their statement of what they are doing, probability in their theory is a logical concept. To reason about this concept is to engage in logical thought, about logical possibilities, and not to make inferences, based on actual observations, about physical events that have some relative frequency in the real world. As they themselves say: "This way of reasoning aims to be deductive" (p. 63). "Events" for them are not physical occurrences in the actual world, but rather logically possible states of affairs that satisfy basic propositions or their negations. Mental models are mental representations of these logically possible states of affairs and are used by people to reason deductively, or at least try to do so in a bounded system, about these logical possibilities.

A logical notion of probability like this one faces well-known problems in the philosophy of science (Howson & Urbach, 1993). One is the problem of explaining how a priori inference about logical probabilities could help us in the real world to predict physical events and to make adaptive, or in some other sense beneficial, decisions on that basis. Johnson-Laird et al. seem to see little value in discussing what might have been adaptive in the evolutionary sense (Johnson-Laird et al., 1999, p. 81), and they do not explain how probability in their sense can be of practical value in some other way. But in my view, they cannot avoid the problem. For after all, why would we expect reasoning of no practical importance to have any psychological significance? Surely, purely a priori reasoning about probability would be a waste of time for problem solving in the real world and little, if any, mental energy would be devoted to it by ordinary people. This is not to deny that logical reasoning can be of practical use, but only to point out that purely logical reasoning cannot have this usefulness on its own. For that purpose, logical inference depends on some nonlogical premises, which are justified by some reliable empirical means. The practical and psychological significance of logical reasoning cannot be revealed if it is studied without relating it to cognitive processes that are not a priori. As a dual process theorist of reasoning (Evans & Over, 1996; Sloman, 1996; Stanovich, 1999; Stanovich & West, 2000), I can express this point by saying that an account of human probability judgement in terms of System 2 logical processes alone must be severely limited. To be of real psychological significance, a study of any System 2 process must be closely related to accounts of System 1 processes of observation and much more directly practical thought. A mental model theory of probability is potentially of great help in understanding people's probability judgements, but only as part of much wider project of understanding how logical thought in System 2 combines with practical thought in System 1.

The model theory

Some of the problems faced by the theory of Johnson-Laird et al. can be most easily illustrated by relating it to an earlier logical concept of probability, that of Wittgenstein (1961, pp. 515–516). Wittgenstein's logical analysis of probability is based on the truth tables for the truth-functional connectives of elementary logic: negation, conjunction, disjunction, and the material conditional. Wittgenstein's definition of probability can best be introduced with examples (Table 8.1).

Suppose that we want to know the probability of q given that p & q holds, $P(q/p \& q)$. Wittgenstein tells us to look at the rows of the truth table in which p & q holds, and to ask in how many of these rows we find q. There is only one row in which p & q holds, the pq row, and q holds there too. By Wittgenstein's definition, $P(q/p \& q)$ is 1. What is $P(q/p \text{ or } q)$? In Table 8.1, which reports the truth table for conjunction and disjunction, there are three rows in which p or q holds, pq, p¬q, and ¬pq, and q holds in two of these, and by Wittgenstein's definition, $P(q/p \text{ or } q)$ is 2/3. Wittgenstein adheres to a principle of indifference, and all rows of a truth table are treated as equally likely, at least in default of any evidence to the contrary. Clearly, this is a definition of a logical concept of probability, depending only on a logical analysis, using truth tables, plus a principle of indifference. A conditional probability of one

Table 8.1 Truth table for conjunction and disjunction

Possible states of p and of q	Truth value of p & q	Truth value of p or q
pq	T	T
p¬q	F	T
¬pq	F	T
¬p¬q	F	F

proposition given another is inferred a priori. It is derived from the number of rows of a truth table in which the first proposition holds as well as the second, and the total number of rows of the table in which the second proposition holds. The conditional probability is simply the ratio of the first of these numbers to the second.

We can now more easily understand the mental models for probability judgement in the theory of Johnson-Laird et al. (1999). These mental models correspond to the rows of truth tables. Consider Table 8.2 (compare Johnson-Laird et al., 1999, p. 68).

This table shows the mental models for conjunction, (inclusive) disjunction, and the material conditional, but it can also be thought of as a partial truth table. What are called mental models in this table are the "initial" mental models of Johnson-Laird and Byrne (1991); people sometimes can and will "flesh out" these initial models to make them the fully explicit models. The three dots in mental models for the material conditional are said to be a "mental footnote" that some models for this connective are initially left implicit. A priori reasoning tells us that there are four logically possible states of affairs for the basic propositions p and q. First, there is the possible state, or model, in which p holds and q holds, the pq state. Second, there is the one in which p holds and *not-q* holds, the p¬q state. Third, the one in which *not-p* holds and q holds, the ¬pq state. Fourth, the one in which *not-p* holds and *not-q* holds, the ¬p¬q state. These four states are logically exclusive and exhaustive, and correspond to the four rows of the full truth tables for the conjunction, disjunction, and material conditional. But the initial mental models, and even the fully explicit models, simply leave out the rows in which conjunction, disjunction, and the material conditional are false. By the "truth principle" of mental model theory, these falsifying states, for any connective, are not represented (Johnson-Laird et al., 1999, p. 68). For example, the three possible states in which p & q is false, p¬q, ¬pq, and ¬p¬q, are not represented as models in which p & q fails to hold. Another example is that the single logical possibility in which the material conditional is false, p¬q, is not represented as a model in which this conditional fails to hold.

Table 8.2 Models for conjunction, disjunction, and the material conditional

Connective	Mental models		Fully explicit models	
p & q	p	q	p	q
p or q	p		p	¬q
		q	¬p	q
	p	q	p	q
If p then q	p	q	p	q
	. . .		¬p	q
			¬p	¬q

The definition of probability in Johnson-Laird et al. (1999) parallels Wittgenstein's definition. Johnson-Laird et al. consider inferences, e.g., where q is inferred from p & q or from p or q, and define the conditional probability of the conclusion given the premise or premises. To determine $P(q/p$ & $q)$ and $P(q/p$ or $q)$, we are to look at the mental models for p & q, and for p or q, and ask how many of these are models of q. By the process that Johnson-Laird et al. describe, which is exactly parallel to Wittgenstein's procedure, $P(q/p$ & $q)$ is 1 and $P(q/p$ or $q)$ is 2/3. Using their definition, we also derive a conditional probability a priori, based on what is basically a truth table analysis plus a principle of indifference. For this logical probability of one proposition given another, we count the number of models of the first proposition and the second, and the total number of models of the second proposition. The conditional probability is again simply the ratio of the first of these numbers to the second.

Wittgenstein's definition of probability implies, notoriously in the philosophy of science, that people cannot use it to learn from experience (Carnap, 1950). Suppose that we are the first visitors to a desert island and consider successively observing that three birds there, of the same new species, are flightless. Let p record the first observation, q the second, and r the third. By Wittgenstein's definition, $P(q/p)$ will be 1/2. This does not seem very intuitive, as surely we would judge it more likely than 1/2 that the second bird of the species was flightless given that the first was. But worse follows: By Wittgenstein's definition $P(r/p$ & $q)$ is still 1/2. We can easily deduce this result from the expanded truth table for the three propositions, p, q, and r, and the 8 (instead of 4) logically possible rows of this expanded table: pqr, pq¬r, p¬qr, and so on. Clearly, this is unacceptable. Two observations should make us more confident than one observation that the next member of the species we observe will be flightless. Moreover, by expanding the observations to 4, and the rows of the truth table to 16, we can convince ourselves, if it is not obvious already, that the conditional probability will always be 1/2 no matter how many possible observations we consider.

The logical concept of probability in Johnson-Laird et al. (1999) suffers from the same problem we have just described in Wittgenstein: We cannot learn from experience if we only make probability judgements in their sense. The argument that this is so is essentially the same, as one would expect from the exact parallel between the mental model definition of probability and Wittgenstein's definition in terms of the rows of truth tables. Johnson-Laird et al. themselves stress that they do not aim to account for what they call non-extensional probability judgement using their concept of probability, but this is a severe limitation. For them non-extensional probability judgements are not only those based on what are usually called heuristics, but all judgements that do not result from the a priori listing of logical possibilities in mental models, in the way that they specify. However, if their extensional notion of probability, like that of Wittgenstein's, does not allow us to learn from experience, then what good is it? Why would people ever think in terms of this logical concept of theirs? Why would they spend mental energy on it? Johnson-Laird et al. do not give us any argument that probability judgements, as defined by them, were ever adaptive in the evolutionary sense, or are a reliable means today of achieving practical goals in the real world.

The difficulty for Johnson-Laird et al. (1999) can be illustrated with their first example of a probability problem that they claim can be solved by deductive logic and what they call extensional reasoning (p. 64). They ask us to assume the following premise:

> If there is a red or green marble in the box, then there is a blue marble in the box.

They then ask us whether it is more likely that there is a red marble or a blue marble in the box. They claim that the valid answer is that it is more likely that there is a blue marble in the box, and back this up with a deductive argument, revealing just how logical their concept of probability is. Their argument is this. There are two logically possible ways in which a blue marble could be in the box, but in only one of these logical possibilities is the red marble in the box, the green marble being in the box in the other logical possibility. Since there are more logical possibilities in which the blue marble is in the box than that the red marble is, it is more "likely", in their logical sense, that the blue one is in the box.

But would it do us any practical good to make this inference? It might be practically impossible, or even impossible by the laws of nature, for the "green marble" to be "in the box" in a realistic problem like this. Even sticking with the exact but rather artificial content of their example, imagine a machine that puts marbles in the box. Perhaps the machine is so constructed that it never puts green marbles in the box. As a matter of practical or mechanical fact, it may be equally likely, in a much more useful sense than that of Johnson-Laird et al., that a red and a blue marble are in the box. Johnson-Laird et al. must make assumptions about the facts to apply their logical concept of probability at all. Just to begin with, they must assume the above conditional as a premise. But we cannot in most realistic and practical problems safely make assumptions merely "for the sake of argument" and then reason only a priori. We must, to have some hope of success, take account of how probable or improbable our premises are in a sense that goes beyond what Johnson-Laird et al. give us. We shall return below to the way in which the mental model theory of probability is greatly limited by being restricted to logical inferences from assumptions, which are premises taken, in effect, to be certain.

Consider now the one element of their analysis that cannot be called logical: the principle of indifference. Johnson-Laird et al. themselves explain very well the problems, or potential "paradoxes", of this principle, which have been so extensively discussed by probability theorists (Howson & Urbach, 1993). Critics of the principle have wanted to know how it can be justified. But Johnson-Laird et al. try to avoid the paradoxes and the questions about justification that these raise, by holding that people only apply the principle to the mental models that they generate. Suppose that we generate the three mental models for *p or q*. Johnson-Laird et al. propose that people naturally and automatically, in default of background knowledge, think of these mental models as equally likely. But why do they do this? What good does it do them, or did it ever do them? Johnson-Laird et al. present experiments in which a significant number of people conform to the principle of indifference, but the probability problems in these experiments are quite artificial and distant from most practical everyday concerns, being about coloured balls in boxes and the like. In most everyday matters we have, or think we have, some relevant knowledge, and so Johnson-Laird et al. would not predict that we would apply the principle in these cases. But if we almost never apply this basic principle of their analysis, and if it does not do us any practical good to apply it, then how much relevance can their concept of probability have to human probability judgement and reasoning, and to ordinary decision making?

For example, suppose someone says, "The proposed new vaporetti in Venice will be powered by diesel or electric motors." All Johnson-Laird et al. can predict about our response to this statement, no matter what our background knowledge and beliefs, is that we will not apply the principle of indifference to it, for all of us do have some relevant background knowledge or beliefs. Some of us may know quite a bit about new proposals for vaporetti and whether these are likely to be approved, while others may perhaps only be able to recall that they have never been on a boat with an electric motor. Some of us may conclude that electric motors are more likely for environmental reasons, or diesel ones because they are cheaper. Most of us might infer that it is highly unlikely that there would be both a diesel and an electric motor, but a few of us might recall that some boats (like submarines) do have both kinds of motor for use in different circumstances. Perhaps the new vaporetti will be like this, so that they are relatively efficient and environmentally sound over long and short distances. There are many probability judgements that people with different background knowledge and beliefs would make in this case. But the account of Johnson-Laird et al. makes no attempt at all to describe how these different people would make their probability judgements on the basis of their individual knowledge and beliefs.

Even when we do not have our own experience or knowledge to bring to bear on a realistic probability problem, evolution may have given us some natural tendency to make useful judgements. For example, we may have some natural tendency to think that species are uniform in certain properties, like being flightless as in kiwis (Nisbett, Krantz, Jepson, & Kunda, 1983). Or we might be like rhesus monkeys and have a natural tendency to think that snakes are dangerous (Cook & Mineka, 1990). These tendencies could show themselves in apparently a priori judgements we would make that it is more probable than not that an unfamiliar bird we observe is like other members of its species in some respect, and that some new species of snake that we come across is dangerous. These judgements would not be truly a priori, but would be based, whether we knew it or not, on sampling that natural selection in effect did for us over evolutionary time. Their existence and usefulness, for reproductive success at least under primitive conditions, would be explained by evolutionary psychology. A principle of indifference will not be applied in these cases, so again when exactly will it be applied for useful judgements and why? Johnson-Laird et al. (1999) are negative about explanations in evolutionary psychology (p. 81), but it would make their theory much more plausible, as an account of a significant aspect of reasoning, if they could explain at least part of it in evolutionary terms.

Evolution and probability

Johnson-Laird et al. (1999) effectively criticise some specific claims that have been made about probability by some evolutionary psychologists. It is instructive to examine the claims and the criticisms. This will help us to go more deeply into the positive as well as negative points in the mental model theory of probability. Evolutionary psychologists, especially Cosmides and Tooby (1995) and Brase, Cosmides, and Tooby (1998), have tried to ground their account of probability in what was useful, in the sense of being adaptive, in the real world. Their degree of success in this enterprise is open to debate, as we will see below, but at least they illustrate very well a step that must be taken to go beyond pure logic in an account of human probability judgement.

The evolutionary argument and its limitations

Some psychologists have used evolutionary arguments to try to support the claim that people are better at frequency judgements than at single-case probability judgements. People could supposedly observe frequencies and make use of them under primitive conditions, but could not observe single-case probability judgements (Gigerenzer, 1993; Cosmides & Tooby, 1996). This frequency hypothesis was meant to be relevant to the debate about how rational people are, by implying that they are rational in solving probability problems about frequencies but not about single-case probabilities. However, it was quickly pointed out that people have long been found to have biases in some experiments about frequencies (see Kahneman & Tversky, 1996, for references). Further experiments have confirmed that expressing probability problems in terms of frequencies is not sufficient for helping people to solve them correctly (Evans, Handley, Perham, Over, & Thompson, 2000; Girotto & Gonzalez, 2001, 2002). Moreover, presenting problems in terms of frequencies is not necessary either. People can solve single-case probability problems if these make the relevant logical or set relations clear (Girotto & Gonzalez, 2001; Sloman & Over, 2003; Sloman, Over, Slovak, & Stibel, 2003).

In the face of these criticisms, there has been a retreat to a much weaker form of the frequency hypothesis. This weaker claim (following Kleiter, 1994) is that people can solve some probability problems when these are expressed in a very specific frequency format: that of natural frequencies obtained by natural sampling (Brase et al. 1998; Gigerenzer & Hoffrage, 1995, 1999; Hoffrage, Gigerenzer, Krauss, & Martignon, 2002). Gigerenzer and Hoffrage (1995) used an example to introduce natural sampling in what they called the "standard menu", and to suggest that this process was adaptive under primitive conditions (pp. 686–687). In their example, an old physician in an illiterate society has "discovered the symptom" of a certain disease in the course of a long life. She recalls examining 1000 patients in her life, finding that ten of these had the disease, and that eight of those ten had the symptom. She also recalls that 95 of the 990 without the disease had the symptom. On this basis, she is supposed to be able to solve the problem of stating the frequency with which someone with the symptom has the disease. She does this by adding 8 to 95, getting 103, and giving the answer, implicitly conforming to Bayes's theorem, as 8 out of 103.

There are two separate claims that are run together by Gigerenzer and Hoffrage, but which must be distinguished (Over, 2002, 2003). Their first claim is that an illiterate person could actually do the described natural sampling under primitive conditions, accurately remember the results, and make unbiased frequency judgements on this basis. This claim, once it is laid out clearly, is most implausible. It is hard to believe that anyone could have the memories in the example. Few lecturers, in a literate and technically sophisticated society, can even recall the total number of student assignments that they have marked, let alone answer relative frequency questions about these, like what proportion of failed student essays had a spelling mistake on the first page. Even trying to recall as many of these student essays as possible can easily lead to biases in the sample, e.g., those associated with the availability heuristic (Tversky & Kahneman, 1973). The same would be true of the illiterate physician, who would find the memory some of her patients much more available than others for reasons that could well produce a biased sample. To presuppose (as do Gigerenzer, 1998; Gigerenzer & Hoffrage, 1995) that this physician could actually make reliable or adaptive probability judgements, by means of the natural sampling described in the example, is to beg the question about human rationality.

To test Gigerenzer and Hoffrage's (1995) first claim, participants "should be required to extract frequencies from actual observations rather than to process symbolic data", as Girotto and Gonzalez, (2001, p. 270) rightly point out. Gigerenzer and Hoffrage do not test participants in this way, presumably because the evidence is already strong that biased judgements would be the result (Kahneman & Tversky, 1996). What Gigerenzer and Hoffrage do test is a second claim they make that people find it easy to process symbolic data when it is given in word problems like their example. They do not appear to notice that their illiterate physician could not solve these word problems. Her language, in what is supposed to be a primitive, non-literate society, is most unlikely even to contain numerals for numbers as high as 103, 990, and 1000.

Gigerenzer and Hoffrage make two further subclaims under their second claim that a certain type of word problem is easy to solve (for literate people as they should add). Their first subclaim is that word problems about natural sampling are easy for people to solve because there is, for evolutionary reasons, a "sort of instinct" for frequency representations (Gigerenzer & Hoffrage, 1995, p. 701) and an "adaptation for frequencies" (Gigerenzer, 1998, p. 11). Their second subclaim is that these word problems, which are about natural frequencies given by natural sampling, are easy to solve because they are computationally simpler than explicitly working through Bayes's theorem using single-case probabilities or normalised frequencies (Gigerenzer & Hoffrage, 1995, 1999). These two subclaims do not fit together coherently. The computational simplicity of the word problems about natural sampling is to do with their elementary logical form and set/subset structure. It is a category mistake to confuse this simplicity with an "adaptation for frequencies". Gigerenzer and his collaborators have for a long time rejected formal reasoning as a significant aspect of human thought and placed all the emphasis instead on "fast and frugal" heuristics. (See the papers collected in Gigerenzer, 2000; Gigerenzer, Todd, & ABC Research Group, 1999. For comment and a reply see Over, 2000a, 2000b, and Todd, Fiddick, & Krauss, 2000.) But it is inconsistent to so downplay logic while stressing the value of computational simplicity in the word problems about natural sampling (Over, 2003).

In these word problems, the four logically possible states of affairs can be laid out perspicuously for us, a fact evident in the tree structure displayed by Gigerenzer and Hoffrage (1995, p. 687) for their example. This is essentially a formal tree in the set theoretic sense, with the four logically possible states, pq, p¬q, ¬pq, and ¬p¬q, being those for having, or not having, the disease and having, or not having, the symptom. These logically possible states are, of course, the ones that appear in the truth table (Table 8.1). For this example, we can even more clearly symbolise these logical possibilities with ds, d¬s, ¬ds, and ¬d¬s. Now after using pure elementary logic to derive these possible states, all we need to do is to weight them in some way to make them relevant to a word problem of the general type we are considering. In the example, this is done by stipulating (and not by remembering) that there are 8 instances of ds, 2 of d¬s, 95 of ¬ds, and 895 of ¬d¬s. If we wish, we can display this information in a formal tree, as Gigerenzer and Hoffrage do in effect. At this point, of course, it is utterly trivial to infer the frequency of disease cases given symptom cases: We merely take the number of instances of ds out of the number of instances of ds plus the number of instances of ¬ds, getting 8 out of 103. But our purely formal ability to perform this inference and calculation does not mean that we are being accurate about some objective frequency. If the samples we are given in the word problem are biased, the logic and computational simplicity of our mental processes are to no avail.

There is no dispute that expressing some problems in terms of certain types of frequency information makes them easy to solve. Tversky and Kahneman (1983) were the first to get results of this kind and to explain them. Their explanation was that frequency information sometimes allows us to solve a probability problem by making its set or class structure transparent. This explanation has basically been repeated, and supported by experiments, in response to the claims about natural sampling. (See Evans et al., 2000; Johnson-Laird et al., 1999; Girotto & Gonzalez, 2001, 2002; Sloman & Over, 2003; and Sloman et al., 2003.) In the example we have just been through, what this means is that, at the last step, the frequency information makes it transparent that the set of instances of ds is a subset of the union of this set and the set of instances of ¬ds. The computational simplicity of the problem follows from the trivial logical and set theoretic steps leading to its solution. This simplicity could hardly have a more elementary formal basis, and it has nothing specifically to do with any "sort of instinct" for frequencies or "adaptation for frequencies".

As noted above, some evolutionary psychologists have claimed that people could never have observed single-case probabilities but only frequencies (Cosmides & Tooby, 1996; Gigerenzer, 1993, 1998; Gigerenzer & Hoffrage, 1995). In the first place, this contention confuses sample frequencies with objective frequencies. Obviously, people can notice and recall some sample frequencies, but an inference is always necessary to have reasonable confidence that a sample frequency is unbiased and reflects an objective frequency. The concept of an objective frequency is difficult to define, and there is controversy about how to do this, in terms of infinite sequences, and whether it can be done at all (Howson & Urbach, 1993). Objective frequencies, defined as infinite sequences, are not in fact directly observable, but inferences have to be made about them from sample frequencies. On the other hand, people do have some access to their degrees of belief about singular propositions: This is presupposed in psychological experiments on confidence and subjective probability. The metaphysical question of whether there are objective single-case probabilities is hardly relevant here. These would be no less directly observable than objective frequencies (see Sloman & Over, 2003).

Suppose that we are given a word problem in which, on a scale of 0 (low) to 10 (high), people express as 8 their confidence that Mary likes John given that John likes Mary, and as 2 their confidence that Mary does not like John given that John likes Mary. The word problem is to say how much more confidence these people have in the former conditional probability than they have in the latter. In symbols, we are asked to compare $P(q/p)$ with $P(\neg q/p)$. This ratio is given by a form of Bayes's theorem, and we can implicitly comply with this form merely by inferring that the people have four times as much confidence in $P(q/p)$ as they have in $P(\neg q/p)$. This judgement, in line with Bayes's theorem, is as trivial as the one about the illiterate physician's supposed memories and yet has no relation at all with frequencies.

Johnson-Laird et al. (1999) point out how their mental model theory can account for the results of experiments on easy frequency word problems. By weighting mental models to indicate degrees of confidence (Stevenson & Over, 1995), they can also explain why we can sometimes find it easy to conform to Bayes's theorem when asked about degrees of confidence in singular propositions. These explanations, using mental model theory, reveal how solving some word problems draws on elementary abilities to perform logical inferences and set operations. These are the same abilities to generate and manipulate mental models, which are used in the theory to account for sentential and syllogistic inference. Gigerenzer (2000, chapter 9) has criticised the goal of trying to devise a system in which formal relations are as clear as possible. He calls this "Leibniz's dream" and attacks the Enlightenment and later logicians and mathematicians for trying to achieve it. But Leibniz inspired Euler, a great Enlightenment figure, to create his circle system (Kneale & Kneale, 1962, p. 349), and this system has often been used to make syllogistic, set theoretic, probabilistic, and other formal relations as clear as possible. As well as this much more general use, Euler circles help people to solve the frequency word problems (Sloman et al., 2003; Sloman & Over, 2003). Perhaps mental model theory can even explain why geometric representations like Euler circles can help people so much to understand formal problems in general (see Johnson-Laird & Byrne, 1991, on Euler circles and mental models).

Johnson-Laird et al. (1999) are rightly critical of current explanations in evolutionary psychology of why frequency word problems are easy, but they also express general scepticism about evolutionary psychology (see Brase, 2002, for a reply). They agree that doing evolutionary psychology can lead to interesting hypotheses about the mind. Yet they proffer no evolutionary hypothesis about why making probability judgements as they describe would have been adaptive, or have any benefit at all in the real world. The evolutionary psychologists at least try to fulfil the obligation of connecting what they say about probability with the real world. (In this connection, note as well what Brase et al., 1998, say about individuation.) True, their attempt to do so is limited, if only because they presuppose that the sample frequencies in their word problems accurately represent objective frequencies. At the very least, they must investigate the extent to which people can infer the existences of biases in sample frequencies and the evolutionary reasons for this. Still, they do recognise their obligation to try to explain why probability judgements as they describe them are beneficial.

A possible way forward for mental model theory

One step that Johnson-Laird et al. should take to fulfil this obligation themselves is to develop the notion that mental models can be weighted in relative probability. Consider the conditional:

If a bird is a kiwi then it is flightless.

The mental models for this conditional should increase in relative probability given the evidence of an observed kiwi that is flightless. Logic does play a rule in this Bayesian confirmation of the conditional, since the confirmation partly results from a logical relation: The conditional and the observation of a bird that is kiwi logically implies that the bird is flightless (Over, 2002, 2003). But logic has to find a place in a system in which there is a place for observation and prior beliefs. There should also be some explanation, in evolutionary psychology, of why observation and some belief-forming mental processes were adaptive and continue to be reliable, to some extent, in contemporary circumstances. We need to raise questions such as "Do we have some reliable tendency to believe, thanks to natural selection, that species are uniform in central properties like being flightless?" This can be done in a dual-process mental system that includes some bounded Bayesian inference about hypotheses and not just about the relative frequencies of objective physical events (Evans & Over, 1996).

Mental model theory in its current form is greatly restricted by being designed to explain deductive inference from given assumptions. This "logicism" (see Oaksford & Chater, 1998, for an extended critique) has been a limitation, until relatively recently, of all major theories of human reasoning (Evans, 2002). Johnson-Laird et al. (1999) had the opportunity to move beyond logicism in their account of probabilistic reasoning, but what we find instead is still more logicism, with only a logical concept of probability on offer. Return again to the first example in their paper:

> If there is a red or green marble in the box, then there is a blue marble in the box.

Johnson-Laird et al. ask us to assume this premise and to make logical deductions from it about probability. There could be no more extreme example of logicism: the belief that we will get an account of an important aspect of ordinary human reasoning through the use of the concepts of deductive logic alone. However, for the reasons I have given, we cannot get very far at all in the study of probabilistic reasoning by using pure deductive logic alone. We cannot even get very far by restricting our study to assumptions, about marbles in a box or, like the evolutionary psychologists, about sample frequencies. We must take account of the fact that few premises in ordinary or, for that matter scientific, contexts can be safely assumed true. Reliable inference depends on taking proper account of the different degrees of uncertainty in premises. Psychologists have started to investigate inference from uncertain premises, and there is no reason why this most common kind of inference should not be covered by mental model theory. But to do that, we must go beyond the default setting of mental models as equally likely and assign them different degrees of uncertainty or probability. (See Politzer & Bourmaud, 2002; Politzer & Carles, 2001; Stevenson & Over, 2001, for some recent papers on inference from uncertain premises, and Stevenson & Over, 1995, on such inference and mental models.)

Johnson-Laird and Byrne (2002) advance principles of semantic and pragmatic "modulation" that can categorically introduce or rule out mental models of premises, but what is needed, more generally, is for the relative probabilities of these models to be increased or decreased. There are signs in their paper that Johnson-Laird and Byrne may be prepared to take this step, but another severe limitation to the current mental model theory of naive probability remains in their paper. This is their analysis of ordinary conditionals and the probabilities of these.

Probability and conditionals

The mental model theory in Johnson-Laird and Byrne (1991) was committed to the material conditional as an adequate representation of the ordinary indicative conditional, as in Table 8.2. See also Table 8.3, which is a truth table for the material conditional.

The mental model account of this ordinary conditional is clearly a truth table analysis of it, making it logically equivalent to the material conditional. A material conditional *if p then q* is itself logically equivalent to *not-p or q*, and so, by this mental models analysis, the ordinary indicative conditional is logically equivalent to *not-p or q*. Many philosophical logicians have long rejected this analysis because of the "paradoxes" it leads to (Edgington, 1995). There are two basic paradoxes that result from supposing that the ordinary indicative conditional is the material conditional, which can be well illustrated by examples in Johnson-Laird and Byrne (1991, p. 74). The first basic paradox is that the following is a valid inference if the ordinary indicative conditional:

Shakespeare wrote the sonnets.
Therefore, if Shakespeare didn't write the sonnets, then Bacon did.

The second basic paradox is that the following is also is a valid inference if the ordinary indicative conditional is a material conditional:

Bacon wrote the sonnets.
Therefore, if Shakespeare didn't write the sonnets then Bacon did.

Table 8.3 Truth values for a material conditional *if p then q*

Possible states of p and of q	Truth values of p and of q		Material conditional: if p then q
pq	T	T	T
p¬q	T	F	F
¬pq	F	T	T
¬p¬q	F	T	T

Johnson-Laird and Byrne (1991, p. 74) point out that one must either give up the truth table analysis of ordinary conditionals or accept these paradoxes as valid. They take the latter option and try to explain away the paradoxes as only apparently paradoxical. There is supposedly only an appearance of paradox here because of a general constraint on deductive inference that applies as much to inferring a disjunction as to inferring a conditional. Consider this example:

> Strasbourg is in France.
> Therefore, Strasbourg is in France or it is in Germany.

According to Johnson-Laird and Byrne (1991, p. 74), this inference should seem paradoxical because it "throws semantic information away", the single premise being more informative than the conclusion. And to throw away information like this violates "one of the fundamental constraints on human deductive competence". But suppose our knowledge of European history and geography is rather poor. We are not completely sure that Strasbourg is in France: We are only confident to a modest extent that it is in France. Given the uncertainty, we might prefer to infer the conclusion above from the single premise and to assert it instead of the premise. The conclusion is weaker, but the advantage is that we can have more confidence in the conclusion than the premise. We would not infer that Strasbourg is in France or in Egypt, but that would be a waste of time by not decreasing our uncertainty, as we are sure that Strasbourg is not in Egypt. There are though good rational grounds for inferring a weaker proposition from a stronger one when we do have significantly more confidence in the former. There is no general problem, due to any "fundamental constraint", about inferring a weaker proposition from a stronger one. The claim that there is can be seen to be unjustified when we move beyond narrow logicism to study the most common type of inference in the real world, inference from uncertain premises.

On the other hand, it is truly counterintuitive to claim, as Johnson-Laird and Byrne (1991) would have had to, that the following inference is valid:

> We will not go to Strasbourg tomorrow.
> Therefore, if we go to Strasbourg tomorrow, then we will be in England.

This inference is valid if the conditional is a material conditional, and the way out of this absurdity is to give up the idea that the ordinary indicative conditional is the material conditional. The paradoxical air of this inference is precisely not the result of inferring a weaker proposition from a stronger one. Suppose that we have absolutely no intention of going to Strasbourg tomorrow and no means of getting there in so short a time. Then the above inference is clearly invalid because its conclusion is extremely improbable while its premise is highly probable. In a valid inference with a single premise, the probability of the premise cannot be greater than the probability of the conclusion. (People do sometimes violate this rule, as Tversky and Kahneman, 1983 showed, but that is another matter.)

Accepting that the paradoxes are valid for the ordinary conditional is logically equivalent to claiming that this conditional is the same as the material conditional. The latest paper by Johnson-Laird and Byrne (2002) on conditionals continues to argue early on (pp. 651–652) that the basic paradoxes are valid, and tries to explain them away in the old way, which does not take account of inference from uncertain premises. However, there are new developments in this latest work that call for further clarification. Johnson-Laird and Byrne (2002) distinguish between what they call "basic conditionals", which are analysed without background knowledge, and non-basic conditionals, which call on background knowledge. An example of a basic conditional would be "if there is a circle then there is a triangle", asserted about some arrangement of shapes we had no prior knowledge of. The examples above, about Shakespeare, Bacon, and Strasbourg, are not "basic conditionals", as we do have background knowledge relevant to their evaluation. Johnson-Laird and Byrne (2002) no longer consider the paradoxes to be valid for nonbasic conditionals, but this is only implied in the paper and not clearly stated.

Johnson-Laird and Byrne (2002) hold that the "core meaning" of the indicative conditional in natural language has the mental models given in Table 8.2. This "core meaning" is that of the "basic conditional". It follows that a basic conditional is a truth functional, material conditional and the paradoxes are valid for it. However, Johnson-Laird and Byrne now accept that not all natural language conditionals are "basic" and truth functional. Indeed they claim (p. 673) that, in general, no natural language connectives (except negation, Johnson-Laird, personal communication) are truth functional. For example, the use of some natural language conditionals can convey, beyond the core meaning, that there is a temporal or spatial relation between what is referred to in their antecedents and consequents, making them nontruth functional. Even some conjunctions and disjunctions can convey such relations, according to Johnson-Laird and Byrne. Strawson (1952) discusses an example in which, he claims, "They got married and had a child" is not logically equivalent to "They had a child and got married". If "and" in such uses means "and then", or if what a speaker intends to convey by "and" is "and then", then we cannot interpret these uses, or what the speaker intends to convey, by a truth functional "and". Johnson-Laird and Byrne take such examples (Johnson-Laird, personal communication) to imply that not even "and" is in general truth functional in natural language.

I interpret Johnson-Laird and Byrne as making the point that we should not be naive about logical form in natural language. There is considerable ambiguity in natural language, and there may be uses of "and" that mean "and then" semantically. There are certainly speakers who pragmatically mean us to interpret their use of "and" as "and then". When we interpret "and" as "and then", the result will not be truth functional, as we have used an intensional tense operator (responsible for the failure of truth functionality) in our interpretation. But then Johnson-Laird and Byrne's mental model theory must be extended to cover the logic of this tense operator. When we do not interpret a use of an ordinary conditional as truth functional, the paradoxes of the material conditional cannot be valid for this interpretation, as the validity of the paradoxes implies truth functionality. It is misleading of Johnson-Laird and Byrne (2002) to argue early in their paper, without qualification, that the paradoxes are valid for the ordinary indicative conditional. They must qualify what they say about the paradoxes to clarify their new position that some uses of the ordinary indicative conditional are not "basic" and fail to be truth functional, and give a mental model account of the logic of these uses. Moreover, Johnson-Laird et al. (1999) and Johnson-Laird and Byrne (2002) do not give us a mental model theory of the probability of the use of a conjunction, a disjunction, or an indicative conditional that is not truth functional in natural language.

Johnson-Laird and Byrne (2002) are committed to the view that most (though not all) natural language uses of connectives "correspond to" (Johnson-Laird's term, personal communication) truth functional connectives. They continue to give mental models for the connectives that are equivalent to the rows of the truth tables, as shown in Table 8.2 (p. 141). Unless many uses of natural language connectives "correspond to" truth functional connectives, the extensional analysis of probability in Johnson-Laird et al. (1999), with its emphasis on logical deduction, would have little application to the minds of ordinary people who express and understand probability judgements in natural language.

A limitation in Johnson-Laird and Byrne (2002) is that their account of basic conditionals is much more detailed and precise than what they say about nonbasic conditionals. There is a mass of empirical data on conditional reasoning, from responses in the selection task to the endorsement rates for different forms of conditional inference (Evans, Newstead, & Byrne, 1993; Evans & Over, 1996, forthcoming). But the explanation of these data that Johnson-Laird and Byrne try to give, going back to Johnson-Laird and Byrne (1991), depends on Table 8.2, which applies only to truth functional basic conditionals. The fully explicit mental models for the conditional in Table 8.2 imply that the conditional is a truth functional, "basic" conditional. Consider the most elementary conditional inference of all, modus ponens, which is inferring q from *if p then q* and p. It is obviously impossible, given Table 8.2, for this inference to be invalid: for its premises to hold when its conclusion fails. But Johnson-Laird and Byrne (2002, pp. 665–666) discuss an example that is supposed to show that modus ponens is invalid for nonbasic conditionals. However, they put nothing in place of Table 8.2 to show which inferences are and which are not valid for nonbasic conditionals. How does one construct mental models of nonbasic conditionals in such a way that the conclusion of modus ponens can fail to hold in mental models of the premises? Johnson-Laird and Byrne do not yet appear to have an answer to this question.

The account Johnson-Laird et al. (1999) and Johnson-Laird and Byrne (2002) give of the probability of a conditional only applies to basic conditionals. They claim support for it (see also Girotto & Johnson-Laird, in press), but it implies that there is no general relation between the probability of a basic conditional, P(*if p then q*), and conditional probability, P(*q*/*p*). There is strong evidence of this relation for indicative conditionals that are rather abstract in content (Evans, Handley, & Over, 2003; Hadjichristidis, Stevenson, Over, Sloman, Evans, & Feeney, 2001; Oberauer & Wilhelm, 2003) and for completely realistic ordinary conditionals (Over & Evans, 2003). Johnson-Laird and Byrne could gain by accepting a relation between the probability of a nonbasic conditional and conditional probability. They would then at least have a proposal about the probability of a nonbasic conditional. And by holding that people represent P(*if p then q*) as P(*q*/*p*), we may be able to explain a great deal about conditional reasoning (Oaksford, Chater, & Larkin, 2000). If Johnson and Byrne did accept this representation, they could justify their claim about a problem with modus ponens and non-basic conditionals. When the conditional is replaced by conditional probability, this inference becomes conditionalisation, e.g., inferring that P(*q*) is high from P(*p*) is high and P(*q*/*p*) is high, and conditionalisation is a defeasible inference that is only justified in certain circumstances (Howson & Urbach, 1993).

There are more questions to be asked about the treatment of subjunctive conditionals in Johnson-Laird and Byrne (2002). According to them, a subjunctive conditional, for example:

If you were to go for a walk then you would get too hot

has the mental models:

Fact:	not walk	not too hot
Counterfactual possibilities:	walk	too hot
	not walk	too hot

For you to assert this subjunctive conditional about me is, by the above, for you to assert two things: first, that it is a fact that I will not go for a walk and will not get too hot; second, that it is possible that I will go for a walk and get too hot and possible that I will not go for a walk and get too hot. This analysis of the subjunctive conditional implies that you have asserted something false if I do, in fact, go for a walk and get too hot. But that is counterintuitive, as your subjunctive conditional warning to me is intuitively confirmed by my going for a walk and becoming too hot. Even more counterintuitive is that the second example:

If you were to go for a walk then you would get too cold

with the mental models:

Fact:	not walk	not too cold
Counterfactual possibilities:	walk	too cold
	not walk	too cold

does not conflict with the first subjunctive conditional, given in the model theory of Johnson-Laird and Byrne. The reason is that I am not going for a walk and am neither too hot nor too cold, and that all the counterfactual possibilities exist. It is possible that I will go for a walk and get too hot, and it is possible that I will go for a walk and get too cold, and so on. As logical possibilities, these possibilities do not conflict with each other. In most actual circumstances, some of these possibilities will be more probable than others. It is far more probable that I will get too hot, than too cold, going for a walk in August in Venice, but this matter of fact is not reflected in the logical analysis of Johnson-Laird and Byrne as it stands, nor in that of Johnson-Laird et al. (1999).

Some analyses in philosophical logic can reflect this fact by applying the notion that my going for a walk and getting too hot is a "closer" or "nearer" possibility to the actual state of affairs in Venice in August than my going for a walk and getting too cold. (Stalnaker, 1968; and Lewis, 1973, have philosophical notions of "closeness", but even they suggest some psychological ways of making this distinction that are grounded in what the actual world is like.) Johnson-Laird and Byrne quickly reject talk of some possibilities being "closer" or "near" to the facts than other possibilities. They do not discuss the psychological evidence that people really do make these distinctions, which can be important even for emotional responses like feeling regret (Kahneman & Miller, 1986). For example, residents of Venice will find going for a walk in August and being hot a "closer" possibility because that has been the more normal or frequent occurrence for them than going for a walk in August and being cold. In some way or other, Johnson-Laird and Byrne must give some account of how some counterfactual possibilities are more probable than others, and that account will have to go far beyond the logical theory of probability in Johnson-Laird et al. (1999).

Legrenzi (1970) said that the interpretation of the negation of an ordinary conditional "remains considerably problematic" (p. 332). Everyone can understand that it is not the case that, if I were to drink lots of water from a Venetian canal, then I would feel much better. At least we can all understand that this negation of a conditional is highly probable. What are the mental models for this negation, and how do those models represent it as highly probable? How does "highly probable" in this sense connect with, not merely logical possibilities in the logicism of Johnson-Laird et al. (1999), but our knowledge of the actual quality of the water in Venetian canals? Legrenzi drew attention to the problem of such negations, and his words still ring true. Representing the negations of ordinary conditionals – indicative, subjunctive, and others – remains problematic, and we can only hope that mental model theory will eventually find a way to move beyond this point.

Conclusion

The mental model theories of Johnson-Laird et al. (1999) and Johnson-Laird and Byrne (2002) are limited by extreme logicism. They are right that there must be a place for logic in any acceptable account of probability judgement, and I also believe that mental models must play a central role in any such account. But there cannot be a theory of a significant aspect of human reasoning – probabilistic, conditional, or other – that consists of little more than laying out logical possibilities as mental models. Some of these mental models must be represented as more likely than others in a way that is connected with what is adaptive or reliable in the real world.

References

Brase, G. L. (2002). Ecological and evolutionary validity: Comments on Johnson-Laird, Legrenzi, Girotto, Legrenzi, & Caverni's (1999) mental model theory of extensional reasoning. *Psychological Review, 109* (4), 722–728.

Brase, G. L., Cosmides, L., & Tooby, J. (1998). Individuation, counting, and statistical inference: The role of frequency and whole-object representations in judgement under uncertainty. *Journal of Experimental Psychology, 127*, 3–21.

Carnap, R. (1950). *Logical foundations of probability*. Chicago: University of Chicago Press.

Cook, M., & Mineka, S. (1990). Selective associations in the observational conditioning of fear in rhesus monkeys. *Journal of Experimental Psychology: Animal Behavior Processes, 16*, 272–389.

Cosmides, L., & Tooby, J. (1996). Are humans good intuitive statisticians after all? Rethinking some conclusions from the literature on judgement under uncertainty. *Cognition, 58*, 1–73.

Edgington, D. (1995). On conditionals. *Mind, 104*, 235–329.

Evans, J. St. B. T. (2002). Logic and human reasoning: An assessment of the deductive paradigm. *Psychological Bulletin, 128*, 972–996.

Evans, J. St. B. T., Handley, S. H., Perham, N., Over, D. E., & Thompson, V. A. (2000). Frequency versus probability formats in statistical word problems. *Cognition, 77*, 197–213.

Evans, J. St. B. T., Newstead, S. E., & Byrne, R. M. J. (1993). *Human reasoning: The psychology of deduction*. Hove, UK: Lawrence Erlbaum Associates Ltd.

Evans, J. St. B. T., Handley, S. H., & Over, D. E. (2003). Conditionals and conditional probability. *Journal of Experimental Psychology: Learning, Memory, and Cognition, 29*, 321–335.

Evans, J. St. B. T., & Over, D. E. (1996). *Rationality and reasoning*. Hove, UK: Psychology Press.

Evans, J. St. B. T., & Over, D. E. (forthcoming). *If: Philosophical and psychological perspectives*. Oxford: Oxford University Press.

Gigerenzer, G. (1993). The bounded rationality of probabilistic mental models. In K. I. Manktelow & D. E. Over (Eds.), *Rationality: Psychological and philosophical perspectives* (pp. 284–313). London: Routledge.

Gigerenzer, G. (1998). Ecological intelligence: An adaptation for frequencies. In D. Dellarosa Cummins & C. Allen (Eds.), *The evolution of mind* (pp. 9–29). New York: Oxford University Press.

Gigerenzer, G. (2000). *Adaptive thinking*. New York: Oxford University Press.

Gigerenzer, G., & Hoffrage, U. (1995). How to improve Bayesian reasoning without instruction: Frequency formats. *Psychological Review, 102*, 684–704.

Gigerenzer, G., & Hoffrage, U. (1999). Overcoming difficulties in Bayesian reasoning: Reply to Lewis and Keren (1999) and Mellers and McGraw (1999). *Psychological Review, 106*, 425–430.

Gigerenzer, G., Todd, P., & ABC Research Group (1999). *Simple heuristics that make us smart*. New York: Oxford University Press.

Girotto, V., & Gonzalez, M. (2001). Solving probabilistic and statistical problems: A matter of information structure and question form. *Cognition, 78*, 247–276.

Girotto, V., & Gonzalez, M. (2000). Chances and frequencies in probabilistic reasoning: Rejoinder to Hoffrage, Gigerenzer, Krauss, and Martignon. *Cognition, 84*, 353–359.

Girotto, V., & Johnson-Laird, P. N. (in press). The probability of conditionals. *Psychologia*, special issue "Reasoning", edited by K. Manktelow and H. Yama.

Hadjichristidis, C., Stevenson, R. J., Over, D. E., Sloman, S. A., Evans, J. St. B. T., & Feeney, A. (2001). *On the evaluation of "if p then q" conditionals*. Proceedings of the 23rd Annual Meeting of the Cognitive Science Society, Edinburgh.

Hoffrage, U., Gigerenzer, G., Krauss, S., & Martignon, L. (2002). Representation facilitates reasoning: What natural frequencies are and what they are not. *Cognition, 84*, 343–352.

Howson, C., & Urbach, P. (1993). *Scientific reasoning: The Bayesian approach* (2nd edn.). La Salle, IL: Open Court.

Johnson-Laird, P. N., & Byrne, R. (1991). *Deduction*. Hove, UK: Lawrence Erlbaum Associates Ltd.

Johnson-Laird, P. N., & Byrne, R. (2002). Conditionals: A theory of meaning, pragmatics and inference. *Psychological Review, 109* (4), 646–678.

Johnson-Laird, P. N., Legrenzi, P., Girotto, V., Legrenzi, M., & Caverni, J.-P. (1999). Naive probability: A mental model theory of extensional reasoning. *Psychological Review, 106*, 62–88.

Kahneman, D., & Miller, D. (1986). Norm theory: Comparing reality to its alternatives. *Psychological Review, 93*, 136–153.

Kahneman, D., & Tversky, A. (1996). On the reality of cognitive illusions: A reply to Gigerenzer's critique. *Psychological Review, 103*, 582–591.

Kleiter, G. (1994). Natural sampling: Rationality without base rates. In G.H. Fisher & D. Laming (Eds.), *Contributions to mathematical psychology, psychometrics, and methodology* (pp. 375–388). New York: Springer-Verlag.

Kneale, W., & Kneale, M. (1962). *The development of logic*. Oxford: Oxford University Press.

Legrenzi, P. (1970). Relations between language and reasoning about deductive rules.

In G. B. Flores d'Arcais & W. J. M. Levelt (Eds.), *Advances in psycholinguistics* (pp. 322–333). Amsterdam: North-Holland.

Lewis, D. (1973). *Counterfactuals*. Oxford: Blackwell.

Nisbett, R. E., Krantz, D. H., Jepson, C., & Kunda, Z. (1983). The use of statistical heuristics in everyday inductive reasoning. *Psychological Review, 90*, 339–363.

Oaksford, M., & Chater, N. (1998). *Rationality in an uncertain world: Essays on the cognitive science of human reasoning*. Hove, UK: Psychology Press.

Oaksford, M., Chater, N., & Larkin, J. (2000). Probabilities and polarity biases in conditional inference. *Journal of Experimental Psychology: Learning, Memory, and Cognition, 26*, 883–889.

Oberauer, K., & Wilhelm, W. (2003). The meaning(s) of conditionals: Experiments with a probabilistic truth-table task. *Journal of Experimental Psychology: Learning, Memory, and Cognition, 29*, 680–693.

Over, D. E. (2000a). Ecological rationality and its heuristics. *Thinking and Reasoning, 6*, 182–192.

Over, D. E. (2000b). Ecological issues: A Reply to Todd, Fiddick, & Krause. *Thinking and Reasoning, 6*, 385–388.

Over, D. E. (2002). The rationality of evolutionary psychology. In J. L. Bermúdez & A. Millar (Eds.), *Reason and nature: Essays in the theory of rationality* (pp. 187–207). Oxford: Oxford University Press.

Over, D. E. (2003). From massive modularity to metarepresentation: The evolution of higher cognition. In D. E. Over (ed.), *Evolution and the psychology of thinking: The debate* (pp. 121–144). Hove, UK: Psychology Press.

Over, D. E., & Evans, J. St. B. T. (2003). The probability of conditionals: The psychological evidence. *Mind and Language, 18*, 340–358.

Politzer, G., & Bourmaud, G. (2002). Deductive reasoning from uncertain conditionals. *British Journal of Psychology, 93*, 345–381.

Politzer, G., & Carles, L. (2001). Belief revision and uncertain reasoning. *Thinking and Reasoning, 7*, 217–234.

Sloman, S. A. (1996). The empirical case for two systems of reasoning. *Psychological Bulletin, 119*, 3–22.

Sloman, S. A., & Over, D. E. (2003). Probability judgement from the inside and out. In D. E. Over (ed.), *Evolution and the psychology of thinking: The debate* (pp. 145–169). Hove, UK: Psychology Press.

Sloman, S. A., Over, D. E., Slovak, L., & Stibel, J. M. (2003). Frequency illusions and other fallacies. *Organizational Behavior and Human Decision Processes, 91*, 269–309.

Stalnaker, R. (1968). A theory of conditionals. *American Philosophical Quarterly Monograph Series, 2*, 98–112.

Stanovich, K. E. (1999). *Who is rational? Studies in individual differences in reasoning*. Mahwah, NJ: Lawrence Erlbaum Associates, Inc.

Stanovich, K. E., & West, R. F. (2000). Individual differences in reasoning: Implications for the rationality debate? *Behavioral and Brain Sciences, 23*, 645–726.

Stevenson, R. J., & Over, D. E. (1995). Deduction from uncertain premises. *Quarterly Journal of Experimental Psychology, 48A*, 613–643.

Stevenson, R. J., & Over, D. E. (2001). Reasoning from uncertain premises. Effects of expertise and conversational context. *Thinking and Reasoning, 7*, 367–390.

Strawson, P. F. (1952). *Introduction to logical theory*. London: Methuen.

Todd, P. M., Fiddick, L., & Krauss, S. (2000). Ecological rationality and its contents. *Thinking and Reasoning, 6*, 375–384.

Tversky, A., & Kahneman, D. (1973). Availability: A heuristic for judging frequency and probability. *Cognitive Psychology*, *5* (2), 207–232.

Tversky, A., & Kahneman, D. (1983). Extensional versus intuitive reasoning: The conjunction fallacy in probability judgement. *Psychological Review*, *90*, 293–315.

Wittgenstein, L. (1961). *Tractatus logico-philosophicus*. (D. F. Pears & B. F. McGuinness, Trans.). London: Routledge.

9 Probabilistic reasoning and combinatorial analysis

Vittorio Girotto and Michel Gonzalez

Introduction

Consider the following problem:

> *The six-chip problem*
> Six chips are in a hat: two are red and round, two are white and triangular, one is red and square, one is white and square. A chip is drawn at random from the hat. If it is red, what is the probability that it is round?

If you are familiar with the probability calculus, you may solve the problem assuming that the prior probability of drawing any chip is 1/6. Given that the prior probability of drawing a red, round chip equals two times 1/6 (i.e., 1/3), and that the prior probability of drawing a red chip equals three times 1/6 (i.e., 1/2), you correctly conclude that if the chip that is drawn is red then the probability that it is round equals (1/3) / (1/2), that is 2/3. What if you are *unfamiliar* with the probability calculus (i.e., if you are in the same condition as almost all members of humankind)? We maintain that in this case too you will correctly solve the problem. The chip that is drawn is one of the three red chips. Since two of them are round, there are two possibilities out of three to obtain a round chip, that is, two chances out of three. Indeed, almost everybody arrives at this correct solution (see Gonzalez & Girotto, 2004), which is an example of an *extensional* evaluation of probability. Individuals reason extensionally about probabilities by considering and enumerating the various possibilities in which an event may occur, and then inferring the chances of its occurrence. For instance, reasoners consider the three possibilities in which they obtain a red chip, and the two possibilities in which it is round. They count each possibility as one chance, and correctly infer that the required solution is two chances out of three. Evidence exists that naive individuals do evaluate probabilities extensionally (see, e.g., Girotto & Gonzalez, 2001, 2002; Johnson-Laird, Legrenzi, Girotto, Sonino-Legrenzi, & Caverni, 1999; Legrenzi, Girotto, Sonino-Legrenzi, & Johnson-Laird, 2003; Sloman, Over, Slovak, & Stibel, 2003). However, the previous results concern problems, such as the six-chip one, in which the initial set of all possibilities (e.g., the set of six chips) was given, and the required probability can be obtained by counting the possibilities in the appropriate sets. In many cases, however, elementary possibilities are not as readily ascertained as in the six-chip problem. Consider the following problem:

The dice problem
We roll two regular dice and then we count the sum of the numbers that turn up. These sums can be: 2, 3, 4 . . . 11, 12. If the sum of the numbers turning up is odd, what is the probability that it is 7?

If you try to solve this problem extensionally in the way you solved the six-chip problem, you may reason as follows. The possible odd sums are: 3, 5, 7, 9 or 11. Given that 7 is one of this five possible results, it follows that the probability of its occurrence is one chance in five. Unlike the six-chip problem, such extensional reasoning does not lead to the correct solution. The enumeration of possibilities is correct (five possible sums are odd numbers), but the resulting probability evaluation is incorrect because these possibilities are not equiprobable. In order to apply a correct extensional treatment to the dice problem, you have to envisage a set of more elementary possibilities all having the *same* chances of occurrence. The key to the solution is to consider the *ways* in which the various sums can be obtained. A roll of two dice produces 7 in three ways: when they turn up 1 and 6, 2 and 5, or 3 and 4. Do the other odd sums occur in the same number of ways? The answer, of course, is no. For instance, the numbers sum to 3 only when the dice turn up 1 and 2. Given that each of these possible ways of producing a given sum has the same chances to occur, if you enumerate all of them, you can correctly evaluate the required probability. In sum, you can solve the dice problem extensionally. Unlike the six-chip problem, however, you have to consider that the result of a two-dice roll is the combination of the possibilities of obtaining the various numbers on each die. That is, you have to construct the set of the relevant, compound possibilities by means of a *combinatorial analysis*. Are individuals unfamiliar with the probability calculus able to solve problems of this sort? More generally, are they able to evaluate a probability extensionally by conducting a combinatorial analysis of possibilities?

   The chapter addresses these issues. In the first part, we examine children's and adults' ability to make combinatorial analyses in probability evaluations, and we describe some historical cases and some empirical results. In the second part, we consider an important source of faulty combinatorial reasoning. In some problems, individuals tend to disregard combinations necessary for a proper extensional treatment, judging them to be irrelevant. We discuss some classical examples of erroneous probabilistic reasoning, attributing them to such a tendency. Finally, we report empirical results showing that participants fail a notorious probability brainteaser, because of the same tendency to disregard appropriate possibilities.

Naive probabilistic reasoning based on combinatorics

In this section, we show that individuals who do not know the probability calculus correctly evaluate chances in problems that call for a combinatorial analysis of possibilities.

Historical evidence

The dice problem calls for an explicit probability judgement. In everyday life, individuals often face decisions that depend on the evaluation of the chances of uncertain events. For instance, individuals play games in which they have to bet on the outcome produced by dice or other devices. A popular dice game in the Middle Ages, mentioned by Dante in his *Divine Comedy*, was called "Zara". It consisted in guessing the outcome of a throw of three dice. The gambler who correctly guessed the sum won the stake. The gambler was not allowed to bet on the lowest (3 and 4) and the highest (17 and 18) sums. When the dice produced one of these sums, the outcome was not considered and the gambler said "Zara". Long before the advent of probability calculus, some writers tried to find the best way to play such a game. Their solutions ranged from the insightful ideas of the fourteenth-century commentators on Dante, such as Jacopo Della Lana (see Girotto & Gonzalez, 2004), to the complete analysis of the anonymous author of the thirteenth-century poem "De Vetula", of Cardano circa 1563, and Galileo circa 1613 (for extensive references, see David, 1962; Franklin, 2001). All their solutions are extensional, and posit that the advantage of a bet depends on the number of ways in which the betted sum can be obtained. For instance, Della Lana recommends the gamblers to bet on the sums that can be obtained in more ways, because these sums must occur more often. His analysis correctly indicated the need to carry out a combinatorial analysis of the possibilities. But Della Lana's account contained some flaws. In particular, he did not take into account the various arrangements of the dice corresponding to a given combination. For instance, he argued that gamblers were not allowed to bet on a sum of 4, given that this outcome could occur only in one way, namely when the dice land 2, 1 and 1, failing to take into account that this combination can be obtained in three possible ways, depending on which of the three dice lands 2. As we will show below, such failures occur in the extensional reasoning of both naive individuals, such as children, and great minds such as Leibniz. All these pieces of evidence show that individuals unfamiliar with probability calculus, such as those living before its development, evaluate chances by means of a combinatorial analysis. In the following section, we show that this conclusion holds also for children.

Developmental evidence

According to the traditional Piagetian view (Piaget & Inhelder, 1951/1975), children are not able to reason correctly about probability. Young children lack the most basic logical abilities necessary to compute a probability ratio. Older children are not able to conduct a combinatorial analysis until the acquisition of complex logical abilities during adolescence. Contrary to this pessimistic view, we have provided evidence that 11-year-children can solve Zara-like problems in which they have to compare the respective chances of two opponents who bet on the sum of a throw of two dice (Girotto & Gonzalez, 2004). When the children compared bets on 12 versus 10, and bets of 10 versus 8, a majority of them correctly identified the player more likely to win. Hence, even children make elementary combinatorial analyses, and judge the event occurring in more possibilities as the more probable. These results corroborated the hypothesis of an early extensional competence. However, they have been obtained only with a single problem, and with children of an age too close to the period (the adolescence) in which, according to the Piagetian view, individuals are supposed to acquire the logical abilities necessary to assess combinatorial possibilities.

In order to confirm and extend our previous findings, we have carried out a further study in which children of various ages (7-year-olds, 9-year-olds, 11-year-olds, and 13-year-olds) tackled two probability problems calling for a combinatorial analysis (Girotto & Gonzalez, 2003). One problem was based on the Zara game. In one version, it reads as follows:

> #### The Zara problem
> As you see, I have a white die and a red die. Each die has six sides, each with a number from 1 to 6. Now I play a game with these two puppets, Paolo and Maria. I throw the dice, and when they land on the table I cover them, so that Paolo and Maria cannot see the sum the dice made. [The experimenter throws the dice and covers them.] Paolo says that I got 3 with the two dice. Maria says that I got 5 with the two dice. According to you, who is more likely to win their bet? [After the participants give their answer, they have to justify it.]

In all versions, the correct answer was to name the puppet who predicted the sum that could be obtained in more ways (in the version above, the puppet that bet on 5).

Unlike the Zara problem, the other problem did not involve numbers. In one version, it reads as follows:

> #### The picture problem
> I have two cards: one of a picture of a lorry and the other of a picture of a fish. I cut each card in half. Here you see the halves of each picture. [The experimenter shows the two pieces of each card.] Now I play a game with

these two puppets, Anna and Beatrice. I hide all the pieces in this bag and I shake it. Now, I take two of them, without looking, and I cover them, so that Anna and Beatrice cannot see the pieces I drew. [The experimenter draws two pieces and covers them.] Anna says that I drew two pieces from two different pictures. Beatrice says that I drew two pieces from the same picture. According to you, who is more likely to win the bet? [After the participants give their answer, they are required to justify it.]

The correct solution was to indicate the puppet that bet on the event that can occur in more ways (i.e., drawing pieces from two different pictures). Most children solved the two problems. For instance, 72 per cent of them solved the above version of the Zara problem, and 65 per cent solved the above version of the picture problem. Considering all versions, children performed better than chance from the age of 9 in the Zara problem, and from the age of 11 in the picture problem.

Children were also tested on their ability to construct combinations. They had to produce the possible combinations for each of the two outcomes, that is the two sums of dice in the Zara problem, and the sorts of combinations of pieces in the picture problem. Considering all versions, from the age of about 9, most children solved this task. For instance, 72 per cent of the children solved the above version of the Zara problem, correctly indicating that the sum 3 is obtained with a 1 and a 2, and the sum 5 is obtained with a 3 and a 2 or with a 4 and a 1. Few children of any age, however, distinguished the two possible arrangements of each combination (e.g., 5 is obtained with a 3 and a 2, or with a 2 and a 3). Similarly, 59 per cent of children solved the above version of the picture problem, correctly enumerating the four possible ways of drawing pieces of two pictures, and the two possible ways of drawing pieces of one picture.

These results extend those obtained with problems that did not demand a combinatorial analysis (e.g., Acredolo, O'Connor, Banks, & Horobin, 1989; Brainerd, 1981), Taken together, these findings contravene the pessimistic view that individuals can assess probabilities from combinations only when they have attained the alleged level of formal operations in the Piagetian framework, that is, around the age of 12 (Piaget & Inhelder, 1951/1975). They also call into question the hypothesis that both children and adolescents are only "capable of assimilating combinatorial procedures with the help of instruction" (Fischbein, 1975, p. 128). More generally, these results corroborate our hypothesis that individuals unfamiliar with probability calculus may correctly reason about uncertain events by considering the different ways in which they may occur.

Conceptual errors in combinatorial probabilistic reasoning

In the above study some participants, particularly in the younger age groups for the Zara problem, failed to produce the entire set of combinatorial possibilities. These errors may be attributed to the limited capacity of working memory to hold possibilities or to the difficulty of working out all the possibilities (see Johnson-Laird et al., 1999). In the present section, we consider another source of errors in combinatorial reasoning, namely, the tendency to disregard some possibilities that appear as irrelevant.

Leibniz and the confused arrangements

The solution of many probability problems asks for a combinatorial analysis in which one has to enumerate possible arrangements. For instance, with two dice, one obtains 11 when one die lands 5 and the other one lands 6, but also when the former die lands 6 and the latter lands 5. The ability to consider arrangements (or permutations) has been considered a hallmark of adult reasoning, given that children allegedly lack the logical competence to do so (Piaget & Inhelder, 1951/1975). Adults, however, sometimes fail to consider arrangements, as pointed out by Legrenzi (1973) and as shown by Girotto and Gonzalez (2003). The same error can be found even in the work of eminent mathematicians, such as Leibniz. In a letter dated 1714, he wrote: "With two dice, it is as doable to throw a twelve as to throw an eleven for each can only be done in one way" (quoted by Dudley Sylla, 1998, p. 50). In fact, one can obtain 12 only in one way, but 11 in two ways. How is it possible that Leibniz, like the children in our studies, failed to consider arrangements? We conjecture that errors of this sort result from the representation of the setting, and not from difficulties in constructing the appropriate combinations. In a justified combinatorial structure, each combination represents an actual and relevant possibility. Any combination corresponding to an observable possibility has to be considered. Sometimes, however, combinations that are relevant are incorrectly disregarded. For instance, one obtains 11 when the two dice land 5 and 6, but which die lands 5 and which die lands 6? One does not know, if the dice are regarded as indistinguishable. If individuals do not consider two combinations such as 5 and 6, and 6 and 5 as corresponding to two distinct possibilities, they may confound them. It is legitimate to treat different arrangements as one and the same possibility, if the domain is one in which they cannot be distinguished as a matter of principle (see the so-called Bose–Einstein statistics for fundamental particles that are not distinguishable). But in a domain such as the throwing of dice, individuals who fail to consider arrangements will produce incorrect probability assessments. They may nevertheless be capable of such an analysis, but merely fail to realise the need for it.

D'Alembert and the fictitious possibility

Conceptual errors in reasoning about possibilities can be more subtle than the failure to distinguish permutations. The famous "error of d'Alembert" falls in this category. Like Leibniz, Jean Le Rond d'Alembert was a brilliant mathematician, interested in the logic of probabilities. In the "Heads or tails" entry of the *Encyclopedia*, d'Alembert (1754) addressed the question: "How much are the odds that one will get heads in playing two successive tosses?" A standard answer relies on enumerating the possible combinations of two tosses, that is:

First toss	*Second toss*
Heads	Heads
Heads	Tails
Tails	Heads
Tails	Tails

Given that three of the four sequences contain a heads, there are three chances out of four of obtaining one head in two tosses. This extensional solution sounds correct. D'Alembert, however, challenged it, arguing that "as soon as heads comes one time, the game is finished, and the second toss counts for nothing". Considering the actual game, there are indeed only three possibilities:

Heads, first	
Tails, first	Heads, second
Tails, first	Tails, second

D'Alembert concluded that there are two chances out of three, and not three chances out of four, of getting heads in two tosses. This solution is based on a correct representation of the actual game. Indeed, as argued by d'Alembert, it is unrealistic to consider the two possibilities in which heads first is followed by a second toss. However, his probability evaluation relies on the unwarranted assumption that the possibilities under consideration are equiprobable. A few years after its first publication, d'Alembert (1757) himself reported in the entry "Wager" of the *Encyclopedia* some objections to his own solution. In modern terms, if each of the three possibilities were equiprobable, then there would be the following probabilities:

First toss	*Second toss*	*Probability*
Heads		1/3
Tails	Heads	1/3
Tails	Tails	1/3

It follows that the probability of tails on the first throw would be 1/3 + 1/3, that is, 2/3. Hence, heads and tails on the first throw would not be equiprobable. D'Alembert minimised the importance of such a paradoxical consequence of his argumentation, and never wholly changed his mind.

D'Alembert's error illustrates a general tendency in human reasoning about probability. Unless they have beliefs to the contrary, individuals reason as if the possible ways in which an event can occur are equiprobable (see Johnson-Laird et al., 1999). In sum, like Leibniz's error, d'Alembert's error shows that conceptual difficulties in considering the suitable combinations, rather than an inability to reason about combinations, may yield erroneous extensional evaluations of probability.

The Monty Hall game: When behaving as if all possibilities were equiprobable leads to wrong decisions

In this section, we show that individuals making errors similar to d'Alembert's misapprehension of possibilities may make wrong decisions. From 1963 to 1990, hundreds of contestants participated in the famous American TV show *Let's Make A Deal*, and played a game whose host was Monty Hall. In this game, a contestant is presented with three closed doors (which we will refer to as X, Y and Z), only one of which hides a valuable prize. The contestant has to choose one door. If he has chosen the right door, he gets the prize. Suppose that he chooses door X, and that you watch the game. If you do not know where the prize is, you can estimate, on the basis of elementary extensional reasoning, that there is one chance in three that the contestant gets the prize. Suppose you hear a person saying, "Door Y does not hide the prize." If you have only this piece of information, you can estimate, again on the basis of an elementary extensional reasoning, that there is one chance in two that the contestant gets the prize, given that he has chosen one of the two doors that hide the prize. Your estimation, however, may be different, if you know the way in which the assertion that door Y does not hide the prize has been established. Suppose that the above person, unaware of the location of the prize, looks behind the chosen door X, and then says, "Door Y does not hide the prize." Given that she has inspected only door X, her conclusion implies that she has seen the prize beyond door X. Therefore, you may conclude that the contestant has certainly won the prize. In sum, different ways of acquiring the same piece of information lead to different probability estimations. This effect of the way information is acquired has been exploited in the original version of the Monty Hall problem (Selvin, 1975a, 1975b). After the contestant had chosen the door, Monty Hall, knowing the location of the prize, opened one door which does not hide the prize and has not been chosen by the contestant, say, Y, to reveal as always that it did not hide the prize, and then offered the contestant the chance of switching to the other unopened door, say, Z. The vast majority of persons presented with this problem, judge that the contestant should stay with the chosen alternative, because in their view X and Z were equally likely to be hiding the prize (see e.g., Friedman, 1998; Granberg & Brown, 1995; Granberg & Dorr, 1998). This solution is intuitively appealing and supported by extensional reasoning: Given that only two doors are left, door X has one chance in two of hiding the prize. The contestants' decision of not switching to door Z, however, is questionable. Suppose that Monty has a 1/2 chance of opening door Y, if the door chosen by the contestant hides the prize (for a discussion of this assumption, see Nickerson, 1999). Given the prior probability that Monty opens door Y is also 1/2, the probability that door X hides the prize is unaffected by the opening of door Y, that is, it remains 1/3. (Denote the presence of the prize beyond door X as X+, and the host's opening of door Y as Yo. According to Bayes's formula, $p(X+|Yo) = p(X+) p(Yo|X+) / p(Yo)$. Given that $p(Yo|X+) = p(Yo) = 1/2$, it follows that $p(Yo|X+) / p(Yo) = 1$. Hence, $p(X+|Yo) = p(X+) = 1/3$, that is, the posterior probability that the prize is beyond door X is the same as its prior probability.) By complementarity of probability, Z, the other, unopened door, has a 2/3 chance to hide the prize.

Can individuals draw these correct inferences? As we have seen, extensional reasoning based *only* on the possible location of the prize leads to the incorrect conclusion that the contestant has one chance in two to win. What if one combines the possible locations of the prize and Monty Hall's decisions? The combination of these two factors leads to a consideration of four possibilities:

Prize	Opening
Door X	Door Y
Door X	Door Z
Door Y	Door Z
Door Z	Door Y

Further combinations are not considered given that Monty Hall never opens door X or a door hiding the prize. Knowing that Monty Hall has opened door Y, the possibilities representing the opening of door Z are eliminated, leaving the following two possibilities

Prize	Opening
Door X	Door Y
Door Z	Door Y

If one bases the probability evaluation on this representation, one is likely to conclude, once again, that door X has one in two chances of hiding the prize. Extensional reasoning based on the above representation results in an incorrect probability assessment, given that the four prior possibilities are *not* equiprobable. Indeed, two of the four possibilities concern the case in which door X hides the prize, and only one concerns the case in which Y (or Z) hides the prize. A key to a correct extensional solution consists in restoring equiprobability by representing the case in which Y (or Z) hides the prize as *two* possibilities (see Johnson-Laird et al., 1999), that is:

Prize	Opening
Door X	Door Y
Door X	Door Z
Door Y	Door Z
Door Y	Door Z
Door Z	Door Y
Door Z	Door Y

Information on the way in which Monty Hall decides to open the door may support such a representation. Consider the following version of the Monty Hall problem, which explicitly provides this information:

The Monty Hall problem (modified version)
In a TV game a contestant is presented with three closed doors (called X, Y and Z), only one of which hides a valuable prize (the others doors hide nothing). The contestant has to choose one door in order to win the prize. The contestant chooses door X. As usual, the host of the game does not show immediately what door X hides. To make the show go on, he opens first another door, which does not hide the prize. He has a card for each door. He does not consult the card of the door chosen by the contestant, and consults the card of one of the other two doors. If the card indicates that the door does not hide the prize, the host opens this door. If the card indicates that the door hides the prize, the host opens the other door. Now, if the host opens door Y, what are the chances that, respectively, door X and door Z hide the prize?

On the basis of this problem statement, one can combine the three possible locations of the prize and the two cards that the host can consult, leading to six equiprobable prior possibilities. For each of these possibilities, one infers which door Monty opens. For instance, if door X hides the prize and Monty consults the card of door Y, he opens door Y. Thus, the six possibilities can be represented as follow:

Monty's action

Prize	Consulting	Opening
Door X	Door Y	Door Y
Door X	Door Z	Door Z
Door Y	Door Y	Door Z
Door Y	Door Z	Door Z
Door Z	Door Y	Door Y
Door Z	Door Z	Door Y

On the basis of the information that the host has opened door Y, one can eliminate some cases, considering the remaining possibilities:

Monty's action

Prize	Consulting	Opening
Door X	Door Y	Door Y
Door Z	Door Y	Door Y
Door Z	Door Z	Door Y

Given that door X hides the prize in only one of these three possibilities, one can conclude that there is one chance in three that door X hides the prize.

In order to test whether an explicit indication of the ways in which the host opens the door may be helpful, we presented the modified version of the Monty Hall problem to two groups of participants: 33 psychology under-graduates at the University of Provence (France) and 33 applicants to a highly selective French School of Engineering. The latter had had a consider-able training in mathematics. In particular, they were familiar with prob-ability calculus. Participants had also to solve a standard version of the Three Prisoner problem. We used it as a control because, like the standard Monty Hall game, it does not provide participants with information about the ways in which data are generated (see Morgan, Chaganty, Dahiya, & Doviak, 1991).

The Three Prisoner problem

Three men, A, B and C, were in jail in a foreign country. The king of the country has decided that one of them is to be set free. The jailer knows the outcome of the king's decision, but he cannot reveal it to the prisoners, who only know that one of them will go free. A asked the jailer, "Since two of the three will stay in prison, it is certain that either B or C will be, at least. You will give me no information about my own chances if you give me the name of one man, B or C, who is going to stay in prison." The jailer accepts this argument and tells A the name of one man who is going to stay in prison. If the jailer says that, between B and C, B is going to stay in prison, what are the chances that A and C, respectively, will be set free?

The solution of this problem is the same as in the Monty Hall problem (i.e., there are, respectively, 1/3 and 2/3 chances that A and B will be freed). As with the latter problem, however, individuals erroneously conclude that the two alternatives have the same probability (A and B have each 1/2 probability to be freed; see Shimojo & Ichikawa, 1989). If information on the host's deci-sion is sufficient to improve extensional reasoning, participants should per-form better on the revised version of the Monty Hall problem than in the Three Prisoner one.

In both problems, which were presented in a counterbalanced order, parti-cipants had to evaluate probabilities by stating a ratio of chances, writing their solution and a justification of it. Table 9.1 shows the patterns of responses produced by the two groups of participants to the problems.

Table 9.1 Percentage of participants in each group assigning correct (1/3–2/3) and equal chances (1/2–1/2) to the alternatives in the modified Monty Hall and Three Prisoners problems

	Problem	
Group	*Modified Monty Hall*	*Three Prisoners*
Engineering applicants		
Correct chances	6	3
Equal chances	79	85
Other evaluation	15	12
Psychology undergraduates		
Correct chances	3	0
Equal chances	88	76
Other evaluation	9	24

The results were straightforward. Most participants in both groups failed the standard Three Prisoner problem, as well as the Monty Hall modified version. The few participants who made a correct evaluation did not justify it in an extensional way. They argued only that the information given to them did not modify the prior probability that the contestant won the prize, or that A was to be freed. In sum, despite an explicit indication of the ways in which data are generated, participants failed the Monty Hall problem (for similar results, see Macchi & Girotto, 1994). This finding suggests that failure to solve the standard Monty Hall game should not be attributed to a tendency to reason about basic possibilities (i.e., the locations of the prize, regardless of Monty Hall's decisions), deriving from a greater difficulty to construct compound possibilities. Our modified version of the Monty Hall game encouraged the use of the combinations necessary to solve the problem. Our participants, especially the applicants, were surely able to construct them. Their failure suggests that the crux of the problem is that these combinations appear as irrelevant to most individuals, so that they resort to more basic possibilities. As a consequence, our participants made incorrect probability evaluations because they treated the basic possibilities as if they were equiprobable.

Conclusions

In this chapter, we have examined combinatorial probabilistic reasoning. Previous studies have established that individuals who are unfamiliar with the probability calculus correctly evaluate the probability of uncertain events by making an extensional analysis of possibilities (e.g., Girotto & Gonzalez, 2001; Johnson-Laird et al., 1999). In more recent studies (Girotto & Gonzalez, 2003) we have extended these results, showing that, from the age of about 9, children can conduct an elementary combinatorial analysis. Likewise, from the age of about 11, they can use a combinatorial analysis to assess the probability of an event. Here, we have shown that the difficulty of reasoning about combinations does not merely reflect the difficulty of constructing them. In some problems, individuals fail to consider all the combinations as relevant to the evaluation of a probability. For example, in the Monty Hall problem, individuals disregard some possibilities that appear as irrelevant (i.e., they consider the case in which a not chosen door hides the prize as one possibility, rather than as a double possibility). In these cases, they construct an alternative representation of possibilities and draw erroneous probability evaluations. For example, in the Monty Hall problem, individuals reason about a set of not equiprobable possibilities as if they were equiprobable. In sum, we have provided evidence that naive individuals, including children, do draw correct probability inferences asking for a combinatorial analysis. They may draw incorrect inferences, but their errors should be attributed to a failure to consider all relevant possibilities, rather than to an intrinsic inability to construct a complete combinatorial structure.

Finally, a personal note: Vittorio Girotto was a student in his first course on psychology at Padua University in October 1976. For the examination, he had to study a book entitled: *Form and content of cognitive processes: The history of an idea*. Its author was the teacher of the course: Paolo Legrenzi. Ten years later, Vittorio and Paolo spent a summer in Aix-en-Provence, designing their first collaborative research. On this occasion, Michel Gonzalez also met Paolo for the first time. Since then, both of us have had the opportunity to meet, discuss, and work with Paolo on many occasions. And both of us have come to appreciate his intellectual and personal qualities – in particular, his penchant for the history of ideas. For this reason, we believe that the historical and empirical evidence collected in this chapter represents an appropriate tribute to Paolo's work.

Acknowledgements

We thank Phil Johnson-Laird for his helpful comments on an earlier version of the chapter, and Marc Loustalot for his help in collecting data on the Monty Hall and Three Prisoners problems. Preparation of this paper was partially funded by a COFIN grant (ex-40%) from MIUR (the Italian Ministry of University and Research).

References

Acredolo, C., O'Connor, J., Banks, L., & Horobin, K. (1989). Children's ability to make probability estimates: Skills revealed through application of Anderson's functional measurement methodology. *Child Development, 60*, 933–945.

Brainerd, C. J. (1981). Working memory and the developmental analysis of probability judgement. *Psychological Review, 88*, 463–502.

d'Alembert, J. (1754). Croix ou pile. In D. Diderot & J. d'Alembert (Eds.), *Encyclopédie ou Dictionnaire raisonné des sciences, des arts et des métiers* (R. J. Pulskamp, Trans.). (Vol. 4, pp. 512–513). Retrieved in web site January 11, 2003 from http://cerebro.xu.edu/math/Sources/Dalembert/croix/croix.html

d'Alembert, J. (1757). Gageure. In D. Diderot & J. d'Alembert (Eds.), *Encyclopédie ou Dictionnaire raisonné des sciences, des arts et des métiers* (R. J. Pulskamp, Trans.). (Vol. 7, pp. 420–421). Retrieved January 11, 2003 from http://cerebro.xu.edu/math/Sources/Dalembert/gageure/gageure.html.

David, F. N. (1962). *Games, gods and gambling. A history of probability and statistical ideas.* London: Griffin.

Dudley Sylla, E. (1998). The emergence of mathematical probability from the perspective of the Leibniz–Jacob Bernoulli correspondence. *Perspectives on Science, 6,* 41–76.

Fischbein, E. (1975). *The intuitive sources of probabililistic thinking in children.* Dordrecht: Reidel.

Franklin, J. (2001). *The science of conjecture. Evidence and probability before Pascal.* Baltimore: Johns Hopkins University Press.

Friedman, D. (1998). Monty Hall's three doors: Construction and deconstruction of a choice anomaly. *American Economic Review, 88,* 933–946.

Girotto, V., & Gonzalez, M. (2001). Solving probabilistic and statistical problems: A matter of information structure and question form. *Cognition, 78,* 247–276.

Girotto, V., & Gonzalez, M. (2002). Chances and frequencies in probabilistic reasoning: Rejoinder to Hoffrage, Gigerenzer, Krauss, and Martignon. *Cognition, 84,* 353–359.

Girotto, V., & Gonzalez, M. (2003). *Early reasoning about chances and possibilities: Historical and developmental evidence.* Paper presented at the 16th Piaget Conference, Geneva 25–27 September.

Girotto, V., & Gonzalez, M. (2004). Extensional reasoning about chances. In W. Schaeken, G. De Vooght, A. Vandierendonck, & G. d'Ydewalle (Eds.), *Mental model theory: Extensions and Refinements.* Mahwah, NJ: Lawrence Erlbaum Associates, Inc.

Gonzalez, M., & Girotto, V. (2004). *Eliciting probabilities: When choices and judgements disagree.* Manuscript submitted for publication.

Granberg, D., & Brown, T. A. (1995). The Monty Hall dilemma. *Personality and Social Psychology Bulletin, 21,* 711–723.

Granberg, D., & Dorr, N. (1998). Further exploration of two-stage decision making in the Monty Hall dilemma. *American Journal of Psychology, 111,* 561–579.

Johnson-Laird, P. N., Legrenzi, P., Girotto, V., Sonino-Legrenzi, M., & Caverni, J. P. (1999). Naive probability: A model theory of extensional reasoning. *Psychological Review, 106,* 62–88.

Legrenzi, P. (1973). Probabilità soggettiva e strategie di pensiero [Subjective probability and thinking strategies]. *Rivista di Psicologia, 67,* 189–204.

Legrenzi, P., Girotto, V., Sonino-Legrenzi, M., & Johnson-Laird, P. N. (2003). Possibilities and probabilities. In L. Macchi & D. Hardman (Eds.), *Thinking: Psychological perspectives on reasoning, judgement, and decision making* (pp. 147–164). Chichester: Wiley.

Macchi, L., & Girotto, V. (1994). *Probabilistic reasoning with conditional probabilities: The three boxes paradox.* Paper presented at the Society for Judgement and Decision Making Annual Meeting, St. Louis.

Morgan, J. P., Chaganty, N. R., Dahiya, R. C., & Doviak, M. J. (1991). Let's make a deal: The players's dilemna. *American Statistician, 45*, 284–288.

Nickerson, R. S. (1999). Ambiguities and unstated assumptions in probabilistic reasoning. *Psychological Bulletin, 120*, 410–430.

Piaget, J., & Inhelder, B. (1975). *The origin of the idea of chance in children.* (L. Leake, Jr., P. Burrell, & H. Fischbein, Trans.). New York: Norton. (Original work published 1951)

Selvin, S. (1975a). A problem in probability (letter to the editor). *American Statistician, 29*, 67.

Selvin, S. (1975b). On the Monty Hall problem. *American Statistician, 29*, 134.

Shimojo, S., & Ichikawa, S. (1989) Intuitive reasoning about probability: Theoretical and experimental analyses of the "problem of three prisoners". *Cognition, 32*, 1–24.

Sloman, S. A., Over, D., Slovak, L., & Stibel, J. M. (2003). Frequency illusions and other fallacies. *Organizational Behavior and Human Decision Processes, 91*, 296–309.

Part V

Social and emotional aspects of decision making

10 Affect and argument

David W. Green

Introduction

Researchers debate the role of reasons and argument in the conduct of affairs. For some, decisions are "often reached by focusing on reasons that justify the selection of one option over another" (Shafir, Simonson, & Tversky, 1993, p. 34). For others, decisions, opinions and attitudes are products of other, perhaps implicit, factors. For instance, although opinions can be retrieved from memory (Eagly & Chaiken, 1993), they may also be constructed on the spot (Hastie & Park, 1986; Iyengar & Ottati, 1996) and so may be affected by information that is temporarily accessible at the time of judgement (Wilson, Lindsey, & Schooler, 2000). In support of this claim, Wänke, Bless, and Biller (1996) asked individuals to write down three or seven arguments either in favour of public transport or against public transport before reporting their attitudes. Participants reported more favourable attitudes when they experienced an easy time in generating positive arguments or a difficult time in generating negative arguments. Haddock (2002) extended this line of research. In his study, individuals wrote down either two or five positive or negative characteristics of Tony Blair (the British Prime Minister at the time). The group was split into those with an interest in British politics and those with no strong interest. For those interested in British politics there was no effect on opinion of the number and type of attributes generated. In contrast, for those with no interest, more favourable opinions followed the generation of positive compared to negative attributes. In addition, attitudes were slightly more positive for those generating two positive attributes compared to five positive attributes and for those generating five negative attributes compared to two negative attributes. In other words, for those with little interest in an issue, it is not only the nature of the generated arguments but also the ease of their generation that is important. But do these data undermine the importance of reasons and argument in judgement and opinion? No. Ease of generation may be a good proxy for the strength of arguments. Expressed differently, difficulty in generation may be a good indicator of the absence of strong arguments and might count as a "fast and frugal heuristic" (Goldstein & Gigerenzer, 2002). But is there any need to postulate a proxy for argument strength? No. Opinion might be directly sensitive to the strength of produced arguments. The requirement to generate five or seven arguments on an issue may elicit weak arguments that deplete the average strength of arguments for the position. If this suggestion proves correct, no proxy, nor any additional, implicit process is needed to explain the results. Opinion is sensitive to the strength of arguments or reasons. Alternatively, both factors may be important and tap different aspects of the process of generating an opinion.

Another important line of attack on the notion that opinions and decision are reason based has been to assert that affect is primary and that the reasons individuals provide for their decisions are mere rationalisations (Zajonc, 1980). Slovic, Finucane, Peters, and MacGregor (2001) proposed that in a complex, uncertain and potentially dangerous world, reliance on affect allows for fast and efficient decisions. They propose an affect heuristic, in which an overall affective impression guides decision or opinion. In support of this claim, Slovic et al. (2001) report that the affective value of elicited images is a good predictor of preferences for visiting different cities, attitudes to different technologies (such as nuclear power, see Finucane, Alhakami, Slovic, & Johnson, 2000), purchasing stock in new companies (MacGregor, Slovic, Dreman, & Berry, 2000) and engaging in behaviours that either threaten health, e.g., smoking, or enhance it, e.g., exercise (Benthin, Slovic, Moran, Severson, Mertz, & Gerrard, 1995).

The basic idea is that in reaching a decision or opinion individuals access an "affect pool". This pool comprises a set of "positive and negative tags consciously or unconsciously associated with representations" (see also Damasio, 1994). Use of the affect heuristic, according to Slovic et al. is "far easier, more efficient than weighing the pros and cons or retrieving from memory many relevant examples". In other words, Slovic et al. oppose the affect heuristic to a decision procedure based on the assessment of reasons. They link this opposition to the idea that everyday decisions derive from two distinct kinds of processes (e.g., Epstein, 1994; Evans & Over, 1996; Sloman, 1996). For instance, Epstein (1994, p. 710) writes: "There is no dearth of evidence in everyday life that people apprehend reality in two fundamentally different ways, one variously labelled intuitive, automatic, natural, non-verbal, narrative, and experiential, and the other analytical, deliberative, verbal and rational." The affect heuristic is allied to an experiential mode of apprehending reality whereas a process of assessing reasons is linked to an analytic and deliberative apprehension. Much of the research based around this distinction of two processes or systems (Stanovich & West, 2003) seems to bolster this opposition in that an analytic process acts to override or suppress experiential responses. However, if there is a need to postulate two processes, these must work together. I consider some evidence for how they might do so in the context of the affect heuristic, but first we need to consider what it would take for the affect heuristic to be effective and efficient.

Efficiency and effectiveness

Slovic et al. (2001) propose that the affect heuristic is effective and efficient compared to a process involving the deliberate weighing of arguments – i.e., reasons for a particular course of action or decision. Consider the efficiency issue. The relative efficiency of these two procedures cannot be assessed independently of a proposal about how reasons are weighed. In fact, evidence suggests that the relative strength of arguments for and against some option is a good predictor of the decisions that individuals reach both when they generate arguments on an issue (e.g., Green, 2000) and when they compre- hend presented arguments (Green & McCloy, 2003). Why should such a process be slower than one based on the summing of affective tags? Next consider the effectiveness issue. In order to be effective can the affect heuristic really operate in opposition to a reason-based process? Certainly the head and the heart may pull in opposite directions but isn't that just to say that one can have an affective reason for some opinion and a cognitive reason for some other opinion?

Implicit cognition research may seem to offer an objection to the attempt to equate an affect-based procedure and one based on reasons. For instance, Greenwald, Pickrell, and Farnham (2002), using the Implicit Association Test (Greenwald, McGhee & Schwartz, 1998), found that after spending 45s studying the names of four members of one of two fictitious teams, partici- pants show implicit liking (as measured by the ease of associating those names with winning) and implicit identification (as measured by the ease of associating those names with self) with the group. On occasions implicit attitudes may indeed diverge from those expressed overtly (e.g., Dasgupta & Greenwald, 2001; McConnell & Leibold, 2001), but the conditions under which this is true remain unclear. In any case, these results do not refute the present proposal. The focus here is on expressed or manifest opinion. Expressed opinion is itself likely to reflect different kinds of reasons of different strengths and may also be moderated by other apparently noncognitive fac- tors such as the ease of generating arguments or reasons. Expressed opinion may also convey ambivalence. For instance, the tone of voice in which an opinion is expressed may signal a degree of reservation or doubt.

The point I wish to make here is that in order to act as an effective proxy for explicit deliberation, the affect heuristic must respect reasons for and against a course of action. There is no reason why it should not do so. Affective tags are attached to specific thoughts and images. A priori, a given option might be attractive in some respects (e.g., it is a nice place to visit) but unattractive in other respects (e.g., it takes 24 hours to get there). On the affect scale then some of a person's initial thoughts, images and feelings will be rated positive and others will be rated negative. The affect heuristic (summing or averaging affective tags) might then be functionally equivalent to a process of integrating arguments for and against some course of action. Such a claim can be simply tested. The set of initial images, feelings and thoughts, will also provide some of the arguments that individuals consider when explicitly deliberating about an issue.

The affect heuristic proposed by Slovic et al. raises questions about the nature of the initial thoughts about an issue and how reflection affects these, if at all. The next section considers the relation between initial thoughts and reflection. The following section considers how overt reflection alters the affect pool.

Initial thoughts and the effects of reflection

Consider one task described in Slovic et al. (2001). Participants are presented with an issue and record in a word or a phrase any images, feelings and thoughts ("initial thoughts" from now on) that come to mind. They rate each one on a five-point affect scale running from −2 (very negative) to +2 (very positive) with 0 as the neutral point. The summed or average value of these ratings predicts opinion or decisions on a range of issues.

The first question is: What is the relation between these initial thoughts and the arguments that individuals would use in discussing the issue with a colleague or friend? A strong claim would be that these initial thoughts are independent of the arguments that individuals would consider explicitly. But, as pointed out above, if the affect heuristic is to be an efficient and effective proxy for explicit deliberation then these two sets must overlap. The second question is: If the two sets do overlap, what is the relation between the affective value of the initial thought and the likelihood that it will be endorsed as an argument? One possibility is that endorsement will increase with a thought's rated affective value. Ignoring whether the rating is positive or negative, endorsement should increase with a thought's absolute affective value. On this proposal, affective ratings are a proxy of the power or strength of arguments. The third question concerns the consistency of the thoughts that are endorsed. Reflection, for purposes of discussion, might lead to the selection of thoughts that are affectively consistent. Baron (1995) suggested that individuals tend to present arguments for their own side of an issue. However, as noted above, individuals can and do represent arguments both for and against a particular decision. In the case of presented arguments in a legal case, for example, individuals may not so much ignore arguments presented for the other side as perceive them as coherently separated from those for the side they favour (see Holyoak & Simon, 1999; Simon, Pham, Le, & Holyoak, 2001). Participants first listed images, thoughts and feelings on an issue (genetically modified crops, GM crops for short) and expressed each one in a couple of words or a phrase. They then rated each one on the five-point affect scale. The study extended the research of Slovic et al. by requiring participants to complete a further two tasks. They ticked which, if any, of these initial thoughts they would use as arguments in discussing the use of GM crops with a friend or colleague. They then listed out any other points and rated these in turn for how emotionally positive or negative they were. The study was carried out in a single session with participants assigned at random either to a condition in which their opinion on GM crops was elicited before the thought-listing task or after it. There were 42 participants in each condition.

Of the total number of arguments, 79 per cent originated in the initial thoughts. The remaining 21 per cent arose on further reflection. Clearly, it is wrong to assume that initial thoughts are independent of those that individuals might use on reflection. Indeed, just to drive the point home, individuals endorsed 68 per cent of the initial thoughts as arguments. As expected, endorsement increased significantly as a function of a thought's rated absolute affective value. Overall, individuals endorsed 50 per cent of initial thoughts rated zero in affective value, 64 per cent of initial thoughts rated 1 in affective value and 77 per cent of those rated 2 in affective value. Initial thoughts were also somewhat more varied than endorsed thoughts. Where at least two of an individual's initial thoughts had an affect rating greater than zero, it was possible to assess their affective consistency, i.e., whether they were all positive or all negative. For initial thoughts, 27 per cent were consistent. For those endorsed as arguments, 60 per cent were consistent – a significant increase on a sign test with 22 out of the 67 participants showing a shift. Less than half of the participants (46 per cent) produced additional arguments, and of these 58 per cent were consistent. Finally, this study explored possible predictors of opinion. Given the incomplete sample providing additional arguments, regression analyses compared as predictors of opinion, the summed affective value of initial thoughts ("initial thoughts") and the summed affective value of initial thoughts endorsed as arguments ("endorsed thoughts"). The regression analyses confirmed expectations. Initial thoughts predicted opinion expressed before the elicitation task whereas endorsed thoughts predicted opinion expressed after the elicitation task.

A second study (described below) included the same tasks and corroborated the key findings. Individuals endorsed 72 per cent of initial thoughts as arguments. and they were also significantly more likely to endorse thoughts with higher absolute affective value. In addition to rating the affective value of their thoughts, individuals in this second study also rated the argument strength of each endorsed thought. The absolute affective value correlated positively and significantly with argument strength (Pearson r = 0.74) again suggesting a close connection between the affective ratings of initial thoughts and assessments of their potential as arguments. Reflecting on the initial thoughts, for the purpose of arguing about the issue, also increased consistency. Finally, as expected, opinion expressed after the elicitation task was predicted by endorsed thoughts.

In sum, these data are consistent with the notion that the affect heuristic is functionally equivalent to a procedure that integrates arguments. There is considerable overlap between initial thoughts and those endorsed as arguments. Reflection achieves two effects: It reduces variety by endorsing thoughts of higher absolute affective value. It also eliminates inconsistencies to a small extent. Nonetheless, a substantial number of individuals (40 per cent in both studies) endorse arguments that are affectively inconsistent. Such a result is understandable given that most individuals were either moderately for or moderately against the use of GM crops. Affective inconsistency, of course, does not entail logical inconsistency (cf. Legrenzi, Girotto, & Johnson-Laird, 2003) because positive affect can be linked to one aspect of the issue (e.g., helping food production in difficult conditions) and negative affect to another aspect of the issue (e.g., interfering with natural world). The next section considers additional effects of reflection arising from its capacity to alter the contents of the affect pool.

Effects of reflecting on a future possibility

How might thinking about an issue change the contents of the affect pool and with it opinion on an issue? The second study examined this issue. Experience tells us that we tend to think about how things could have been different when things go wrong (Kahneman & Tversky, 1982). In particular, we tend to think about how we could have behaved differently when things go wrong (Girotto, Legrenzi, & Rizzo, 1991). Counterfactual "if only" thinking influences various emotions such as regret (e.g., Gilovich & Medvec, 1994) as well as judgements of causality (e.g., N'Gbala & Branscombe, 1995). Is there evidence that counterfactual thinking affects opinion? Hetts, Boninger, Armor, Gleicher, and Nathanson (2000) cite earlier work by Gleicher and colleagues. As part of a presentation on AIDS to students at a community college in the United States, speakers either led students to consider a circumstance where they had unprotected sexual intercourse and subsequently contracted HIV, or led them them through a review of the important facts about AIDS and exhorted them to use condoms as an effective way to avoid contracting HIV. Relative to those in the review group, participants who implicitly anticipated counterfactual regret had a more positive attitude to the use of condoms and were more inclined to use them. Hetts et al. explicitly manipulated the nature of the anticipatory counterfactual regret and confirmed, for a noncontroversial issue, that participants chose to act in a way that minimised the chance of them experiencing the specified regret. In terms of the notion of an affect pool, anticipatory regret (a consequence of counterfactual thinking) works by adding positive tags to an action that avoids the regret.

However, it is important to consider in more detail the nature of the mental representations involved in thinking counterfactually. To do so, it is useful to contrast counterfactual "if only" thinking with semifactual "even if" thinking (e.g., Johnson-Laird & Byrne, 1991; McCloy & Byrne, 2002). McCloy and Byrne (2002) proposed that individuals understand a counterfactual of the form "if only p, q" (e.g., "if only I had caught the train, I would have made the meeting") by keeping in mind a conjectured possibility of p and q (catching the train and making the meeting) and the presupposed fact, *not-p* and *not-q* (not catching the train and not making the meeting). In contrast, individuals understand a semifactual of the form, *"even if p, not-q"* (e.g., "even if I had caught the train, I would have missed the meeting") by envisaging the conjectured possibility of *p, not-q* (catching the train and missing the meeting) and the presupposed fact, *not-p and not-q* (not catching the train and missing the meeting). Consistent with this analysis, McCloy and Byrne (2002) showed that generating "even if" thoughts decreased judged emotion compared to a condition where individuals generated counterfactual "if only" thoughts or produced no thoughts at all. "Even if" thinking can reduce emotional reactions to negative outcomes (such as "regret" and "feeling bad") whereas counterfactual "if only" thinking can increase them. "Even if" thinking can also reduce the perceived causal importance of an event. In a second study, they confirmed that individuals focus on different imaginary alternatives when they generate "if only" thoughts compared to "even if" thoughts. In the former case, they focus on alternatives that would lead to a different outcome. In the latter case they focus on an imaginary alternative that would lead to the same outcome.

Turning to the present concerns, the basic idea is that there could be two distinct kinds of effect: one associated with the conjectured world and one associated with the presupposed world. In the example above, in the conjectured "if only" world, positive feeling is associated with catching the train. In contrast, in the presupposed world, negative feeling is associated with missing the train. How sensitive is opinion to these contrasts?

In the second study I addressed these three questions:

(1) Does a conjectured future possibility affect current opinion?
(2) Is current opinion insulated from the affect associated with a presupposed future world?
(3) How do such effects arise?

The study comprised a set of tasks. Participants first imagined a scenario in which there had been a large volcanic eruption in 2040 that threatened worldwide famine. They listed their thoughts, expressed in a word or in phrase, and rated their affective value. Next, they imagined they were attending a meeting to decide what to do. They overhear a couple of people talking about the banning of research into GM crops in 2020 and start to think about whether or not things could have been different. In one condition, participants listed out and rated their "if only" thoughts. For exposition's sake, this will be termed the benefit condition because it was supposed that thinking counterfactually would lead individuals to identify a benefit of research into GM crops that might improve the outcome. In a second condition, individuals listed out and rated their "even if" thoughts. Here individuals were not expected to identify any benefit of GM crop research and so this will be termed the no benefit condition. Finally, they were asked to list out their thoughts associated with GM crops in today's world and carried out the other tasks described in the first study.

Effects of a conjectured future possibility

With these materials, the presupposed future world is one in which GM crop research is banned. The conjectured future world is one, like the current world, where research on GM crops is not banned. The expectation therefore was that participants in the benefit condition who explicitly mentioned GM crop research would be more pro GM crops in the current world than those in the no benefit condition. Individuals who mention GM crops entertain a future circumstance focused around the critical issue (cf. Legrenzi, Girotto, & Johnson-Laird, 1993) and so in the benefit condition, for instance, associate GM crops with positive affect. Others who do not mention GM crops have no grounds for acting in this manner.

In the study, just under half of the participants (45 per cent: 34/75) mentioned GM crops. As predicted, for these participants opinion was significantly more pro GM crops in the benefit condition (where they thought counterfactually) than in the no benefit condition (where they thought semi-factually). The difference was 1.59 scale points, on average. In contrast, for those who did not mention GM crops, there was no significant difference between the two conditions (0.30 scale points, on average). This effect of the conjectured possibility on current opinion supports the idea that reflection can add affective tags to the affect pool or equivalently induce a reason to weight opinion in a particular way.

In line with the research by McCloy and Byrne (2002), participants in the benefit condition also felt more regret than those in the no benefit condition at the banning of GM crop research by an average of 1.53 scale points (on a nine-point regret scale). In contrast, and in line with expectation, there was no effect of conditions for those who did not mention GM crops (–0.59 scale points, on average).

Effects of the presupposed world

Consider next how listed thoughts in the two conditions might differ in the presupposed future world. Participants in the benefit condition should feel angry that GM crop research was banned. In contrast, those in the no benefit condition should be more resigned and less negative. In fact, affective value did vary as a function of condition and GM crop reference. As expected, where participants mentioned GM crops, those in the benefit condition compared to those in the no benefit condition rated their thoughts significantly more negatively (by an average of 2.12 scale points). In contrast, and contrary to expectation, those participants who made no reference to such research showed the opposite pattern rather than a weaker version of the same effect. Individuals in the no benefit condition, compared to those in the benefit condition, rated their thoughts significantly more negatively by 1.73 scale points. One post-hoc possibility is that those who did not mention GM crops despaired in the no benefit condition (there was nothing anyone could have done to change matters) but retained a shred of hope in the benefit condition.

Predictors of opinion

In order to examine whether the conjectured and presupposed worlds independently influence current opinion, it is necessary to partial out effects associated with current arguments, anticipated regret and the extent to which participants think about the future anyway. In general, individuals are more regretful about a negative event when they consider a counterfactual action that changes that event compared to one that does not. However, Boninger, Gleicher, and Stratham (1994) showed that this tendency was modified in individuals who routinely consider future consequences. Participants high in the Consideration of Future Consequences (CFC) were not more regretful when the counterfactual action changed the outcome compared to when it did not.

The 12-item Consideration of Future Consequences (CFC) questionnaire (Stratham, Gleicher, Boninger, & Scott Edwards, 1994) is a validated measure of this individual difference. I asked participants to complete it after an experimental task. Participants rate each item on a five-point scale that runs from 1 (extremely uncharacteristic of me) to 5 (extremely characteristic of me). For instance, one item reads: "Often I engage in a particular behaviour in order to achieve outcomes that may not result for many years." Another reads: "I think that sacrificing now is usually unnecessary since future outcomes can be dealt with at a later time." On the questionnaire, a higher score indicates a greater concern with the future consequences.[1]

The linear regression analysis on the full sample included the following five predictor variables: condition (i.e., conjectured possibility), CFC score, regret, endorsed thoughts (i.e., the affect value of those initial thoughts endorsed as arguments), and affect in the presupposed world. It explained 62 per cent of the variance in opinion. All predictors were significant bar affect in the presupposed world which was not. More pertinent are the regression

---

1 In the present context, the expectation was that high-CFC participants, compared to low-CFC participants, would be less affected by the thought manipulation condition. A further analysis, identifying individuals who scored above or below the median on the CFC questionnaire, showed that the effect of the thought manipulation varied somewhat as a function of CFC score. Low-CFC scorers (i.e., those scoring below the median) showed a greater effect of condition on opinion. However, a similar analysis of the regret ratings showed no effects. Conceivably, the effects of CFC score on regret are more apparent when there is an explicit outcome manipulation as in Boninger et al. (1994).

results of the two subsets. (The results for the subsets remain the same if, on the grounds of sample size, the predictors are reduced to three, viz. condition, affect in the presupposed world and affect of initial argument.) For the subset who did not mention GM crops in the thought manipulation task, the same predictors explained 47 per cent of the variance overall, but only endorsed thoughts significantly predicted opinion. Ratings of regret were marginally predictive but affect in the presupposed world was not significant. In contrast, for those who mentioned GM crops in the thought manipulation task, the same predictors explained 78 per cent of the variance in opinion. All predictors were significant, bar the CFC score that was marginal. Individuals scoring high on the CFC questionnaire were more pro GM crops than those scoring lower on the questionnaire. For those who mention GM crops in the thought manipulation task, there are two effects of thinking about a future world on current opinion: one effect is attributable to the conjectured future possibility and the second is attributable to the presupposed future world. These effects arise even when the effects of current arguments and anticipatory regret are partialled out. The next section reviews the main findings and considers the implications for the claim that the affect heuristic is functionally equivalent to a procedure based on the integration of reasons.

Implications and further issues

The affect heuristic yields an opinion by integrating affective tags (positive or negative) associated with the issue in question. Such tags reside in an affect pool. The rhetoric surrounding the affect heuristic opposes its decision procedure to a procedure based on reasons and links its power to an experiential, intuitive system rather than to an analytic and reflective system. This chapter has advanced an alternative thesis: The affect heuristic is functionally equivalent to one based on the integration of arguments or reasons (e.g., to a procedure that assesses the relative strength of arguments for and against an option). In fact, it was argued that this must be so if the heuristic is to be efficient and effective. A great merit of the notion of an affect pool is that both the fruits of experience and the outcomes of reflection on an issue can enter the affect pool using the common currency of an affective tag varying in value.

The alternative thesis is supported by a number of findings. First, there is considerable overlap between initial thoughts on an issue (here GM crops) and the arguments that individuals make in discussing the issue with a friend or colleague. Second, reflection for the purposes of arguing about an issue selects from that initial set as a function of absolute affective value and this value correlates strongly with rated argument strength. Third, reflection induced by considering future worlds also affects opinion. When individuals envisage a future benefit associated with GM crops, opinion is more positive than when they envisage no such future benefit. In other words, a conjectured future possibility enters a positive tag into the affect pool in one case but not in the other. All these findings are consistent with the functional equivalence of an affect-based and a reason-based procedure.

One puzzle for such a view is the finding that expressed opinion is also affected by how individuals feel about the presupposed future world in which research into GM crops is banned. Unlike the effects of the conjectured future possibility it is not obvious what reason-based equivalent can be given. It is as if an affective tag has been associated with just thinking about the issue. If future work using other scenarios confirms such an effect, then the claim of functional equivalence will need to be amended. At a minimum, the present findings support the collaboration of the experiential and reflective systems. The nature of this collaboration warrants further study. First, the supposition here has been that initial thoughts are attributable to an implicit experiential system and the endorsement of thoughts is a product of a reflective system. Certainly, the instructions in the task encourage immediate and uncensored responses and inspection of these responses (e.g., fields of wheat, giant tomatoes, Frankenstein foods, unnatural crop yields) suggests that the participants adhered to the instructions. But initial thoughts may also be generated reflectively. Second, to claim there is collaboration between the experiential and the reflective systems is not to propose that reflection yields normative responses (cf. Evans & Over, 1996; Stanovich & West, 2000). There is nothing, in principle, it seems to me, that is particularly normative, or nonnormative in allowing a future fiction and one's responses to it to guide current opinion, especially when there are many such fictions. However, where those fictions are plausible and relevant it is surely adaptive to take them into account and vary present opinion and action so as to achieve the best possible outcome.

Conclusion

This chapter has questioned the notion that the affect heuristic is radically distinct from a decision procedure based on reasons. There is a close correspondence between affect ratings and endorsement of initial thoughts as arguments. Reflection can increase consistency, but it can also, when individuals imagine future worlds, increase ambivalence in a way that under-mines a strong equivalence of the affect heuristic and a procedure based on the assessment of reasons. Articulating the nature of the collaboration between reflective (explicit) processes and nonreflective (implicit) processes may be the best way to proceed in order to develop an adequate theory of expressed opinion and decision.

Acknowledgements

My thanks to the editors for helpful comments on an earlier draft of this chapter.

References

Baron, J. (1995). Myside bias in thinking about abortion. *Thinking and Reasoning, 1*, 221–235.

Benthin, A., Slovic, P., Moran, P., Severson, H., Mertz, C. K., & Gerrard, M. (1995). Adolescent health-threatening and health-enhancing behaviors: A study of word association and imagery. *Journal of Adolescent Health, 17*, 143–152.

Boninger, D. S., Gleicher, F., & Stratham, A. (1994). Counterfactual thinking: From what might have been to what may be. *Journal of Personality and Social Psychology, 67*, 297–307.

Damasio, A. R. (1994). *Descartes' error: Emotion, reason, and the human brain.* New York: Avon.

Dasgupta, N., & Greenwald, A. G. (2001). On the malleability of automatic attitudes: Combating automatic prejudice with images of admired and disliked individuals. *Journal of Personality and Social Psychology, 81*, 800–814.

Eagly, A. H., & Chaiken, S. (1993). *The psychology of attitudes.* Fort Worth, TX: Harcourt Brace Jovanovich.

Epstein, S. (1994). Integration of the cognitive and psychodynamic unconscious. *American Psychologist, 49*, 709–724.

Evans, J. St. B. T., & Over, D. E. (1996). *Rationality and reasoning.* Hove, UK: Psychology Press.

Finucane, M. L., Alhakami, A., Slovic, P., & Johnson, S. M. (2000). The affect heuristic in judgements of risks and benefits. *Journal of Behavioral Decision Making, 13*, 1–17.

Gilovich, T., & Medvec, V. H. (1994). The temporal pattern to the experience of regret. *Journal of Personality and Social Psychology, 67*, 357–365.

Girotto, V., Legrenzi, P., & Rizzo, A. (1991). Counterfactual thinking: The role of events controllability. *Acta Psychologica, 78*, 111–133.

Goldstein, D. G., & Gigerenzer, G. (2002). Models of ecological rationality: The recognition heuristic. *Psychological Review, 109*, 75–90.

Green, D. W. (2000). Argument and opinion. In J. García-Madruga, N. Carriedo, M. J. González-Labra (Eds.), *Mental models in reasoning* (pp. 57–67). Madrid: UNED.

Green, D. W., & McCloy, R. (2003). Reaching a verdict. *Thinking & Reasoning, 9*, 307–333.

Greenwald, A. G., McGhee, D. E., & Schwartz, J. L. K. (1998). Measuring individual differences in implicit cognition: The implicit association test. *Journal of Personality and Social Psychology, 74*, 1464–1480.

Greenwald, A., Pickrell, J. E., & Farnham, S. D. (2002). Implicit partisanship: Taking sides for no reason. *Journal of Personality and Social Psychology, 83*, 367–379.

Haddock, G. (2002). It's easy to like or dislike Tony Blair: Accessibility experiences and the favourability of attitude judgements. *British Journal of Psychology, 93*, 257–267.

Hastie, R., & Park, B. (1986). The relationship between memory and judgement depends on whether the judgement is memory-based or on-line. *Psychological Review, 93*, 258–268.

Hetts, J. J., Boninger, D. S., Armor, D. A., Gleicher, F., & Nathanson, A. (2000). The influence of anticipated counterfactual regret on behavior. *Psychology and Marketing, 17*, 345–368.

Holyoak, K. J., & Simon, D. (1999). Bidirectional reasoning in decision making by constraint satisfaction. *Journal of Experimental Psychology: General, 128*, 3–31.

Iyengar, S., & Ottati, V. (1994). Cognitive perspective in political psychology. In R. S. Wyer, Jr. & T. K. Srull (Eds.), *Handbook of social cognition* (Vol. 2, pp. 143–187). Hillsdale, NJ: Lawrence Erlbaum Associates, Inc.

Johnson-Laird, P. N., & Byrne, R. M. J. (1991). *Deduction*. Hillsdale, NJ: Lawrence Erlbaum Associates, Inc.

Kahneman, D., & Tversky, A. (1982). The simulation heuristic. In D. Kahneman, P. Slovic & A. Tversky (Eds.), *Judgement under uncertainty: Heuristics and biases* (pp. 201–211). Cambridge: Cambridge University Press.

Legrenzi, P., Girotto, V., & Johnson-Laird, P. N. (1993). Focusing in reasoning and in decision-making. *Cognition, 49*, 37–66.

Legrenzi, P., Girotto, V., & Johnson-Laird, P. N. (2003). Models of consistency. *Psychological Science, 14*, 131–137.

McCloy, R., & Byrne, R. M. J. (2002). Semifactual "even if" thinking. *Thinking and Reasoning, 8*, 41–67.

McConnell, A. R., & Leibold, J. M. (2001). Relations among the implicit association test, discriminatory behaviour and explicit measures of racial attitudes. *Journal of Experimental Social Psychology, 37*, 435–442.

MacGregor, D. G., Slovic, P., Dreman, D., & Berry, M. (2000). Imagery, affect, and financial judgement. *Journal of Psychology and Financial Markets, 1*, 104–110.

N'Gbala, A., & Branscombe, N. R. (1995). Mental simulation and causal attribution: When simulating an event does not affect fault assignment. *Journal of Experimental Social Psychology, 31*, 139–162.

Shafir, E., Simonson, I., & Tversky, A. (1993). Reason-based choice. *Cognition, 49*, 11–36.

Simon, D., Pham, L. B., Le, Q. A., & Holyoak, K. J. (2001). The emergence of coherence over the course of decision-making. *Journal of Experimental Psychology: Learning, Memory, and Cognition, 27*, 1250–1260.

Sloman, S. A. (1996). The empirical case for two systems of reasoning. *Psychological Bulletin, 119*, 3–22.

Slovic, P., Finucane, M., Peters, E., & MacGregor, D. G. (2001). The affect heuristic. In T. Gilovich, D. Griffin, & D. Kahneman, (Eds.), *Intuitive judgement: Heuristics and biases* (pp. 397–420). Cambridge: Cambridge University Press.

Stanovich, K. E., & West, R. F. (2000). Individual differences in reasoning: Implications for the rationality debate? *Behavioral and Brain Sciences, 23*, 645–726.

Stanovich, K. E., & West, R. F. (2003). Evolutionary versus instrumental goals: How evolutionary psychology misconceives human rationality. In D. Over (Ed.), *Evolution and the psychology of thinking* (pp. 171–230). Hove, UK: Psychology Press.

Stratham, A., Gleicher, F., Boninger, D. S., & Scott Edwards, C. (1994). The Consideration of Future Consequences: Weighing immediate and distant outcomes of behaviour. *Journal of Personality and Social Psychology, 66*, 742–752.

Wänke, M., Bless, H., & Biller, B. (1996). Subjective experience versus content of information in the construction of attitude judgements. *Personality and Social Psychology Bulletin, 22*, 1105–1113.

Wilson, T. D., Lindsey, S., & Schooler, T. Y. (2000). A model of dual attitudes. *Psychological Review, 107*, 101–126.

Zajonc, R. B. (1980). Feeling and thinking: Preferences need no inferences. *American Psychologist, 35*, 151–175.

11 Reasoning together: From focusing to decentring

Fabrizio Butera and Céline Buchs

Introduction

Focusing is a pervasive phenomenon occurring in reasoning and decision making, which has been thoroughly described by Legrenzi, Girotto, and Johnson-Laird (1993). It consists in the fact that reasoners seem to restrict their thoughts to what is explicitly represented in their mental models. Legrenzi and his colleagues have demonstrated that this phenomenon is a very general one, and concerns such domains as deductive reasoning, decision making and counterfactual thinking. Focusing is believed to be an inevitable consequence of the use of models in reasoning and depends on the fact that individuals construct very few explicit models when reasoning, focus on these models, and ignore other alternatives. However, this effect can be inhibited. In the above cited article, Legrenzi et al. also propose, and demonstrate, that the effects of focusing can be reduced by any manipulation that leads individuals to flesh out alternative models.

In the present chapter, we make this idea more specific, and introduce the notion of decentring, a mechanism supposed to reduce the focusing effect, since it leads individuals to take into account alternative models and points of view. We show how decentring can be induced both by a manipulation of the representation of the task and by confronting individuals with a source of social influence. This latter phenomenon is important, because reasoning often takes place in situations in which reasoners encounter diverging models, alternative viewpoints, and conflicts with people with whom they are working.

Egocentrism, decentring, and related concepts

Decentring has been known for a long time in the psychological literature. In Piaget's early writings, and all through his career, egocentrism and decentring appear to be central mechanisms in the development of the intellect (cf. Inhelder & Piaget, 1958; Piaget, 1963). Egocentrism is a mechanism that resembles focusing: It consists in considering one's own judgement as the only possible one, overlooking alternative ones. For instance, a 5-year-old child considers that the left and right hands of the person standing in front of him/her are those that directly correspond to his/her left and right hands. Decentring occurs in later stages of development, and relates to the ability to take different perspectives; i.e., the ability to understand, for instance, that a person who views a scene from a different point of view sees things differently. In this respect, decentring allows individuals to understand that their own point of view is not the only possible one, and to consider other alternatives. However, and critical for our contention, Piaget's decentring *occurs* with development. After a stage of its complete absence (up to 4–5 years old), there follows a stage in which children recognise that different points of views can exist, but they have no mastery over them. Development into a third and final stage (starting from 8 years old) allows children to co-ordinate different points of view, and to understand what others think.

Contrary to Piaget, there is an abundant evidence that egocentrism is still present in reasoning and judgement well after the age of 8, and that it is important to develop means of decentring to overcome the effects of focusing. This evidence is so abundant that Greenwald has described the self as the "totalitarian ego" (1980). Indeed, it appears that individuals encode events in memory only from their own point of view (Tulving, 1972); that they are convinced that they influenced events which are in fact aleatory (illusion of control, Langer, 1975); that they recall information confirming their expectations better than disconfirmatory information (Mischel, Ebbesen, & Zeiss, 1976); that they judge messages as more persuasive if the messages are in line with their opinions than if they oppose their opinions (Greenwald, 1969); that they judge other people on the basis of the first description (primacy effect, Luchins, 1958); and so on. This incomplete list shows that phenomena related to some kind of egocentrism still occur in adults, as – by the way – demonstrated by the focusing effects described by Legrenzi et al. (1993). Clearly, there is a need for decentring. In line with this idea, many authors have argued that it is possible to reduce people's egocentrism, with a significant benefit for problem solving, judgement, accuracy and reasoning. They all converge in recognising that *confrontation* with somebody else's position can lead to decentring and result in increased attention to alternatives.

Johnson and Johnson (1995), for instance, have shown the link between controversy and perspective taking (see also Tjosvold, 1998; Tjosvold, Johnson, & Fabrey, 1980), a form of decentring. Controversy is a discussion between two or more partners in which opposing opinions clash; it has been shown that controversy promotes perspective taking, the understanding of another's knowledge and reasoning (see also Kohlberg, 1969). Perspective taking, in turn, results in benefits for learning, interpersonal relations, as well as for cognitive and moral development (Johnson & Johnson, 1995). For instance, groups who received perspective-taking instructions produced significantly more creative solutions than groups who received egocentric instructions (Falk & Johnson, 1977). Moreover, perspective-taking instructions increased perceived co-operation, trust, attraction, satisfaction among group members, and effective communication. Perspective taking as a process of information exchange has also been proved to stimulate individual change toward more accurate judgements (Johnson, 1977).

In a similar vein, Wicklund has described "multiple perspectives" as a tool for reducing self-serving biases, restrictive goal orientations, and for promoting the acquisition of new repertoires (Wicklund, 1999; Pantaleo & Wicklund, 2001). Multiple perspectives are a form of perception in which "people can recognise that an event can be viewed, defined and perceived in more than one manner, through several focal points" (Wicklund, 1999, p. 667).

Beyond the above conceptions, one theory is particularly relevant for our argument: the socio-cognitive perspective proposed by Doise and Mugny (1984). This perspective is relevant for two interrelated reasons. The first reason is that these authors demonstrated that confronting a child with a diverging point of view (a socio-cognitive conflict) can lead the child to abandon an egocentric mode of problem solving in such Piagetian tasks as conservation of length, conservation of liquids, spatial orientation. The change occurs prior to the Piagetian stage of "co-ordination", which is supposed to be necessary for its appearance. Thus, confrontation with a source of "influence" can lead to decentring. The second reason is that this research has shown that not every source of influence can induce decentring, and that the effects are found with an influence source of same status (in terms of competence) as the participants, or even of lower status. When children are confronted with a higher status source, no progress is observed, and they maintain their egocentric mode of problem solving. With a high-status source, the difference in power is overwhelming and threatens the children's competence. This leads to mere compliance without internalising the source's position, thereby maintaining the children's original point of view. With a low-status source, children are not threatened and can find a solution to the divergence between their position and the source's position. Hence, they decentre and create the basis for development (see also Butera & Mugny, 1995).

In the remainder of this chapter, we present a set of studies that illustrate how decentring can overcome focusing effects such as confirmation bias, and how decentring can be induced by confronting participants with a source of influence, provided that its status does not threaten their competence.

Confirmation bias and decentring

To study decentring as a result of social influence, we developed a line of research to investigate confirmation bias, a form of focusing effect (Butera, Legrenzi, & Mugny, 1993; see also Butera & Mugny, 2001). Indeed, research on hypothesis testing has shown a systematic tendency towards confirmation: Individuals who have to test their hypotheses tend to use procedures that support these hypotheses, even in tasks in which disconfirmation would be more diagnostic (e.g., Gorman & Gorman, 1984; Mynatt, Doherty, & Tweney, 1977; Wason, 1960; but cf. Klayman & Ha, 1987). What is interesting for the purpose of this chapter is that several authors agree that confirmation as a "bias" is due to a lack of activation, analysis and articulation of alternative solutions to a problem (e.g., Johnson-Laird, 1983; Kruglanski & Mayseless, 1988; McDonald, 1990). In fact, it has been noted that disconfirmation is possible when reasoners consider alternative solutions (Gorman & Carlson, 1989).

Our general claim is that hypothesis confirmation and disconfirmation are reasoning processes specific to particular social situations (Butera, Legrenzi, Mugny, & Pérez, 1991–1992). Indeed, hypothesis testing most often takes place during situations of social confrontation; i.e., in situations where one may be confronted with the alternative hypothesis proposed by someone else. In particular, social psychologists have shown that exposure to a majority's model or proposal induces conformity (Moscovici, 1980) and cognitive functioning of a convergent type, i.e. confined to the use of information at hand (Nemeth, 1986; Nemeth, Mosier, & Chiles, 1992). These results suggest that the majority's proposal induces individuals to take it into account in formulating their own hypothesis. Convergent thinking should then bias individuals to take into account only the elements and characteristics of this hypothesis. Thus, when individuals test a hypothesis, they should consider positive examples of the hypothesis under test. In short, individuals should be oriented toward the use of confirmation in social situations that inculcate an expectation of conformity to the majority.

Furthermore, research in social influence has shown that when a model is given by a minority source, individuals are not motivated to adopt it (Moscovici, 1980) because the source does not guarantee the validity of its proposal (Nemeth, 1986). Thus, when individuals must come to a reliable solution to a problem, they are unlikely to trust a minority source. Minorities accordingly induce divergent thinking, which is a form of decentring proposed by Nemeth (1986) to account for the cognitive processes of problem solving when faced with a minority source. Hence, "minorities stimulate a greater consideration of other alternatives" (p. 25). In fact, several studies have shown that individuals faced with a minority source do search for alternatives (e.g., De Dreu, De Vries, Gordijn, & Schuurman, 1999; Nemeth & Kwan, 1985). Moreover, a study by Huguet, Mugny, and Pérez (1991–1992) suggests that minority influence induces decentring; i.e., the possibility of taking into account several points of views when formulating a judgement. We propose that individuals confronted with a minority proposal should be less motivated to adopt it and more likely to choose or to formulate an alternative hypothesis. Hence, in the case of hypothesis testing, minority influence elicits mechanisms that question the limits of a hypothesis, and in turn the use of negative instances to test the hypothesis; i.e. instances that are not compatible with the hypothesis under test, with the aim of disconfirmation. In fact, the use of disconfirmation is linked to the ability to imagine an alternative hypothesis, since it is difficult for individuals to try to disconfirm the only available hypothesis.

Minority influence and decentring

In our experimental paradigm, the participants have to discover the rule underlying triads of numbers triad (e.g., 2–4–6; see Wason, 1960). They were asked to formulate a hypothesis and to propose a triad to test it. *Before* being allowed to answer, the participants were informed of the hypothesis and of the triad proposed to test it either by the majority (82 per cent) or a minority (12 per cent) of previous participants. In fact, we used the same hypothesis in both cases: "each new number is greater than the previous one". In other words, the participants experienced a social influence. In the first experiment (Legrenzi, Butera, Mugny, & Pérez, 1991), the triad proposed by the majority or minority source was either confirmatory (e.g., 8–10–12), or disconfirmatory (e.g., 12-10-8) with respect to the source's hypothesis. The results showed that more participants used the source's hypothesis in the majority condition, and that more participants formulated new hypotheses when the minority used a confirmatory strategy. Although the participants' main strategy in all conditions was confirmation, more participants used disconfirmation when this strategy was used in the initial triad proposed by the source, which corroborates the results of Gorman and Gorman (1984). More importantly, when the source used confirmation for testing the hypothesis, the participants' strategy depends on whether the source was the majority or the minority. When the majority used confirmation, the participants almost never used disconfirmation, whereas when the minority used confirmation, the participants used disconfirmation more often, and these participants proposed the highest rate of new hypotheses. In a second experiment (Butera, Legrenzi, Mugny, & Pérez, 1991–1992), also using a 2–4–6-like task, a minority source again induced participants to formulate new hypotheses and to use disconfirmation more often than a majority source.

A minority source evidently elicits decentring, and a majority source elicits focusing. We accordingly devised an experiment to test whether a majority source induces more conformity (imitation) and more confirmation because it produces focusing, and whether a minority source elicits alternative hypotheses and disconfirmation because it produces decentring (Butera, Mugny, Legrenzi & Pérez, 1996). We manipulated two variables. The first variable was the nature of the source, either a majority or a minority; and the second variable, which concerned the representation of the task, was whether the participants were told that the task allowed one single correct answer (the focusing condition) or several possible answers (the decentring condition).

The results showed, as in the previous experiments, that the nature of the source induced differential effects. The representation of the task induced differential effects too – it is the mediating variable accounting for the source's effects. Indeed, an interaction showed that the participants given the majority view tended to accept the source's hypothesis and to use confirmation more when the task was represented as having a single solution than when it was represented as having several solutions. Moreover, the participants given a minority view tended to consider alternative hypotheses (different from those of the source) and to use disconfirmation more when the task was represented as having several solutions than when it was represented as having a single solution. In sum, a majority source may threaten individuals, since an apparent unity of opinion calls for conformity and for confirmation as a sort of self-protection: Confirmation asserts self-competence. Conversely, a minority source does not threaten individuals or their competence, and it allows decentring and disconfirmation.

Competence threat and focusing

We have argued that the differential effect of majority and minority sources results from different levels of threat to the individual's competence. However, in the previous experiments, the status of the source was not directly related to the competence of the source (though Nemeth, 1986, has noted that people generally assume that a majority is correct and a minority is incorrect). The following experiment (Butera, Mugny, & Tomei, 2000, study 1) had two aims. On the one hand, it aimed to show that the influence effects discussed above are found when the competence of the source is directly manipulated. The participants in this experiment – whose procedure is identical to the previous ones – were accordingly presented with information from either an expert or a novice, which thereby explicitly referred to their level of competence. On the other hand, the experiment aimed to show both that a low status source has a decentring effect and that a high status source has a focusing effect. Hence, the experiment introduced a control condition in which there was no source of influence. We predicted that the novice source should induce more disconfirmatory testing than the control, and that the expert should induce more confirmatory testing than the control. But these effects were expected only when the participants judged under uncertainty, because certainty should reduce the participants' dependence upon the source. We manipulated certainty by leading the participants to think that responses to the task were highly predictable, i.e., almost certainty, or highly unpredictable, i.e., most uncertain.

There was a significant interaction between the two variables corroborating our hypotheses. Under certainty, the status of the source had no impact, and neither the low-status nor the high-status source yielded results that differed reliably from those in the control condition. Under uncertainty, the two expected differences appeared: The low-status source induced more disconfirmation than the control condition, whereas the high-status source induced less. This experiment not only shows the beneficial effect of a low-status source when the competence of the source is directly asserted, but it also shows that the high-status source can enhance the focusing effect. Indeed, this condition produced significantly more confirmation of hypotheses than the control condition. This result suggests that the focusing effect is linked to a threat to participants' competence. In threatening situations, such as a conflict with a high-status source that undermines individuals' competence, they can be motivated to stick to the few models that they have constructed. This phenomenon could occur for two compatible reasons: on the one hand, threatened individuals have fewer cognitive resources to allocate to the task because their attention is concentrated on the conflict (see also Wicklund, 1999); on the other, individuals who focus on their own models and ignore alternatives are likely to think that they are right and to have an enhanced perception of their own competence.

Reducing the high-status source focusing effects

So far, we have shown that low-status sources can induce decentring and so reduce confirmation bias, whereas high-status sources induce focusing and enhance the use of confirmation. The following experiment (Butera, Gardair, Maggi, & Mugny, 1998, study 3) aimed to test the hypothesis that if decentring can be induced through the nature of the task, it should reduce the focusing effect (the high rate of confirmation) of a high-status source. We therefore predicted that inducing decentring should allow a high-status source to lead to an increased use of disconfirmation in comparison with a condition where decentring was not induced. It was also hypothesised that the induction of decentring should not have any effect on the influence of a low-status source, because this source induces decentring in itself. The experimental design thus involved the status of the source (high versus low) and the decentring procedure (present versus absent). The dependent variable was, as in the previous experiments, the confirmatory versus disconfirmatory strategy used in hypothesis testing.

The experiment manipulated decentring in the following way. Half of the participants in the decentring conditions looked into a black box through a hole and saw a square. The other half of the participants looked through another hole and saw a triangle. The participants then had to exchange information about what they saw and to guess what was in the box. In fact no one succeeded, and most of the participants just reported what they had seen. Finally, the experimenter opened the box to reveal a pyramid. This outcome was used to explain the importance of taking into account other individuals' information, even if it seems incompatible. In sum, the decentring manipulation allowed the experimenter to enhance the idea that perspective taking is valuable, even when the other's position seems wrong. Half of the participants received the decentring instructions, and half of the participants were in a control condition that did not receive the decentring instructions

As we predicted, when the source was of low status the decentring procedure produced the same disconfirmation rate as in the control condition. But with a high-status source decentring led to more disconfirmation than in the control condition. Moreover, in the decentring conditions high- and low-status sources induced the same amount of disconfirmation. In sum, this study reveal two important mechanisms. First, even if high-status sources induce a focusing effect (as shown in the previous study), the effect is not inevitable and decentring can compensate for this focusing. Second, a low-status source induces decentring by itself because no differences in disconfirmation rate appeared when decentring was induced independently.

Generality

Decentring appears to be a robust phenomenon. However, its generality can be challenged on two counts. First, are its effects dependent on context? Indeed, they could depend on the specific experimental paradigm in our experiments. The studies do use roughly the same methodology. Yet decentring is *not* specific to the methodology. The evidence comes from an experiment in which, unlike the previous studies, the participants interacted with the influence source. Instead of reading the information from the source about a single hypothesis and test, the participants were confronted with the source throughout the experiment, which used several tests and hypotheses. Nevertheless, the experiment replicated the decentring effect induced by a low-status source (Butera, Caverni, & Rossi, 1999, study 1). The second question that can be asked is whether these effects depend on the specific 2–4–6 hypothesis testing task used in our experiments. But again we know that the answer is negative. The evidence comes from an experiment on decision making that examined moderating factors of the pseudodiagnosticity bias, which is also a focusing effect (Maggi, Butera, Legrenzi, & Mugny, 1998; Maggi, Legrenzi, Mugny, & Butera, 2001). This experiment showed that when the source of influence is of a low status, pseudodiagnosticity is at its lowest. Hence, the decentring effect induced by a low-status source seems to be a general effect. It appears with different methodologies and it compensates for different focusing phenomena, including confirmation bias and pseudodiagnosticity.

Conclusions

In this chapter we presented an account of social factors that intervene in reasoning. More specifically, we presented a line of research that shows the influence of information from a social source on inductive reasoning. We argued that if confirmation bias is a case of focusing in human reasoning, then decentring should be an effective tool to reduce this effect because decentring consists in taking into account models and views other than one's own. However, our studies showed that not every source of influence can induce decentring and thereby reduce the confirmation bias. The effect seems to occur only with low-status sources, whether they are a minority and/or low competence. Conversely, the studies showed that a high-status source maintains or even enhances focusing. Our interpretation of this phenomenon is that a conflict with a high-status source implies a threat to the individual's competence: If the competent person is right, then the individual is wrong and therefore incompetent. This threat, in turn, is likely to orient the individual's reasoning towards a strategy of self-protection. Focusing is such a strategy because an exclusive consideration of your own point of view, coupled with a strategy of confirmation, helps you to maintain confidence in your own competence. This account could explain why confirmation is such a frequent strategy, since reasoning is generally at work in settings in which competence is highly relevant and might be threatened by others. These settings include experiments in a psychological laboratory, and even the work of a scientific research team. The bias is not intrinsic to the confirmatory behaviour, but arises from the constraints imposed by the environment (see Butera, Legrenzi, & Oswald, 1997a, 1997b). A low-status source is less threatening and leads to decentring, which has a strong defocusing effect. Contrary to the view that egocentrism is no longer a problem after childhood, the pervasiveness of focusing effects shows that decentring is needed even in adults. This chapter has shown how information from a non-threatening social source can fulfil this role. It leads to reasoning strategies that take into account other alternatives.

Acknowledgements

We wish to thank Paolo Legrenzi, who was at the inception of most of the work presented in this chapter. This work was supported by the Swiss National Foundation for Scientific Research and by the "Avenir" fund of the French Rhône-Alpes Regional Council.

References

Butera, F., & Mugny, G. (1995). Conflict between incompetencies and influence of a low-competence source in hypothesis testing. *European Journal of Social Psychology, 25*, 457–462.

Butera, F., & Mugny, G. (2001). Conflicts and social influences in hypothesis testing. In C. De Dreu & N. De Vries (Eds.), *Group consensus and minority influence: Implications for innovation* (pp. 160–182). Oxford: Blackwell.

Butera, F., Legrenzi, P., Mugny, G., & Pérez, J. A. (1991–92). Influence sociale et raisonnement. [Social influence and reasoning]. *Bulletin de Psychologie, 45*, (405), 144–154.

Butera, F., Legrenzi, P., & Mugny, G. (1993). De l'imitation à la validation: Études sur le raisonnement. [From imitation to validation: Studies on reasoning.] In J. A. Pérez & G. Mugny (Eds.), *Influences sociales: La théorie de l'élaboration du conflit* (pp. 99–120). Neuchâtel, Paris: Delachaux et Niestlé.

Butera, F., Mugny, G., Legrenzi, P., & Pérez, J. A. (1996). Majority and minority influence, task representation, and inductive reasoning. *British Journal of Social Psychology, 35*, 123–136.

Butera, F., Legrenzi, P., & Oswald, M. (1997a). Is context a bias? *Swiss Journal of Psychology, 56*, 59–61.

Butera, F., Legrenzi, P., & Oswald, M. (Eds.). (1997b). *Contexts and biases*. Bern: Hans Huber.

Butera, F., Caverni, J. P., & Rossi, S. (1999). Social interaction in inductive reasoning. In S. Bagnara (Ed.), *Proceedings of the Second European Conference on Cognitive Science* (pp. 179–184). Siena: Università di Siena.

Butera, F., Gardair, E., Maggi, J., & Mugny, G. (1998). Les paradoxes de l'expertise: Influence sociale et (in)compétence de soi et d'autrui. [Paradoxes of expertise. Social influence and self and other's (in)competence]. In J. Py, A. Somat, & J. Baillé (Eds.), *Psychologie sociale et formation professionnelle: Propositions et regards critiques* (pp. 109–123). Rennes: Presses Universitaires de Rennes.

Butera, F., Mugny, G., & Tomei, A. (2000). Incertitude et enjeux identitaires dans l'influence sociale. [Uncertainty and identity stakes in social influence]. In J. L. Beauvois, R. V. Joule, & J. M. Monteil (Eds.), *Perspectives cognitives et conduites sociales* (*Vol. 7*, pp. 205–229). Neuchâtel, Paris: Delachaux et Niestlé.

De Dreu, C. K. W., De Vries, N. K., Gordijn, E. H., & Schuurman, M. S. (1999). Convergent and divergent processing of majority and minority arguments: Effects on focal and related attitudes. *European Journal of Social Psychology*, *29*, 329–348.

Doise, W., & Mugny, G. (1984). *The social development of the intellect*. Oxford: Pergamon Press.

Falk, D. R., & Johnson, D. W. (1977). The effects of perspective-taking and egocentrism on problem solving in heterogeneous and homogeneous groups. *Journal of Social Psychology*, *102*, 63–72.

Gorman, M., & Carlson, B. (1989). Can experiments be used to study science? *Social Epistemology*, *3*, 89–106.

Gorman, M., & Gorman, M. E. (1984). A comparison of confirmatory, disconfirmatory and control strategy on Wason's 2–4–6 task. *Quarterly Journal of Experimental Psychology*, *36A*, 629–648.

Greenwald, A. G. (1969). The open-mindedness of the counter-attitudinal role player. *Journal of Experimental Social Psychology*, *5*, 375–388.

Greenwald, A. G. (1980). The totalitarian ego. Fabrication and revision of personal history. *American Psychologist*, *35*, 603–618.

Huguet, P., Mugny, G., & Pérez, J. A. (1991–1992). Influence sociale et processus de décentration. [Social influence and decentring processes]. *Bulletin de Psychologie*, *45*, 155–163.

Inhelder, B., & Piaget, J. (1958). *The growth of logical thinking from childhood to adolescence*. New York: Basic Books.

Johnson, D. W. (1977). The distribution and exchange of information in problem-solving dyads. *Communication Research*, *4*, 283–298.

Johnson, D. W., & Johnson, R. (1995). *Creative controversy: Intellectual conflict in the classroom* (3rd edn.). Edina, MN: Interaction Book Company.

Johnson-Laird, P. N. (1983). *Mental models*. Cambridge: Cambridge University Press.

Klayman, J., & Ha, Y.-W. (1987). Confirmation, disconfirmation and information in hypothesis testing. *Psychological Review*, *94*, 211–228.

Kohlberg, L. (1969). Stage and sequence: The cognitive-developmental approach to socialization. In D. Goslin (Ed.), *Handbook of socialization theory and research* (pp. 347–380). Chicago: Rand-McNally.

Kruglanski, A. W., & Mayseless, O. (1988). Contextual effects in hypothesis testing: The role of competing alternatives and epistemic motivations. *Social Cognition*, *6*, 1–20.

Langer, E. (1975). The illusion of control. *Journal of Personality and Social Psychology*, *32*, 311–328.

Legrenzi, P., Butera, F., Mugny, G., & Pérez, J. A. (1991). Majority and minority influence in inductive reasoning: A preliminary study. *European Journal of Social Psychology*, *21*, 359–363.

Legrenzi, P., Girotto, V., & Johnson-Laird, P. N. (1993). Focusing in reasoning and decision making. *Cognition*, *49*, 37–66.

Luchins, A. (1958). Definitiveness of impression and primacy-recency in communication. *Journal of Social Psychology*, *48*, 275–290.

McDonald, J. (1990). Some situational determinants of hypothesis-testing strategies. *Journal of Experimental Social Psychology*, *26*, 255–274.

Maggi, J., Butera, F., Legrenzi, P., & Mugny, G. (1998). Relevance of information and social influence in the pseudodiagnosticity bias. *Swiss Journal of Psychology*, *57*, (3), 188–199.

Maggi, J., Legrenzi, P., Mugny, G., & Butera, F. (2001). Socio-cognitive biases in the choice of candidates. In F. Butera & G. Mugny (Eds.), *Social influence in social reality* (pp. 9–22). Göttingen: Hogrefe & Huber.

Mischel, W., Ebbesen, E. B., & Zeiss, A. M. (1976). Determinants of selective memory about the self. *Journal of Counsulting and Clinical Psychology*, *44*, 92–103.

Moscovici, S. (1980). Toward a theory of conversion behavior. In L. Berkowitz (Ed.), *Advances in experimental social psychology* (Vol. 13, pp. 209–239). New York: Academic Press.

Mynatt, C. R., Doherty, M. E., & Tweney, R. D. (1977). Confirmation bias in a simulated research environment: An experimental study of scientific inference. *Quarterly Journal of Experimental Psychology*, *29*, 85–95.

Nemeth, C. (1986). Differential contributions of majority and minority influence. *Psychological Review*, *93*, 23–32.

Nemeth, C., & Kwan, J. (1985). Originality of word associations as a function of majority vs. minority influence. *Social Psychology Quarterly*, *48*, 277–282.

Nemeth, C., Mosier, K., & Chiles, C. (1992). When convergent thought improves performance: Majority versus minority influence. *Personality and Social Psychology Bulletin*, *18*, 139–144.

Pantaleo, G., & Wicklund, R. A. (2001). *Prospettive multiple nella vita sociale*. [Multiple perspectives in social life]. Padua: Decibel-Zanichelli.

Piaget, J. (1963). *The psychology of intelligence*. New York: Routledge.

Tjosvold, D. (1998). Cooperative and competitive goal approach to conflict: Accomplishments and challenges. *Applied Psychology: An International Review*, *47*, 285–313.

Tjosvold, D., Johnson, D. W., & Fabrey, L. (1980). Effects of controversy and defensiveness on cognitive perspective taking. *Psychological Reports*, *47*, 1043–1053.

Tulving, E. (1972). Episodic and semantic memory. In E. Tulving & W. Donaldson (Eds.), *Organization of memory* (pp. 381–403). Oxford: Academic Press.

Wason, P. C. (1960). On the failure to eliminate hypotheses in a conceptual task. *Quarterly Journal of Experimental Psychology*, *12*, 255–274.

Wicklund, R. A. (1999). Multiple perspectives in person perception and theorizing. *Theory and Psychology*, *9*, 667–678.

12 Heuristics and biases in attitudes towards herbal medicines

Erica Carlisle and Eldar Shafir

Introduction

Herbal medicines such as Echinacea, Ginkgo, Ginseng, Kava, and St. John's Wort have become a major commodity in the US. In 1998, Americans spent $3.87 billion on herbals (Ernst, 2000). This is a remarkable sum, given that it is more than a tenth of what Americans spent out of pocket on all prescription drugs ($30.4b, Centers for Medicare & Medicaid Services, 1998), and more than half of the amount they spent at the box office on movies that same year ($6.9 billion). Eisenberg, Davis, Ettner, Appel, Wilkey, Van Rompay, and Kessler (1998) conducted surveys of alternative medicine use in 1990 and 1997, and found that rates of use had increased for all 16 alternative therapies they studied, including chiropractic, homeopathy, and acupuncture, and that of the 16, herbal medicines showed the largest increase. In a nationally representative survey that we have conducted and to which we return below, 56 per cent of American adults reported having used herbal medicines. This figure does not include the use of ordinary vitamins and minerals, such as vitamin C or calcium. (The industry uses the term "herbal medicines" to refer to such remedies as Echinacea, Ginkgo, and St. John's Wort and to dietary supplements such as amino acids. In what follows, we shall abide by that convention.)

Despite the fact that millions of people use herbal medicines, neither the US government nor any other agency regulates herbal products. The 1994 Dietary Supplement Health and Education Act removed herbal medicines and nutritional supplements from the aegis of the Food and Drug Administration (FDA) (Josefson, 2001), which can only investigate herbals and supplements if there is a formal complaint. Under the 1994 law, manufacturers of herbal medicines and supplements do not have to test their products for effectiveness or for safety, in contrast to the rigorous clinical trials the FDA requires for pharmaceutical drugs. Pharmaceutical drugs may not always prove effective, but at least they contain known, tested, and approved ingredients. Consumers, who are typically reluctant to ingest substances they cannot trust, have no such assurance when they take herbal medicines. Given the lack of effectiveness testing or safety controls, why are people so positively inclined towards taking herbal medicines? This topic, involving an applied problem with potentially significant financial and social repercussions and a dose of suspect reasoning, is reminiscent of the sort of issues that have characterised Paolo Legrenzi's research throughout the years. We thus decided to first summarise our explorations in this area in this volume, in Paolo's honor.

We designed a telephone survey for a nationally representative sample of American adults to begin to answer this question. The survey was conducted between April and June 2002 by the Survey Research Centre at Princeton University. Respondents were selected using random-digit dialling, and our final sample size was n = 531. In the descriptive statistics presented below, the data have been weighted so as to render the sample representative of the national population in terms of gender, age, education, census region, and race/ethnicity, as per the Census Bureau Annual Demographic File (March 2001, Current Population Survey). The complete survey results will be published elsewhere (Carlisle & Shafir, 2003).

Of our respondents 56 per cent reported having used a herbal medicine or dietary supplement. This figure is at the high end of what other studies have found, but rates of use are on the rise. We asked our respondents who had used herbals to estimate the number of herbal medicines (not different brands) they had tried in the last year. The modal response was one, but with a wide range, including one in five who had used more than five kinds and one in 16 who had used ten or more herbals in the last year (see Table 12.1). We

Table 12.1 Reported use of herbals in a representative national survey.

How many herbals have you taken in the past year? (Free response)

Response	*Per cent*
Don't know	3
0	17
1	23
2	17
3	11
4	10
5–9	13
10–40	6

How often have you taken a herbal in the past two months?

Response category	*Per cent*
Not at all	44
One time only	7
Monthly	7
Bi-weekly (once every 2 or 3 weeks)	7
Weekly (once or twice a week)	8
Daily (more than 3 times a week)	25
Don't know	1
Refused to answer	0.2

also asked about frequency of use in the preceding two months. As Table 12.1 shows, many people had not used a herbal during the recent past, but more than a quarter were using them on a daily basis. The vast majority, 81.6 per cent, reported intending to take herbals in the future.

A large number of Americans are using herbal medicines on a regular basis, and intend to continue doing so. In what follows, we explore some of the decision heuristics that may underlie consumers' attitudes towards herbal medicines. We begin with evidence – culled from various surveys – that suggests a heuristic reliance on the notion of "naturalness" in people's perception of herbal medicines. In general, "natural" things tend to be perceived as mild, less potent, less effective, and possibly less intrusive. We show that people's general expectation that herbal medicines will prove less effective than prescription counterparts paradoxically leads to a more positive evaluation of the possibly limited effects of herbals. Finally, we document several biased beliefs and attitudes, including greater risk seeking and perceptions of illusory correlations in users' evaluation of herbal medicines. We conclude with some general remarks concerning the naturalness heuristic and its implications.

The "naturalness" heuristic

If you ask a herbal medicine user why she takes herbal medicines, the answer you are most likely to get is "because they're natural". In this section, we present survey data demonstrating the prevalence of this attitude, as well as its potentially powerful impact on people's choices. We are not the first to argue for a bias towards things "natural". Spranca (1993), for example, presented people with descriptions of three drinking waters that were identical except for their histories. While all were chemical free, one emerged that way from its source, one was filtered through bedrock, and one had been filtered by humans. Participants rated these waters as decreasingly attractive, and were willing to pay more than a 50 per cent premium for the naturally pure water over the ones that had been filtered. Spranca concluded that people were subject to a naturalness bias because, having agreed that the waters were chemically identical, they still strongly favoured the "natural" alternative. In a different line of research concerned with the role of affect in decision making, Slovic, Finucane, Peters, and MacGregor (2002) have observed that the term "natural" evokes quick positive emotions in people.

A recent survey of 2000 American adults reports that naturalness was the most common reason for using herbal medicine rather than a prescription or an over-the-counter medication (cited by 43 per cent and 47 per cent of respondents, respectively). The second most popular reason, "fewer serious side effects", received only half as many endorsements as did "prefer natural or organic products" (*Prevention Magazine*, 1999). Yet when they were asked about the amount of regulation to make sure supplements do not harm people, 59 per cent said there was "not as much as there should be" (Henry J.

Kaiser Family Foundation & Harvard School of Public Health, 1999). Nonetheless, in another poll, 66 per cent said they would continue using a dietary supplement even if the FDA reported that it was ineffective (Kaiser Family Foundation, Kennedy School of Government, & National Public Radio, 1999). Although people apparently know that herbals and dietary supplements are not well regulated and would like to see regulation improve, they seem to base their decision to take herbals on the appearance of naturalness, rather than on scientific testing or reported effectiveness.

Other sensible suggestions about the popularity of herbal medicine have not been borne out by the data. For example, people generally do not turn to herbal medicines because they are dissatisfied with traditional medicine or because they have stopped seeing regular doctors (Astin, 1998). Instead, the three main predictors of individuals who were alternative medicine users in Astin's oft-cited study were that they had been classified as "cultural creatives" (a demographic group committed to environmentalism, feminism, spirituality, personal growth, and self-expression), they held a holistic philosophy of health, and they had had a "transformational" experience. Again, the use of alternative medicines seems to be based not on cost–benefit analyses of health, treatment effectiveness, or expense. Rather, it seems to be based on a philosophical stance, the primary feature of which is "naturalness".

We have conducted a series of studies intended to test the naturalness hypothesis. These focus on conditions under which people choose natural medicines over other alternatives and on potential differences in the types of choices made by people who value naturalness compared to those who do not. The studies with Princeton University students are replicated with findings from our survey of American adults.

To explore attitudes about safety and the use of herbals, we asked 264 Princeton undergraduates to complete a survey on medical issues. Participants addressed issues ranging from the safety and regulation of herbal and prescription drugs to personal use of them. Selected items culled from the survey can be found in the Appendix. Consider, for example, Question 3 in the Appendix, about the safety of herbal medicines. The majority of respondents consider herbals safe primarily because they are natural. This is corroborated by the first free response question in the Appendix, where over 43 per cent of respondents reported herbals safe due to their being natural, more than 30 percentage points ahead of any other reason. Similarly, in Question 12, 44 per cent of participants indicated naturalness as their primary reason for using herbal medicines.

The mildness of herbals does not seem to be a very important feature to herbal users, compared to naturalness. In our student survey, we asked participants how much they agreed or disagreed with the statements "Herbal products are natural" and "Herbal products are typically mild". As expected, most agreed with both. Respondents then rated how important it was to them that herbals are natural and that they are mild. We then regressed herbal use on the following four items: Agree Natural, Agree Mild, Importance of

Naturalness, and Importance of Mildness. The only variable that significantly predicted herbal use was Importance of Naturalness ($\beta = 0.179$, $t = 2.54$, $p<0.01$), indicating a significant relation between using herbals and feeling it was important that they are natural, but no relation with feeling it was important that they are mild ($\beta = -0.036$, $t = -0.529$, $p = 0.59$). These results control for the simple endorsement of herbals as natural and mild, neither of which significantly predicts use (Agree Natural: $\beta = 0.112$, $t = 1.66$, $p = 0.10$; Agree Mild: $\beta = 0.032$, $t = 0.493$, $p = 0.62$.)

We were interested in differences among participants depending on how they prioritise naturalness. Hence, we divided the participants into three groups based on reported use of herbal medicines and reasons for their use. The first group was all non-users, the second group was people who reported using herbals for reasons other than their being natural (non-natural users), and the third group was those who used herbals because they are natural (natural users). We expected the motivation and perceptions of natural users to differ from those of both non-natural users and non-users, since natural users should rely on the naturalness heuristic in a way that the other two groups do not.

Natural users indeed seem to show different attitudes than non-natural users and non-users. A contrast test comparing natural users to the other two groups was significant for many items on the survey. As shown in Table 12.2, the results indicate that natural users see herbals as more effective than do the other two groups. They also see them as more natural and, as expected, rate naturalness as more important.

Table 12.2 Selected results from student survey, comparing means of natural users to non-natural users and non-users.

	Non-users $N = 144$	Non-natural users $N = 78$	Natural users $N = 42$	Contrast test t	sig.
1. Agree or disagree: herbals are natural. (-2 = Disagree, $+2$ = Agree)	0.78	0.96	1.38	3.27	0.001***
2. How important is it to you that herbals are natural? (1 = Not Imp., 5 = Very Imp.)	2.9	3.17	3.88	3.96	0.000***
3. When used to treat similar symptoms, are herbals or prescriptions more effective? (-3 = Herbal, $+3$ = Prescription)	1.91	1.69	1.21	2.74	0.006***

Note: The contrast compares natural users to remaining two groups. All overall one-way ANOVAs were significant.

We examined the relations between the items above. A regression of the naturalness ratings (item 1) on the effectiveness ratings (item 3) reveals a positive association among natural users, a lower association for non-natural users, and a negative relation for non-users. In other words, people who value naturalness expect effectiveness to increase with it, whereas those who do not value naturalness expect effectiveness to decrease with higher naturalness. Remarkably, the above distinctions between the two types of users, natural and non-natural, suggest that a dichotomy based on people's behaviour, in this case herbal medicine use, fails to capture differences in perceptions that emerge from different attitudes towards naturalness.

The contrasts above mirror findings of "consistency" in the social psychology literature, in which people's judgements tend to correlate with their values or with other judgements in indefensible ways. For example, those opposed to capital punishment tend also to believe that it is ineffective, and this correlation grows stronger, not weaker, after individuals see disconfirming evidence (Lord, Ross, & Lepper, 1979). Similarly, natural users among our respondents appear to expect a positive relation between naturalness and effectiveness that is hard to justify, runs contrary to the general expectation that pharmaceuticals ought to prove more effective, and is an expectation that is not shared by others.

Like the undergraduates, American adults in our survey reported using herbals largely because they are natural (with over 40 per cent listing "natural" as their single main reason). We then divided respondents into the same three groups: non-herbal users (n = 211), non-natural users (n = 191), and natural users (n = 128). Table 12.3 displays selected items from the survey, along with mean responses from each group. Again, there are significant differences between natural users and the remaining two groups. Natural users are significantly more likely than others to report positive attitudes towards herbals, to agree that herbals are safe to give to children, and to prefer a herbal even when it is as strong as a prescription. The national survey

Table 12.3 Unweighted responses to telephone survey items of American adults, comparing means of natural users to non-natural users and non-users

	Non-users	Non-natural users	Natural users
1. In general, do you see herbal products as safe or unsafe?	2.31_a	2.17_a	1.74_b
2. Herbal products are mild.	2.67_a	2.71_a	2.39_b
3. Herbal products are natural.	1.74_a	1.71_a	1.34_b
4. Do you agree or disagree that it is safe to give herbals to children?	3.59_a	3.16_b	2.81_c

Note. All responses are on five-point scales, either from 1 = safe to 5 = unsafe or from 1 = agree to 5 = disagree. Different subscripts indicate significant differences using contrasts. All overall one-way ANOVAs are significant. All Ns between 111 and 211.

findings generally mirror those from our student survey and, in particular, support the idea that people who use herbal medicines are largely motivated by naturalness.

Most respondents are aware that the US government does not require testing of herbal products for safety or effectiveness (Appendix, Questions 4 & 5). At the same time, 85.2 per cent of the students say that it is at least moderately important to them that an organisation such as the FDA regulates herbal medicines (Appendix, Question 6). This suggests that the decision to use herbals cannot be seen as a form of protest against government involvement. These findings raise the question of whether people might prefer a medical treatment that combined the naturalness of herbals with the rigorous safety and effectiveness standards of prescriptions. To test this possibility, we asked three groups of Princeton students about their willingness to take a particular medication. Some read about a prescription drug manufactured by a pharmaceutical company; others read about a herbal drug made from the leaves of a South American tree, and the rest read about a hybrid: a drug made by a pharmaceutical company from the leaves of a South American tree. As predicted, participants reported greater willingness to take the hybrid than either of the other products (one-way ANOVA, $F(2, 252)$ = 3.15, $p<0.04$; a contrast comparing the hybrid to the herbal and the prescription, $t(252) = 2.5$, $p<0.01$.)

In summary, the main reason most people consider herbals safe and like to use them is that they are natural. Furthermore, preference for naturalness is correlated with other choices people make, suggesting that naturalness functions as a general cue. Ideally, our participants preferred not to relinquish safety and effectiveness for the sake of naturalness, but no real alternative is presently available that corresponds to the hypothetical hybrid drug. Nevertheless, people continue enthusiastically to consume herbal medicines. What are some factors that might account for this continuing trend?

Illusions of effectiveness

The advantage of low expectations

Despite the ever-growing popularity of herbal medicines, most people have lower expectations of them than they do of prescription drugs. In our sample of students, 80 per cent thought prescriptions are more effective, and in our sample of American adults, 60 per cent thought so (with 26 per cent indifferent or with no opinion). These expectations may be partly driven by the very fact that prescription medicines are highly regulated and controlled in comparison to herbal medicines, which are easily available over the counter in food stores and pharmacies. As a result, people are likely to conclude that herbals are weaker than prescription drugs, with lower overall effectiveness. In many cases, this may be true, but because herbals are neither standardised nor tested in clinical trials, consumers can not be certain. Cases of serious side effects and deaths from herbal use have been reported, including the case of a woman who required a liver transplant as a result of damage from taking kava kava (Grossman, 2002) and a number of cases of death from taking ephedra (Haller & Benowitz, 2000).

We hypothesised that such differing expectations would alter the perceived effectiveness of herbals and prescriptions. Expectations yield perceived norms, which may need to be adjusted in the face of the evidence (Kahneman & Miller, 1986). When people encounter moderate levels of effectiveness in herbals, they may perceive the effects as large compared to their low prior expectation. In contrast, the same evidence for prescription drugs could be interpreted as a smaller effect in light of high prior expectations.

To test this hypothesis, 250 Princeton students were presented with clinical trial data purportedly testing a treatment drug against a placebo (as in Figure 12.1). The "data" were identical for all respondents, half of whom were told the treatment was a herbal drug, and the other half were told that it was a prescription drug. Participants rated the efficacy of each drug compared to the placebo on a seven-point scale. As expected, despite the identical data, the herbal was rated significantly more effective than the prescription drug, $t(248) = 2.64$, $p<0.009$. In addition, participants reported greater willingness to try the treatment when they thought it was a herbal than when they thought it was a prescription drug, $t(248) = 2.42$, $p<0.016$.

People typically hold herbal medicines to lower standards than prescription drugs. As a consequence, evidence that shows only moderate effectiveness for a prescription medicine is perceived as more effective for a herbal alternative. The difference in expectations is understandable, but the impact on perceived efficacy is notable. Paradoxically, the common expectation that herbal medicines are limited in effectiveness yields a more positive evaluation of their effects. It will be interesting to see whether the trend reverses as the popularity of herbals increases and expectations rise.

Illusory correlations

Everyone seems to share the general expectation that prescription drugs are stronger and more effective than herbals. There are other beliefs, however,

	Received treatment	Received placebo
Average amount of sleep	5.8 hours	5.2 hours
Number of people who slept at least 7 hours	29/100	17/100

Figure 12.1 Materials used in clinical trial study

that herbal drug users and non-users are not likely to share. Users, after all, believe in herbals in ways that many non-users do not. When faced with ambiguous information about whether some treatment cured a disease, people often encode and then interpret the information in accord with their prior theories (e.g., Jennings, Amabile, & Ross, 1982), seeing trends that are not there, simply because they expect to see them (e.g., Redelmeier & Tversky, 1996). One common form of theory-driven misperceptions are "illusory correlations" (Chapman & Chapman, 1975), in which expected correlations are perceived that are not really there. In an attempt to explore the potential differences between herbal users and non-users, we tested their perception of trends in relevant medical data.

A short survey was completed by 105 students, which included questions about their herbal medicine use, including variety and frequency. Later, they were invited to view on a computer screen a series of 40 slides, each presenting two pieces of information about a hypothetical patient: whether the person took a prescription or a herbal medication, and the number of days (between one and nine with an average of four) it took that person to recover. Of the slides 20 concerned herbal medicines and 20 concerned prescriptions. The two sets of slides – for herbals and for prescriptions – were otherwise identical. After viewing the slides, participants estimated the average number of days to recover for someone who took the herbal medicine and for someone who took the prescription.

Participants were grouped into three categories, based on whether they had never used herbals (non-users n = 48), had used them only once or twice (infrequent users n = 25), or used them regularly (regular users n = 31). Because their responses were essentially the same, the non-users and the infrequent users were combined in Figure 12.2. These two groups concluded that the herbal drug required slightly more time for recovery than the prescription. The regular herbal users, on the other hand, saw the herbal drug leading to a faster recovery than the prescription. This interaction proved significant in a repeated measures ANOVA (on all three groups), $F(2, 101) = 4.231, p<0.017$.

In this study, regular herbal users perceived the herbal drug as more effective than it really was, and the prescription drug as less effective than it really was. The opposite held true for non-users and infrequent users, who underestimated the effectiveness of herbals but overestimated the prescription. Of course, based on these data alone, we cannot tell whether people perceive herbals as effective when they use them, or use herbals because they see them as effective. In any event, our participants perceived different patterns in the same data, and those patterns were predicted by their opinions about herbals. To gauge effectiveness in a domain such as herbal medicine, people tend to rely on personal experience rather than published studies. The information presented in this experiment is similar to (if not clearer than) that available to an individual who is sick, takes a medication, and waits to see how long she takes to recover. The results of our study suggest that, barring severe cases,

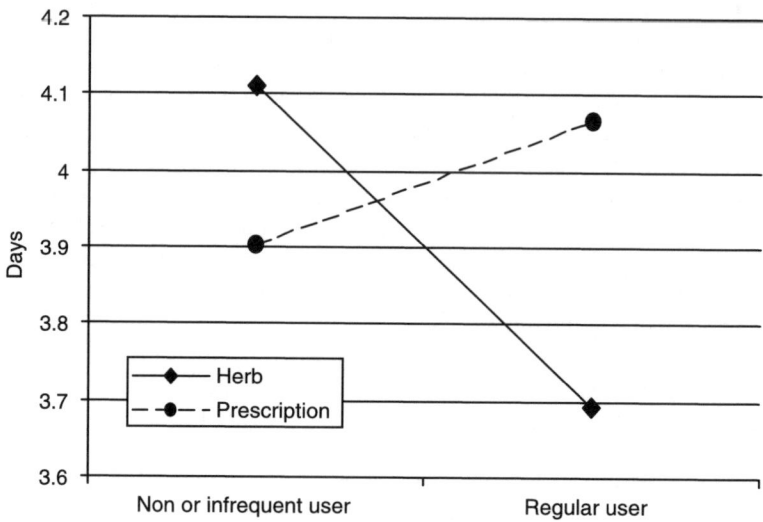

Figure 12.2 Average number of estimated days to recover, as a function of herbal use

conducting one's own series of clinical trials is likely to yield pretty much the results one expects to find.

Greater risk

Naturalness is the primary feature that consumers appreciate in herbal medicines, which they expect to be mild and less potent than prescriptions. As a result, they can be overly impressed by the small effects of herbals, and more prone to perceive rates of effectiveness that are not there. Once they have opted for what appeared as a natural and thus less risky medication, might they now be compelled to take even greater risks in order to stick with their preferred "natural" alternatives? If herbal users become so attached to naturalness that they are willing to accept a high degree of risk to attain it, this would run counter to the initial appeal behind naturalness, which was its harmlessness. The next study aimed to explore this possibility.

People often overgeneralise from certain features of a category to all category members, even in cases where many members deviate from the category norm (e.g., Moshinsky & Bar-Hillel, 2002; Stevens & Coupe, 1978). We suggest that a similar phenomenon might occur with herbal medicines. Once people consider the category of natural things as safe and attractive, then many members of that category benefit from an added perceived element of safety and attractiveness. This can lead to a willingness to accept risk from natural items, even risky natural medicines, because they are natural, and thus (mis)perceived as safe.

We asked 127 Princeton students to choose between hypothetical herbal and prescription drugs with varying levels of side effects and effectiveness. High likelihood of side effects and low levels of effectiveness constitute "risk" in the domain of medicines. All participants made two series of six choices (one series about effectiveness, the other series about side effects). Each series was designed so that one drug stayed at a constant level of effectiveness (or side effects), while the other varied. Thus, in one condition the pharmaceutical remained 99 per cent effective while the herbal's effectiveness gradually decreased over the six choices. The reverse was true in the other condition. For side effects, one drug had a 1 per cent likelihood of causing side effects, while the other's likelihood gradually increased.

We found herbal medicine users willing to accept lower effectiveness (M_{users} = 1.76, $M_{nonusuers}$ = 0.48, $t(57)$ = 3.47, $p<0.001$ where higher means reflect lower effectiveness) and more side effects (M_{users} = 1.21, $M_{nonusuers}$ = 0.32, $t(57)$ = 2.63, $p<0.01$) from a herbal drug than were the non-users. Conversely, non-users were willing to accept lower effectiveness (M_{users} = 0.87, $M_{nonusuers}$ = 1.80, $t(66)$ = 2.87, $p<0.005$) and more side effects (M_{users} = 1.00, $M_{nonusuers}$ = 1.94, $t(66)$ = 2.79, $p<0.007$) from pharmaceutical drugs than were herbal users. In addition, we analysed the results separately for natural and non-natural users, as in the previous study. The natural users were willing to accept even more risk than the rest of herbal users, Mann-Whitney U = 16.5, $p<0.04$. It appears that users are willing to accept higher levels of risk from natural options, despite the fact that the original appeal behind "natural" was its harmlessness. "Naturalness" thus seems to constitute a heuristic shortcut in choices regarding medical treatments. It originates from greater caution but can eventually lead to a biased acceptance of greater risk.

An alternative explanation for these results is that people are willing to accept what looks like greater risk because thinking about herbals brings to mind less serious side effects. To test this explanation, we asked participants to list the first four side effects that had come to mind when they were making their choices, and then to rate these for seriousness. There was no difference between the ratings in the two conditions, herbal and prescription. We then asked a separate group of 18 participants to rate for seriousness each of the 42 side effects listed by the original participants. Again there were no differences between the side effects that respondents in the herbal and the prescription conditions had generated.

A compelling example of the resulting willingness to tolerate risk is provided by one of the items on our national survey. As summarised in Table 12.4, natural users were more likely than other users to report that they felt it was safe to give herbal medicines to children ($\chi^2(2)$ = 10.1, $p<0.006$). Herbal medicines never tested on adults have not been tested on children either.

Naturalness as part of the course of nature

We are currently exploring the possibility that part of the attractiveness of herbal medicines is the perception that the effects of "natural" substances fall

Table 12.4 Percentage of respondents who feel it is safe to give herbals to children

	Non-users	Non-natural users	Natural users
Safe to give herbals to kids	41	53	58
Not safe to give to kids	59	47	42
Total N	202	155	106

under the natural scheme of things, unlike the effects of more artificial substances. A similar suggestion has been made about natural disasters:

> The concept of an act of god implied that something was wrong, that people had sinned and must now pay for their errors. But the idea of natural disaster may have implicitly suggested the reverse, that something was right, that the prevailing system of social and economic relations was functioning just fine. (Steinberg, 2000, page 19)

According to this reasoning, we suggest, harm that comes from natural medicines should be perceived as though it was preordained, more like an omission than a commission, requiring lesser compensation, causing less regret, etc., than equivalent harm from pharmaceutical drugs.

In a preliminary study, we have corroborated this hypothesis. We asked 216 Princeton students to consider two people who had the same medical problem. One had taken a herbal medicine, the other a prescription, and both had developed serious complications, including possible liver damage. Participants (not divided based on use status) then rated the anticipated emotions resulting from the complication. As shown in Table 12.5, there was strong agreement that the prescription drug taker in comparison with the herbal drug taker was more upset, felt more regret, deserved greater compensation, and had interfered more with the natural course of things (chi-squares all significant). Natural medicines appear to be interfering less with natural processes, and thus generate weaker sentiments of anger and regret than do their synthetic counterparts.

Other products

Our research concentrates on herbal medicines, but we expect the appeal of naturalness to extend to other items, notably foods. A quick trip through any American grocery store today finds the phrase "all natural" used to sell everything from ice cream and shampoo to toilet cleaners, cigarettes, and charcoal. To the extent that naturalness extends across domains, we expect its appeal in foods to be particularly strong among natural users of herbal medicines.

We asked 150 Princeton students to complete ratings of appeal, naturalness and preference for four beverages: Diet Coke, Arizona Iced Tea with Ginseng

Table 12.5 Percentages of participants who selected either the natural medicine taker or the prescription medicine taker in response to the following items

	Chose natural medicine taker %	Chose prescription medicine taker %
1. Who do you think is more upset about his bad reaction to the treatment?	36	64
2. Who do you think deserves more compensation for damages?	12	88
3. Who do you think is more likely to feel that this allergic reaction was just meant to be?	83	17
4. Who do you think feels more strongly that what happened to him was unfair?	20	80

extract, Coca-Cola Classic, and Snapple Vibrance Starfruit Orange Fruit drink with rosemary, beta carotene and Echinacea. These drinks were chosen because two seem particularly "unnatural" (the sodas) and two seem more "natural," due to the added herbal supplements. All four are easily available in the Princeton student stores.

As expected, Diet Coke received the lowest ratings of naturalness, followed by Coca-Cola; Snapple and Iced Tea tied, which was rated the most natural. Herbal users and non-users did not differ on these ratings. However, they did differ in their choices. Once again, we divided participants into natural users, non-natural users, and non-users of herbal medicines. We combined the two sodas together and the two "natural" drinks together to simplify the analysis, and we found a significant relation between group membership and beverage choices, $\chi^2(2) = 6.64, p = 0.03$. As shown in Table 12.6, natural users are more likely to choose a natural drink over a soda, whereas non-users are more likely to choose a soda over a natural drink, with non-natural users falling in between.

As before, we expected the correlation between appeal and naturalness to be highest for natural users, as they are the ones relying most on naturalness in making their choices. The simple bivariate correlations between ratings of appeal and ratings of naturalness across all participants were significant for

Table 12.6 Percentage of natural users, non-natural users, and non-users who chose the soda or the natural drink

	Soda	Natural drink	Total N
Non-users	55	45	102
Non-natural users	46	54	30
Natural users	22	78	18

Table 12.7 Correlations between ratings of appeal and naturalness

	All	*Natural users*	*Non-natural users*	*Non-users*
Iced tea	0.35***	0.70**	0.05	0.33**
Coca-Cola	0.27**	0.43▶	0.34▶	0.18▶
Snapple	0.29***	0.67**	0.16	0.22*

Note: ▶ marginally significant, $0.10 > p > 0.05$; *$0.05 > p > 0.01$; **$0.01 > p > 0.001$; ***$p < 0.001$.

three of the four beverages (all but Diet Coke). These correlations were modest in size, ranging from 0.27 to 0.35. For natural users, however, the correlations were significantly higher, and for non-users they were significantly lower, as shown in Table 12.7. For iced tea, the correlation changed from 0.70 for natural users to 0.33 for non-users. Similarly for Snapple, the correlation was 0.67 for natural users and 0.22 for the non-users. People who use herbal medicines primarily because they are natural display a strong relation between how appealing and how natural they then judge drinks to be. Once naturalness plays a prominent role in people's judgements, their preferences can be predicted in different domains.

Discussion: Anatomy of a heuristic

We have presented evidence from a variety of different studies suggesting that some people use the concept of naturalness in a heuristic fashion, leading them to perceive "natural" products as less risky and more appealing. Consequently, they occasionally exhibit bias, making questionable choices in order to obtain the desired "naturalness". However, there are a number of remaining difficulties for this proposal of a "naturalness heuristic".

The affect heuristic

The naturalness heuristic may be a special case of the more general "affect" heuristic. The affect heuristic (Slovic et al., 2002) concerns quick emotional responses people have that tend to guide their judgements and choices. For example, the positive affect associated with a large sum of money tends to prompt people to play the lottery, despite the very small odds of winning. Slovic et al. suggest that "natural" invokes positive affect for consumers, and it is this positive affect that leads people to prefer naturalness. It is likely that "natural" generates positive affect, but there is no inherent reason why that should be so. After all, arsenic, botulism, E. coli, and anthrax are all natural, but not associated with positive affect. Evidence shows that under certain circumstances, people will reject a natural item (juice that touched a sterilised cockroach) in favour something artificial (plastic cockroach), suggesting that affect towards natural items is not uniformly positive (Rozin, Millman, & Nemeroff, 1986).

We conclude that the affect heuristic is likely to play a role in the domain of herbal medicines, but it cannot fully account for the prevalence and attractiveness of "naturalness," which in the biological world is frequently associated with negative outcomes. Furthermore, although the affect heuristic could guide choices, it cannot explain the biased perceptions we have documented; nor does it explain why naturalness has become positively valenced only recently. We are currently conducting archival research to explore the perception of "naturalness" in print media throughout the last century.

The single-feature heuristic

The naturalness heuristic may best be conceptualised as a special example of a more general "single-feature" heuristic. As suggested by the findings above, those who are attracted by naturalness sometimes allow a product's being natural to overwhelm other potentially important considerations. Choices or judgements that are based on a single feature – naturalness in the present case, and possibly other features in other circumstances – may be quick and compelling, but they may often generate excessive bias towards the salient feature.

Versions of the single-feature heuristic arise also in work on stereotyping and person perception. Researchers believe that person perception begins with fast, automatic judgements based on a few easily identifiable features, such as gender and race (as the current debate over racial profiling by the police makes vivid). Perceivers may then re-evaluate their categorisation based on other features, if they have the time, motivation, and attentional resources (e.g., Fiske, Lin, & Neuberg, 1999). While there are important differences between impressions of other people and judgements of consumer products, the general processes seem to have much in common. Tools that have been used to study stereotyping (see Fazio & Olson, 2003, for review), such as the Implicit Association Test (IAT), could just as easily be applied to natural and synthetic medicines. We would expect that participants would react more quickly to the pairing of natural with pleasant and synthetic with unpleasant than vice versa.

The idea of a single-feature heuristic shares similarities also with the "Take the Best" heuristic (Gigerenzer & Goldstein, 1999), where just one cue is used unless it fails to differentiate between the options. Whereas that work focuses on the use of cues in judgement, the present interpretation refers to the reliance on preferred features in choice. It accounts for a consumer who looks at two tubes of toothpaste and buys the one that is "natural", with insufficient regard for other features such as price, quality, or taste.

Individual and cultural differences

There are undoubtedly other variables that may predict reliance on "naturalness" in the use of herbal medicine, such as an individual's education or cultural background. We are not aware of relevant cross-cultural data, but naturalness is likely to prove less salient in cultures that have traditionally used herbal medicines or where this industry has not yet developed. Work by Nisbett and colleagues shows differences in the use of other heuristics among cultures, including differences between Americans and East Asians in the fundamental attribution error (Choi & Nisbett, 1998; Choi, Nisbett, & Norenzayan, 1999; Norenzayan, Choi, & Nisbett, 2002), the hindsight bias (Choi & Nisbett, 2000), covariation detection (Ji, Peng, & Nisbett, 2000), and response scale framing (Ji, Schwarz, & Nisbett, 2000). These differences are attributable to differences in social norms between cultures. Naturalness may have a similar standing, underused by certain segments of the population, but overused by a subgroup of Americans who are particularly prone to related norms and beliefs.

Conclusion

Herbal medicines are very popular and getting more so. In this chapter, we have explored some basic phenomena in the decision-making and heuristics literature that might shed light on consumers' attitudes towards herbal medicines. Survey evidence suggested a reliance on the notion of "naturalness", which leads herbal medicines to be perceived as mild, less potent, less effective, and less intrusive. The common expectation that herbal medicines will prove less effective was shown paradoxically to lead to a more positive evaluation of their potentially limited effects. We documented several biased beliefs and attitudes, including the perception of illusory correlations in the evaluation of the effectiveness of herbal medicines. We also documented greater tolerance among herbal users towards the risks they pose, and a greater reported willingness to administer untested herbal drugs to children. Finally, we suggested that naturalness further contributes to the attractiveness of herbal medicines by making them appear as part of the course of nature, rather than an interference with natural processes.

We conclude that people rely on "naturalness" as a heuristic, that the extent of this reliance differs among individuals, and that it may vary across cultures. The naturalness heuristic is likely to be a culturally dependent manifestation of a more common single-feature heuristic, in which decision makers rely heavily on a salient feature of interest. Hence, understanding the appeal of naturalness may shed light both on important cultural differences, on the use of heuristics in decision-making, and on their impact on highly consequential decisions.

Acknowledgements

This research was supported by National Science Foundation grant 0112284 and by a grant from Merck & Co., Inc. This research is based in part on the doctoral dissertation work submitted by the first author to Princeton University.

Appendix

Frequencies of responses to items on the student survey.

Questionnaire item	Responses	Frequencies %
1. In general, what is your attitude towards herbal medicines? For this survey, we intend the phrase herbal medicines to include herbs such as Echinacea, Ginkgo, and St. John's Wort and dietary supplements such as garlic, ginger, and amino acids, but not vitamins or minerals like vitamin C and calcium.	Positive (strongly & slightly)	58.1
	Neutral	25.4
	Negative (strongly & slightly)	26.5
2. In general, do you see herbal products as safe or unsafe?	Very/moderately safe	43.9
	Somewhat safe	34.8
	Somewhat unsafe	15.2
	Very/moderately unsafe	6.1
3. People think that herbal products are safe for a number of different reasons. Here you can see a list of some reasons. Which one of them is most important to you? Please check one. (n = 172)	Are mild	19.8
	Are natural	51.7
	Are regulated	6.4
	Recommended by a doctor	6.4
	Have been used for centuries	15.7
4. As far as you know, does the government require herbal products to be tested for effectiveness?	Yes	17.0
	No	83.0
5. As far as you know, does the government or some other group monitor herbal products for safety?	Yes	48.9
	No	51.5
6. How important is it to you that herbal drugs be regulated by a group such as the FDA?	Not important	4.2
		10.6
	Moderately	24.2
		30.3
	Very important	30.7
7. How important is it to you that prescription drugs be regulated by a group such as the FDA?	Not important	0.4
	Moderately	0
		2.3
		8.0
	Very important	89.4
8. When used to treat similar symptoms, do you think herbal or prescription drugs are more effective? (n = 263)	Herbals	5.4
	Same	14.4
	Prescriptions	80.2
9. Have you ever taken herbal medicines such as Echinacea, Ginkgo, or St. John's Wort or dietary supplements such as garlic, ginger, or amino acids?	Yes	45.5
	No	54.5

Questionnaire item	Responses	Frequencies %
10. How many different herbal medicines, not just different brands, have you tried? (n = 120)	One	35.0
	Two	27.5
	Three or more	37.5
11. In the past two months, approximately how often have you taken a herbal medicine? (n = 119)	None	10.9
	One time only	44.5
	Monthly	16.0
	Bi-weekly	11.8
	Weekly	7.6
	Daily	9.2
12. People who use herbal medicines have different reasons for doing so. Here is a list of some reasons. Which one of these reasons is the most important reason for you? Please check one (n = 96)	Easy to obtain	19.8
	Mild	5.2
	Cheap	0
	Natural	43.8
	Safe	2.1
	Effective	29.2

Note: N = 264 unless otherwise specified.

Free-response questions and corresponding responses from student survey

1. Answer this if you just responded with "Somewhat, Moderately or Very safe." In general, you see herbal medicines as safe. Why do you feel this way? Please summarise your main reason in a sentence. (n = 208)	Unusable	4.8
	Effective/beneficial	2.4
	Natural/organic	43.3
	Positive personal experience	10.1
	Haven't heard of problems	12.0
	Doctor recommended	0.5
	Have been used for centuries	3.8
	Mild/not that strong	3.4
	FDA approved/tested	2.4
	On the market	4.3
	They cause no harm	13.0
2. Answer this if you just responded with "Somewhat, Moderately or Very unsafe." In general, you see herbal medicines as unsafe. Why do you feel this way? Please summarise your main reason in a sentence. (n = 54)	Unusable	16.7
	Unproven effectiveness	18.5
	Unregulated by FDA	51.9
	Heard are unsafe through media	9.3
	No substances are safe	3.7

Note: Responses were coded by two judges, and agreement was over 90 per cent across all items. Disagreements were resolved through discussion.

References

Astin, J. A. (1998). Why patients use alternative medicine. *Journal of the American Medical Association, 279* (19), 1548–1553.

Carlisle, E., & Shafir, E. (2003). Consumers' attitudes towards herbal medicines: An RDD survey of American adults. Manuscript in preparation.

Centers for Medicare & Medicaid Services. (1998). *Table 9 Personal Health Care Expenditures, by Type of Expenditure and Source of Funds: Calendar Years 1994–2001*. Office of the Actuary, National Health Statistics Group. Retrieved March 6, 2003, from http://www.cms.hhs.gov/statistics/nhe/historical/t9.asp

Chapman, L. J., & Chapman, J. P. (1975). The basis of illusory correlation. *Journal of Abnormal Psychology, 84* (5), 574–575.

Choi, I., & Nisbett, R. E. (1998). Situational salience and cultural differences in the correspondence bias and actor–observer bias. *Personality and Social Psychology Bulletin, 24* (9), 949–960.

Choi, I., & Nisbett, R. E. (2000). Cultural psychology of surprise: Holistic theories and recognition of contradiction. *Journal of Personality and Social Psychology, 79* (6), 890–905.

Choi, I., Nisbett, R. E., & Norenzayan, A. (1999). Causal attribution across cultures: Variation and universality. *Psychological Bulletin, 125* (1), 47–63.

Eisenberg, D. M., Davis, R. B., Ettner, S. L., Appel, S., Wilkey, S., Van Rompay, M., & Kessler, R. C. (1998). Trends in alternative medicine use in the United States, 1990–1997. *Journal of the American Medical Association, 280* (18), 1569–1575.

Ernst, E. (2000). Prevalence of use of complementary/alternative medicine: A systematic review. *Bulletin of the World Health Organization, 78* (2), 252–257.

Fazio, R. H., & Olson, M. A. (2003). Implicit measures in social cognition research: Their meaning and use, *Annual Review of Psychology, 54*, 297–327.

Fiske, S. T., Lin, M., & Neuberg, S. L. (1999). The continuum model: Ten years later. In S. Chaiken & Y. Trope (Eds.), *Dual-process theories in social psychology* (pp. 231–254). New York: Guilford.

Gigerenzer, G., & Goldstein, D. G. (1999). Betting on one good reason: The Take the Best heuristic. In G. Gigerenzer, P. M. Todd, & ABC Research Group (Eds.), *Simple heuristics that make us smart* (pp. 75–95). New York: Oxford University, Press.

Grossman, L. (2002). The curious case of Kava. *Time*, 8 April, 58.

Haller, C. A., & Benowitz, N. L. (2000). Adverse cardiovascular and central nervous system events associated with dietary supplements containing ephedra alkaloids. *New England Journal of Medicine, 343* (25), 1833–1838.

Henry J. Kaiser Family Foundation, & Harvard School of Public Health. (1999). *Health News Interest Index Poll* [Database in Lexis-Nexis, Roper Centre for Public Opinion Research]. Princeton Survey Research Associates. Retrieved January 15, 2002 from http://web.lexis-nexis.com/universe/form/academic/s_roper.html?_m=adee0af9718598bc7864096fb6bfdbc8&wchp=dGLStS-lSlAl&_md5=697f1bd9cc6f-9d001330892b518f2061

Jennings, D. L., Amabile, T. M., & Ross, L. (1982). Informal covariation assessment: Data-based versus theory-based judgements. In D. Kahneman, P. Slovic, & A. Tversky (Eds.), *Judgement under uncertainty: Heuristics and biases* (pp. 211–230). Cambridge: Cambridge University Press.

Ji, L. J., Peng, K., & Nisbett, R. E. (2000). Culture, control, and perception of relationships in the environment. *Journal of Personality and Social Psychology, 78* (5), 943–955.

Ji, L. J., Schwarz, N., & Nisbett, R. E. (2000). Culture, autobiographical memory, and behavioral frequency reports: Measurement issues in cross-cultural studies. *Personality and Social Psychology Bulletin, 26* (5), 585–593.

Josefson, D. (2001). US moves to tighten law on health supplements. *British Medical Journal, 323*, 654.

Kahneman, D., & Miller, D. T. (1986). Norm theory: Comparing reality to its alternatives. *Psychological Review, 93* (2), 136–153.

Kaiser Family Foundation, Kennedy School of Government, & National Public Radio. (1999). *Dietary Supplement Survey* [Database in Lexis-Nexis, Roper Centre for Public Opinion Research]. Retrieved January 15, 2002 from http://web.lexis-nexis.com/universe/form/academic/s_roper.html?_m=adee0af9718598bc7864096fb6bfdbc8&wchp=dGLStS-lSlAl&_md5=697f1bd9cc6f9d001330892b518f2061

Lord, C. G., Ross, L., & Lepper, M. R. (1979). Biased assimilation and attitude polarization: The effects of prior theories on subsequently considered evidence. *Journal of Personality and Social Psychology, 37* (11), 2098–2109.

Moshinsky, A., & Bar-Hillel, M. (2002). Where did 1850 happen first – in America or in Europe? A cognitive account for a historical bias. *Psychological Science, 13* (1), 20–26.

Norenzayan, A., Choi, I., & Nisbett, R. E. (2002). Cultural similarities and differences in social inference: Evidence from behavioral predictions and lay theories of behavior. *Personality and Social Psychology Bulletin, 28* (1), 109–120.

Prevention Magazine (1999). *Special Nutritionals Survey* [Database in Lexis-Nexis, Roper Centre for Public Opinion Research]. Princeton Survey Research Associates. Retrieved June 26, 2002 from http://web.lexisnexis.com/universe/form/academic/s_roper.html?_m=adee0af9718598bc7864096fb6bfdbc8&wchp=dGLStS-lSlAl&_md5=697f1bd9cc6f9d001330892b518f2061

Redelmeier, D. A., & Tversky, A. (1996). On the belief that arthritis pain is related to the weather. *Proceedings of the National Academy of Sciences, USA, 93*, 2895–2896.

Rozin, P., Millman, L., & Nemeroff, C. (1986). Operation of the laws of sympathetic magic in disgust and other domains. *Journal of Personality and Social Psychology, 50* (4), 703–712.

Slovic, P., Finucane, M., Peters, E., & MacGregor, D. G. (2002). The affect heuristic. In T. Gilovich, D. Griffin, & D. Kahneman (Eds.), *Heuristics and biases: The psychology of intuitive judgement* (pp. 397–420). New York: Cambridge University Press.

Spranca, M. D. (1993). *Some basic psychology behind the appeal of naturalness in the domain of foods*. Unpublished manuscript, Berkeley, CA.

Steinberg, T. (2000). *Acts of God: The unnatural history of natural disasters in America*. New York: Oxford University Press.

Stevens, A., & Coupe, P. (1978). Distortions in judged spatial relations. *Cognitive Psychology, 10*, 422–437.

Author index

Subject index